C000145223

Norfolk Record Society
Volume LXXVII for 2013

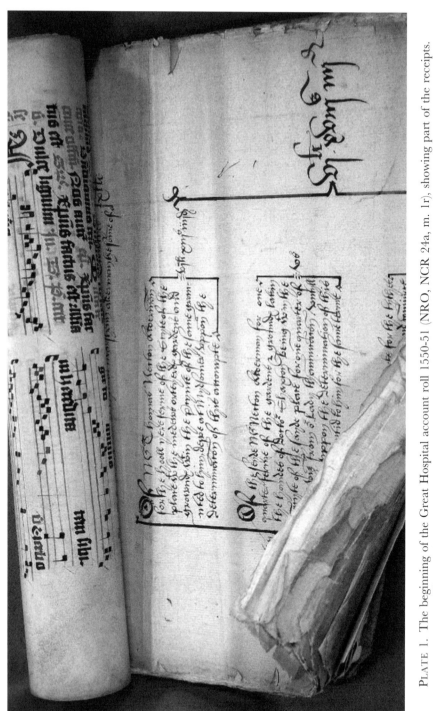

PLATE 1. The beginning of the Great Hospital account roll 1550-51 (NRO, NCR 24a, m. 1r), showing part of the receipts. The roll is bound in a leaf from a medieval service book. (Photograph: Carole Rawcliffe)

HEALTH AND HYGIENE
IN EARLY-MODERN NORWICH

◆

Account rolls of the Great Hospital, Norwich,
1549–50 and 1570–71

ELLIE PHILLIPS

The Norwich River and Street Accounts
1557–61 and 1570–80

ISLA FAY

Norfolk Record Society

Volume LXXVII for 2013

First published in 2013
by the Norfolk Record Society

ISBN 978-0-9556357-6-2

Produced by John Saunders Design & Production, Eastbourne
Printed and bound in Great Britain by
T J International Ltd, Padstow, Cornwall

To Carole Rawcliffe

for her support and kindness to us both

Contents

List of Figures and Plates

General Introduction

By the sixteenth century Norwich had become the most wealthy and most populous of English provincial towns, a position it retained until well into the eighteenth century. The late sixteenth-century city council's innovatory solutions to the problems of poor relief are well known (see, for example, John F. Pound, ed., *The Norwich Census of the Poor 1570*, Norfolk Record Society, xl, 1971). But, as the accounts edited in this volume show, the council was also active in other fields. The dissolution of the medieval hospital of St Giles provided an opportunity for the city to take over the running of the establishment in 1547. Renamed 'The Howse of the Poore on Holme Street' or 'Goddes Howse' (only later 'the Great Hospital') the new regime did away with the liturgical practices that had come to play an increasing rôle in the old hospital of St Giles and replaced these with the purely secular maintenance of forty poor persons and the support of a grammar school, making God's House (as Dr Phillips says) the pre-eminent charitable establishment in the city.

At the same time the civic authorities were addressing another Norwich problem. The state of the River Wensum and the cleanliness of the streets had been a matter of concern throughout the medieval period. After some minor innovations, the city government decided to deal with the matter once and for all, and in 1552 set up a new committee with powers to raise money and tackle abuses. The accounts of this river and street committee make up the latter part of this volume.

We are indebted to the Norwich Town Close Estate Charity for their generous help with our publication costs. Thanks are also due to the Norfolk Record Office for permission to publish the images used in Plates 1 and 2 and to the Trustees of the Great Hospital and Ms Brigid Land for the use of the illustration on the dust cover.

ELIZABETH RUTLEDGE, *General Editor*

Account rolls of the Great Hospital, Norwich, 1549–50 and 1570–71

EDITED BY ELLIE PHILLIPS

Introduction

Ever since its foundation by Bishop Walter Suffield in *c.*1249, the Great Hospital in Norwich – known in the medieval period as the hospital of St Giles and after the Dissolution as God's House – has provided its residents with physical and spiritual succour. Few other charitable institutions in Europe can match its record of continuous care to the present day.[1] The Great Hospital is also unusual among medieval English hospitals because extensive architectural and documentary evidence survives. In 2011, UNESCO, the United Nations Educational, Scientific and Cultural Organisation recognised the value of its medieval records by awarding them UN Status.[2] The numerous documentary sources are extremely detailed and include a long run of account rolls, which provide a fascinating insight into the day-to-day management of a large urban institution. The two account rolls (1549–50 and 1570–71) and supplementary documentary sources edited here reveal how the medieval hospital of St Giles not only survived the Dissolution, but became the city's pre-eminent charitable establishment.[3]

[1] Further material about the Great Hospital/ the hospital of St Giles can be found in C. Rawcliffe, *Medicine for the Soul: The Life, Death and Resurrection of an English Medieval Hospital* (Stroud, 1999) and in E.M. Phillips, *Charitable Institutions in Norfolk and Suffolk c. 1350–1600* (University of East Anglia, Unpublished PhD thesis, 2001). A model of the hospital and additional information is available online at http://www.thegreathospital.co.uk/. For more on medieval hospitals in general, see N. Orme and M. Webster, *The English Hospital 1070–1570* (New Haven and London 1995), B. Bowers, ed., *The Medieval Hospital and Medical Practice* (Aldershot and Burlington, USA, 2007), and S. Sweetinburgh, *The Role of the Hospital in Medieval England: Gift-Giving and the Spiritual Economy* (Dublin, 2004). The name 'The Great Hospital' was used as early as 1720: K.I. Sandred and B. Lindström, *Place Names of Norfolk, Part One*, English Place-Name Society LXI (1989), pp.59–60.

[2] The records are held at the Norfolk Record Office (hereafter NRO), among the Norwich City Records (hereafter NCR).

[3] 'Dissolution' is here used to mean the process by which religious houses, including hospitals, were suppressed following various Acts of Parliament from 1533 to 1547 and is therefore more specific than the general term 'Reformation'. The Dissolution Acts of 1536 and 1539 established the rationale for dissolving religious houses based upon evidence in the 1535 survey of religious institutions, the *Valor Ecclesiasticus*, but a host of other Acts paved the way for the break with Rome and subsequent transfer of wealth to the Crown.

The Foundation of St Giles' Hospital

At least twenty-two hospitals had been established in Norfolk, including five in Norwich, by the time Suffield founded St Giles' in 1249.[4] Many were founded for an apostolic thirteen patients and most cared for the sick poor (rarely women) or lepers, with a few catering to the transitory needs of pilgrims. Hospitals were generally dedicated to saints associated with healing miracles or patron saints of particular diseases. Although also dedicated to the Trinity, the Virgin Mary and to St Anne, Suffield called his new hospital by the name of St Giles, the patron saint of lepers, cripples and nursing mothers. Founding a hospital was a major financial undertaking only possible for a wealthy minority. The £200 Suffield bequeathed to St Giles' hospital, in addition to income from estates, grain and livestock, was but a small part of his overall expenditure in purchasing the site and setting up the institution.[5] The question of how extensively such hospitals served the general population is problematic, as, in addition to their 'statutory' duties outlined by the founder, many provided intermitent assistance when funds permitted. Bishop Suffield described this type of assistance when drawing up and revising his foundation charter:

> And in this hospital there will be an ark of the Lord [*a poor box*] from which poor people passing by shall receive alms and free charitable assistance every day according to the means of the hospital.[6]

Medieval hospitals were not, however, intended to relieve wholesale suffering. It was accepted that the poor and sick were a permanent feature of society and even had a role to play as beneficiaries of other people's charity. The idea of selectivity when dispensing alms had long been established and would be further refined during the sixteenth-century; hospitals had always drawn their inmates from specific sections of society, while excluding others.

St Giles', like many other medieval hospitals, drew upon the model provided by the Augustinian Rule, which prioritised moderation, discipline and solicitude for those in need. Suffield's first carefully worded foundation charter of 1249 reflects this approach; the master, four priests, four lay brothers and four sisters were to live a life of apostolic poverty and dedication to caring for up to thirty sick poor men each of whom was to be 'received kindly and taken care of honestly'.[7] The lay brothers undertook manual work and dealt with business concerns outside the hospital but were also expected to attend services. Provision was made for 'all the poor priests of the diocese of Norwich, who are broken with age or bedridden with constant sickness so that they

---

[4] C. Rawcliffe, *The Hospitals of Medieval Norwich* (Norwich, 1995).

[5] Rawcliffe, *Medicine for the Soul*, p.25. The hospital's finances in the pre-Reformation period are discussed on pp.65–102.

[6] Rawcliffe, *Medicine for the Soul*, p.244.

[7] Rawcliffe, *Medicine for the Soul*, p.243.

cannot celebrate divine service', and who were to 'be received in the hospital to dwell there as long as they live'. Seven poor but promising scholars were, moreover, to be selected by the schoolmaster, 'properly taught in grammar' and fed daily.[8] Suffield specified that an additional thirteen poor people were to receive good quality food including meat or fish or cheese and eggs and, in the cold winter months, might consume it in front of a fire in the hospital.

With the exception of the nursing sisters, who had to be over fifty years of age, women were banned from lodging in the hospital. Lay brothers and sisters were strictly segregated. In establishing an age limit, Suffield aimed to reduce opportunities for sexual misconduct and avoid the potential physical and moral pollution caused by menstruating women that had long been identified by medical authorities. Other clauses in the charter dealt with the management of the hospital, its possessions and income, the election of the master, his duties and rights, and the conduct and dress of the brethren and sisters. A second version of the charter, confirmed in 1257, made few significant alterations to the first, but its focus on maintaining standards of behaviour suggests the possibility that some laxity had crept in. No further revision of the charter took place until the city authorities acquired the hospital in 1547, when a tripartite document was drawn up between them, the Crown and the master, Nicholas Shaxton.[9]

All medieval charity, including the endowment of hospitals, was underpinned by a belief in the efficacy of the Seven Comfortable Works, or the Seven Corporeal Works of Mercy, established in St Matthew's Gospel (Matthew 25: 32–36). Offering food and drink, shelter, clothing and alms to those in need and visiting prisoners was believed to hasten progress through Purgatory and provided a powerful incentive to help the less fortunate.[10] Establishing a hospital encompassed the majority of these Works, but such a major investment was beyond the means of the majority. While wealthy donors such as William Dunwich helped the hospital of St Giles to extend the care on offer by supporting five sick paupers, more modest donations to established institutions also benefitted the donor. In exchange for the 4d bequeathed by Rose Eton in 1528 to the 'pore systers' of St Mary's hospital, Great Yarmouth, the latter were expected to pray for Rose's soul.[11] Prayers for the dead were an effective medicine for sick souls; and in the spiritual, as in the medical, market place people purchased the best remedies they could afford.

[8] Rawcliffe, *Medicine for the Soul*, pp.243–4.

[9] Appendix 1. Transcript kindly provided by Professor C. Rawcliffe.

[10] J. Le Goff, *The Birth of Purgatory*, translated by A. Goldhammer (Aldershot, 1990), discusses in great detail the development and acceptance of Purgatory as a tenet of Christian belief from the twelfth century onwards. The idea that Purgatory was not simply a place of intense suffering and was thus to be feared, but instead offered a much welcomed second chance at redemption is mooted by C. Burgess, '"A Fond Thing Vainly Invented": An Essay on Purgatory and Pious Motive in Later Medieval England' in S.J. Wright, ed., *Parish, Church and People* (London, 1988), pp.56–84.

[11] NRO, Norwich Consistory Court, Maryett f.13.

Although an important aspect of hospitals such as St Giles' was the celebration of masses and performance of the liturgy, medical care in its broadest sense was not neglected. Patients were not attended by salaried practitioners until the city authorities assumed control in 1547 following the Dissolution, but the provision of regular food and drink, bed rest, warmth and respite from hard work reflected the prevailing holistic view of the body derived from Greek theories of well-being.[12] However, medicine for the soul took precedence over medicine for the body, and the metaphor of Christ the heavenly Physician was well established.[13] Augustine of Hippo (d.430) evoked the image of *Christus Medicus* in numerous sermons to describe the way in which Christ, like the good physician, cured the sick (sinners) of their diseases (sin). Few English medieval hospitals offered professional medical care, and St Giles' was not unusual in prioritising the spiritual well-being of residents and benefactors.

Pre-Dissolution Change

In the period between 1249 and the transfer of St Giles' to the civic authorities in 1547, forty-one hospitals were founded in Norfolk.[14] From the mid fourteenth century, however, the number of new foundations in the county was substantially lower than in previous centuries. The cumulative effects of the Black Death and successive outbreaks of plague left the aged, sick and disabled with fewer relatives to support them, but simultaneously provided increased opportunities for wage-labourers as the demand for their services grew. In this unstable environment, few new institutions were founded. The changed social and financial landscape which emerged at this time meant that landowners, the earlier patrons of charitable institutions, faced a crisis as their income from rents plummeted. Hospitals were forced to seek alternative sources of revenue to compensate for their own falling receipts. One response, adopted by the hospitals of St Giles, Norwich, and St Saviour, Bury St Edmunds, was to concentrate even more money on the provision of liturgical services for which charges could be made. Other strategies adopted by the master of St Giles included selling corrodies (a form of sheltered accommodation for the affluent aged), providing board and lodging for senior clergy, and housing fee-paying boys who studied at the nearby grammar school. A delicate balance had to be struck between immediate survival and promoting long-term benefits without straying too far from the founder's original intentions. St Giles' hospital certainly promoted new spiritual services to attract wealthy donors, but it continued to serve humbler parishioners in the parish church of St Helen's and maintain some of its charitable functions (although not as extensively as Suffield might have wished). Moreover, the widespread

---

[12] P. Horden, 'A Non-natural Environment: Medicine without Doctors and the Medieval European Hospital' in Bowers, *The Medieval Hospital*, pp.133–46.

[13] C. Rawcliffe, *Medicine and Society in Later Medieval England* (Stroud, 1997), pp.17–21.

[14] Calculations based on Phillips, 'Charitable Institutions in Norfolk and Suffolk'.

accusations of mismanagement, scandal and corruption in established English hospitals – most notoriously that of St Mary Bethlem in London, and leading to a parliamentary enquiry in 1414 – never included St Giles'. An analysis of lay and clerical wills drawn up between 1370 and 1532 in Norwich reveals that most believed that charity should begin at home, often clearly defined as the parish, but that the hospital of St Giles still remained a popular choice of beneficiary.[15] The broad base of support for the hospital was supplied in no small measure by the city's ruling elite, and such loyalty (or commendable foresight) was to prove vital at the Dissolution.

Dissolution

Henry VIII's financial survey of ecclesiastical property, the *Valor Ecclesiasticus*, provided a preliminary 'snap-shot' of hospital provision in 1535, a year after he declared himself supreme head of the English Church.[16] The entry for St Giles' hospital records an anticipated net annual income of £173. This esti-mate was unrealistically high and did not allow for uncollected arrears, which would have further reduced its profitability. In inflating the hospital's pre-dicted income (which was actually rapidly diminishing) the master may have hoped to stress the viability of the hospital and ensure its continuity. The strat-egy appeared to work, as St Giles' survived the first round of dissolutions which followed a year later, but it was not able to resist official scrutiny for much longer.

Between 1538 and 1540, as large and long-established hospitals such as St Leonard's in York fell to the Crown, the hospital of St Giles formally surren-dered to King Henry.[17] The fate of dissolved institutions had not been deter-mined in the early Dissolution Acts and often depended upon their attractiveness to Henry's courtiers, many of whom benefitted from subsequent asset-stripping. Despite the reformers' claims that hospitals had long ceased to care for the poor, their loss was not unlamented. Attached to the 1546 Chantry Certificate for the hospital of St Saviour in Bury St Edmunds is a petition in which the townspeople complained of the lack of 'eny hospytall [for the] power inhabytant [which] dayly theare moultiplyent'.[18] The threat of losing St Giles' numerous assets, coupled to an awareness of the growing problem posed by the city's poor, prompted the MP for Norwich, William Rogers, to take action. He suggested that the mayor's court should make formal suit to King Henry with a view to acquiring the hospital. By the spring of 1547, following laborious and expensive lobbying, the hospital finally

---

[15] N. Tanner, *The Church in Late Medieval Norwich* (Toronto, 1994), pp.132–7.

[16] *Valor Ecclesiasticus*, 6 vols (London, 1810–1834), vol. 3, pp.291–2.

[17] The exact date is unclear as the year is not given in the original document, only the day and month. See Rawcliffe, *Medicine for the Soul*, p.201 and p.301 n.69 for further explanation.

[18] The National Archives (hereafter TNA), Court of Augmentations: certificates of colleges, chantries and similar foundations, E/301/45 f.8v.

passed to the city.[19] The transformation of the hospital of St Giles into 'The Howse of the Poore on Holme Street', or 'Goddes Howse', is specified in the 1547 refoundation charter[20] and followed in these account rolls.

After the Dissolution: Establishing God's House

The first payment recorded in the first account of the refounded hospital was from Nicholas Shaxton, whose term as master began during the takeover in 1547.[21] Shaxton had been a royal almoner with close links to Anne Boleyn and Archbishops Cranmer and Latimer before their fortunes turned. His time at God's House was not to be a peaceful end to a tumultuous career because in the summer of 1549 an uprising led by Robert Kett brought chaos to the city.[22] Negotiations between the protestors and the mayor of Norwich, Thomas Codde, failed and by August Shaxton had fled the city and much of the hospital property on and around Holme Street lay in ruins. The 1549–50 account notes that income was lost from property made 'destitute ... by reason of the comoycion and brynnyng of the houses there'. Though the hospital's priest, John Fisher, endeavoured to feed the residents by begging for food, the rebellion presented longer-term financial problems for the hospital. Fisher was unable to meet certain obligations because the 'hooll street [Holme Street]... is brente by the rebelles', and further examples of devastation appear throughout the roll.[23] Despite this setback, income from properties and land in the city totalled £33 9s 4d for the year.

The hospital's first endowments in Calthorpe, Costessey, Cringleford, Hardley, Seething and South Walsham had been made by 1251, but successive masters added to the portfolio and particular care was taken to consolidate holdings around the precinct itself.[24] The Lathes, which lay just outside St Augustine's gate to the north of the city, for example, had been acquired in 1280, and by 1549 formed part of the package rented by Thomas Codde at an annual farm of £4 15s. The hospital's numerous properties, which included the evocatively titled 'rede mersh nighe unto Carrowe place called Paradyse', provided wood for fuel, hay and grazing for cattle, and timber for building, as well as a secure rental income.

Although much of the hospital's income was derived from estates that had

---

[19] By this time Henry had died and Edward VI had succeeded. A detailed account of the process of petitioning and eventual surrender of the hospital to the city can be found in Rawcliffe, *Medicine for the Soul*, pp.190–214.

[20] See Appendix 1.

[21] After the death of the previous master, Robert Codde. For Shaxton's biography see Rawcliffe, *Medicine for the Soul*, pp.210–14.

[22] A. Wood, 'Kett's Rebellion' in C. Rawcliffe and R. Wilson, eds, *Medieval Norwich* (London, 2004), pp.277–99.

[23] Mm 1r, 2r, 4r, 12r.

[24] The medieval hospital's acquisitions are described in detail in Rawcliffe, *Medicine for the Soul*, chap. 3, 'Estates and Finances'.

been held for centuries, a new source of revenue is recorded in the 1549–50 account roll. Although it escaped dissolution, St Giles' still fell victim to the asset strippers who sought to capitalise from the dismemberment of religious houses. Tiles, bricks and timber from the hospital precinct were sold off to be reused as building materials, and the considerable sum of £25 was received from Thomas Morley for the 'quere [*chancel*] with the pavemente' (paving slabs). The chancel was no longer needed for elaborate liturgical ceremonies and the civic authorities proposed to use the space to house a grammar school. As Bishop Latimer noted: 'the founding of monasteries [*and hospitals*] argued Purgatory to be, so the putting of them down argueth it not to be'.[25]

Leadership and Management

In the post-Dissolution period God's House was a civic institution and, therefore, important duties were carried out by aldermen appointed by the corporation. The auditors responsible for signing off the hospital's accounts were elected by the mayor and aldermen and were themselves either aldermen or members of the Common Council.[26] In Norwich, as in other major urban centres, ambitious officials transferred between posts, including those at God's House, as they rose up the civic hierarchy. Overall responsibility for the management of the hospital lay with the master. Covenants drawn up between the city authorities and each successive master provide invaluable detail about both parties' responsibilities.[27] Payment for purchasing victuals for the forty residents and their keepers, together with sufficient wood and coal, was made in advance so that the keeper always held money in hand. He was charged with supporting the residents 'in sycknes and in helth', along with their 'four women keepers', and for supplying them with suitable food. Perhaps anticipating the conflict that invariably arises in closed communites, the master (and his wife) were instructed that they should 'gently use and intreate the seid forty pore people and every of them at all tymes, withowt eny correccion or beating of them', and, as a final resort, 'to complayne to the surveyours of their mysdemeansours'. A book was to be kept listing all admissions into the house, as well as departures and deaths, presumably to ensure that the full quota of residents was always maintained. Bequests and gifts of 'bedding, shettis, shirtes and smockes, lynnen and woollen or monye' were to be recorded in a second book. Although the master was appointed by the authorities, a harmonious relationship could not be guaranteed. A graphic entry in the Mayor's Court Book, which highlights the difference between policy (the covenant) and practice, records:

> Whereas Master Mayour yestardaye [*9 December 1561*] was at the hospital with the too surveyours and called before hym Sir John Cawse, mynister there, and

[25] D.M. Palliser, 'Popular Reactions to the Reformation during the Years of Uncertainty 1530–70' in F. Heal and R. O'Day, eds, *Church and Society in England: Henry VIII to James* I (London and Basingstoke, 1977), pp.35–56.

[26] T. Hawes, *An Index to Norwich City Officials 1453–1835* (Norfolk Record Society, lii, 1986).

[27] For the 1566 agreement see Appendix 2.

examined hym for his boke of Christenying and buryall and desyrd to se yt, to whome answer was made there was none kepte. And then Master Mayour called Vyncent Tesmonde and his wyfe and examined them what boke they kepte of souche gyftes and benyvolence of lynen and woollen and other gyfts as have bene given to the same, and it was answeryd that they kepte none. Insomoche as the sayde Sir John Cawse, Vyncent Tesmond and his wife answeryd Master Mayour with stowte wordes, whiche Master Mayour rehersed openly in the courte, Vincent Tesmond beyng present, for the whiche wordes Vincent Tesmond sub-myttith hym selfe to th'order of this howse.[28]

Acts of charity

The main charitable purpose of the reformed hospital was to maintain forty poor persons and this is reflected in the accounts. Covering the naked had been one of the Seven Works of Mercy enjoined upon the pre-Reformation faithful and, even though the theological rationale behind the act had changed, it remained a charitable act laden with symbolism. 'Necessaries for the poore' in the 1549–50 account roll included 8s 9d spent on 'shoes boughte for the poore', and 'a bedstedde' purchased for 12d. In 1571 the civic author-ities noted with distaste that beggars in the city who displayed their 'flesh … eaton with vermyne and corrupte diseases … cared not for apparel', despite the cold.[29] Although sores, ulcers and other physical ailments were loathsome to behold, disgust at the symptoms of disease went beyond mere revulsion, because physical degeneration could (as was the case with the beggars) also represent moral decay. Moreover, the presence of semi-naked beggars in public places constituted a highly visible reminder of the failure of the civic authority to manage and support its poor.[30] Many of the larger medieval hos-pitals required their residents and staff to wear distinctive clothing, which not only served to advertise the generosity of the patron, but also indicated the wearer's social rank.[31] At God's House, thirteen of the forty residents wore gowns bearing the livery of the Company of St George to indicate both their allegiance to, and the generosity of, the Company, which had longstanding connections with the hospital.[32] Clothing the poor extended to the provision of bedding; and the mattresses and sheets at God's House undoubtedly exceeded the standards experienced by many of the city's poor.

The 'dyettes of forty poore folks with officers and kepers' came to around £91 and were similar to what was consumed by the majority of Norwich cit-

[28] NRO, NCR 16a/7, Mayor's Court Book 1555–1562, p.551.
[29] W. Hudson and J.C. Tingey, eds, *The Records of the City of Norwich*, 2 vols (Norwich, 1906–10) vol. 2, p.344.
[30] For an overview of this aspect of the city's history, see M. Pelling, *The Common Lot: Sickness, Medical Occupations and the Urban Poor in Early Modern England* (Harlow, 1996) and J. Pound, *The Norwich Census of the Poor* (Norfolk Record Society, xl, 1971).
[31] Orme and Webster, *The English Hospital*, pp.125–6.
[32] NRO, NCR 17b, Company of St George, Book 2, 1452–1602, p.197/94 (dual numbering).

izens in being fairly basic and dictated by availability and price. Bread and ale were standard hospital fare throughout England. This fact is reflected in the 1566 covenant between the incoming master, William Oliver, and the civic authorities, which states: 'they shalbe fedd with no courser bread then whole wheat bread withowt either rye or barley to be putt and myxed thereith' (Appendix 2). The ubiquity of bread as a staple meant that better quality and more finely milled grain was preferred, but the extent to which this preference could actually be exercised is questionable. Entries in the Mayor's Court Book, which record the current price of various foodstuffs, prosecutions for the sale of contaminated meat or fish, and vigilance in the matter of underweight or adulterated diary products, reflect the city authorities' constant concern with the quality of produce.[33] The hospital accounts refer to the purchase of a grinding stone for the mill, and control of the milling process may have helped to avoid problems commonly associated with adulterated flour. It is probable that fruit and vegetables from the hospital's own gardens and diary products from the 'milch cow' mentioned in a later account roll also formed part of the residents' diet, though they went unrecorded by the accountant.

Medical Care

The treatment on offer in God's House reflected what was available elsewhere as barbers and surgeons 'provided the staple of medical practice' in the city.[34] The 1549–50 account roll records payments of 66s 8d to 'Thomas Reignoldes surgeon to the poore this yere' and of 13s 4d to 'Belton barbour to the poore'. Surgeons were better qualified than barbers and could therefore demand a higher salary, though both received substantially less than would a qualified physician. The master of God's House was committed by his covenant to care for the poor in both sickness and in health, yet the accounts show that payments to medical practitioners and for medical treatment (as we would today understand it) never constituted a major outgoing. Whether this was the result of an admissions policy favouring comparatively healthy applicants, or simply reflects the presence of men and women whose complaints were chronic rather than acute, is difficult to tell. For the majority of residents, rest in warm, comparatively clean surroundings and regular food may have proved sufficient.

Caring for the sick was well established as a charitable act of particular relevance to women but it is impossible to know whether those who accepted such arduous and unremunerative employment were motivated by altruism or poverty. Women were active in nurturing roles, including midwifery, elsewhere in the city and formed an important part of the medical 'pool' from which the civic authorities could draw.[35] Payments in later accounts show that

[33] NRO, NCR 16a/8, Mayor's Court Book 1562–69, p.614.
[34] Pelling, *The Common Lot* explains the availability and hierarchy of medical practitioners, pp.203–58.
[35] Pelling, *The Common Lot*, chapter 8, 'Nurses and Nursekeepers: Problems of Identification in the Early Modern Period', discusses the role of female practitioners, pp.179–202.

female practitioners attended the poor in God's House, and, when specialist knowledge was required, the sexual divisions that usually obtained were temporarily blurred.

The 1549–50 account roll does not refer to specific diseases or medical conditions, although later rolls mention treatment of the 'pockes', the examination of a suspected leper, drawing of teeth, and several instances of ulcerated legs. The 'pockes', or French Pox, as syphilis was then known, was a debilitating and contagious disease which could render its victims unable to work for extended periods, as well as requiring specialised medical treatment and long-term nursing, all of which constituted a serious drain on the civic purse.[36] A transfer to one of the city's five former *leprosaria*, which the civic authorities also managed, might be arranged for those residents of God's House whose condition proved too demanding.

Education

The transition from chancel and choirboys to schoolhouse and scholars reflected contemporary concerns; educating members of the Commonwealth, as opposed to commemorating the dead, was now of primary importance. Expenditure on salaries included the substantial amount of £10 to the newly appointed schoolmaster, Walter Hawes. The 1547 re-foundation charter made provision for:

> one scholemaster and one ussher under hym suffityently lerned in the lateng tong and mete and hable … to teche and lerne chyldren th'art or scyence of grammar.[37]

The master, who was now selected by the mayor, aldermen and two surveyors, was expected to be 'a man hole in body honest and vertuous and lerned in good and cleane Latyn literature and allso in greeke, of sound religion [*and*] a graduate of som Universitie', capable of teaching 100 pupils, ten of them fee-payers.[38] In the following year the schoolmaster's salary was increased to £13 6s 8d and an additional teacher was employed. Education had always been part of the hospital's remit and remained an important function of God's House once it had been transferred to the city.

The 1547 Act for the Dissolution of Chantries linked improvements in education with the demise of 'superstitious' practices, and instruction in the catechism was an important part of the drive to install doctrinal orthodoxy. The civic authorities' efforts to establish the hospital school reflected humanist ideals and may have been influenced by Continental poor relief schemes, which incorporated education into wider programmes of care for the poor. When drawing up the ordinances for the poor relief scheme in Ypres in 1526

---

[36] For an overview of the disease, see J. Arrizabalaga, R.K. French and J. Henderson, *The Great Pox: the French Disease in Renaissance Europe* (New Haven and London, 1997).

[37] See Appendix 1.

[38] H.W. Saunders, *A History of Norwich Grammar School* (Norwich, 1932), p.138.

(which served as a model for many European schemes), Jan Luis Vives noted that, by selecting diligent teachers, magistrates would 'secure for the city over which they rule a great boon at small cost'.[39] There was no shortage of advice regarding the wider benefits of education to the Commonwealth; and a copy of one of the most influential and frequently reprinted works on this topic, Thomas Elyot's *The Boke Named the Governour* (1531), was owned by Nicholas Shaxton.[40] Then, as now, educating the young was an expensive business, and the Norwich authorities sought a good return for their investment.

Staff

Staffing arrangements are revealed in the 1549–50 account roll: payments were made to the master (Nicholas Shaxton), a curate and minister to the poor (John Fisher), a schoolmaster and an usher, a cook, five female keepers (nurses) and medical staff comprising a barber and a surgeon. In addition, the authorities employed administrative staff such as the receiver (or collector), who managed the finances and was responsible for drawing up the annual accounts, and surveyors who dealt with administrative and legal issues, together with various casually-employed individuals.

Actual 'hands on' care of the poor at God's House was a female preserve, this allocation of labour being typical of medieval and post-Dissolution hospitals. The 1547 re-foundation charter stated that four women were to 'make the beddes, wasshe and attend upon the seid poore persons'. The only mention of the nurses as individuals in the account rolls from between 1549 and 1600 appears in 1549–50, where they are described as keepers and their names are recorded as Ellen, Avelyn, Margaret Chapman, Elizabeth Cooke and Alice Norgate.[41] The women's work would have been laborious, especially the constant laundering.[42] That the sexual division of labour was generally unfavourable to women may be seen in John Fisher's complaint of 1550, in which he criticised the male residents for being unwilling to assist with the burial of the dead, as a consequence of which this onerous task fell to the women.[43] Little is known about the qualities the keepers were expected to possess or their reasons for embracing hospital life.

The Development of God's House

Analysis of the 1549–50 account reveals that the civic authorities' ambitious aim of turning St Giles' hospital into the centrepiece of the city's poor relief scheme had largely been achieved. At the same time, the division between

[39] F.R. Salter, ed., *Some Early Tracts on Poor Relief* (London, 1926), p.18.

[40] Rawcliffe, *Medicine for the Soul*, p.221.

[41] M. 14v.

[42] C. Rawcliffe, 'A Marginal Occupation? The Medieval Laundress and her Work', *Gender and History* 21, issue 1 (April 2009) pp.147–69.

[43] Hudson and Tingey, *Records of Norwich* vol. 2, p.388.

the deserving and the undeserving poor and their respective roles within the Commonwealth became more clearly delineated. By 1570, concern about the shiftless poor prompted renewed action.[44] The 1570–71 account roll was drawn up at a crucial time in the history of civic and national responses to endemic poverty. The Norwich Census of the Poor undertaken in 1570 revealed that around a quarter of the city's eleven thousand residents suffered some form of deprivation.[45] Un- or under-employment, ill-health, dependency upon alms, old age and the demands of childcare were factors that could propel a family from relative hardship to destitution. The Census also reported the large number of professional beggars attracted to the city by the generosity of its citizens. Indiscriminate charity resulted in an army of paupers who were, according to the civic authorities, not only idle, but brought up their children as social parasites.[46]

Completion of the Census allowed the civic authorities to understand the full extent of the problem they faced, and in the following year the Mayor's 'Orders for the Poor' were issued. Having summarised the task in hand, they set out proposals to deal with the social evils of 'synnes, vice and cryme'. The scheme had four main features: the sick were to be cared for until they were able to recommence work; children were to be educated or trained; the work-shy were to be punished; and employment was to be provided for people who had genuinely, but unsuccessfully, sought it. Continental poor relief schemes had hitherto been careful to distinguish between the respectable 'naturally abashed and ferful' and 'lustye beggers', and to deal more sensitively with the former.[47] The preamble to the 'Orders' warned that poverty and attendant ill-health suffered by the poor would inevitably cause a financial disaster. 'In fewe yeres', its authors predicted, 'a great parte of the revenues of the citie will skarse suffice to mayteyne them'.[48] Against this background, the payment recorded in the 1570–71 account roll to Edmond Smyth for 'forcying certeyne Egyptyans' (evicting 'gypsies')[49] from the city reflected contemporary concerns regarding the potential dangers posed by the vagrant poor.

As well as addressing the immediate problem of homeless beggars, the civic authorities looked to the future and made provision for twelve children, who were to be raised and educated in God's House before being apprenticed to a suitable trade. Though the actual number of children assisted by the scheme was relatively small, the contrast between the hospital's former role in training choristers to perform the liturgy and the new rationale of creating productive members of the commonwealth reflected an ideological and religious trans-

---

[44] For a discussion of attitudes to the poor c.1530–1553 and responses to problems in the later sixteenth century, see M. Keniston McIntosh, *Poor Relief in England 1350–1600* (Cambridge, 2012), chaps 5 and 7.

[45] Pound, *Census of the Poor*, pp.7–12.

[46] NRO, NCR 20c, Mayors Book of the Poor 1571–79, preamble, no page numbering.

[47] Salter, *Early Tracts on Poor Relief*, pp.54–9.

[48] NRO, NCR 20c, Mayor's Book of the Poor 1571–79, preamble.

[49] M. 9r.

formation. By 1570, the schoolmaster's salary had risen to £20 and that of the usher or sub-master to £13 6s 8d. The schoolmaster, Stephen Lymbert, augmented his income by preaching in various churches, and must have been an impressive orator because he was selected by the authorities to make a speech to honour Queen Elizabeth as she progressed through Norwich in 1578.[50] The educational value of sermons was as important in the later sixteenth century as it had been earlier, though John Fisher's complaint of 1550 showed that the residents of God's House had not always greeted the prospect with enthusiasm. He criticised the men and women who 'wyl nat cum to the sermunnys at Chryst Chyrch [*Norwich Cathedral*], do the best I cane, wan they ar able to goo al the cyte ouer and sume of them the cuntry also'.[51] The pedagogic role of God's House also extended to higher education through its management of an endowment made by Matthew Parker, Archbishop of Canterbury. The account roll records a payment of £8 to the master and fellows of Corpus Christi College, Cambridge to support three scholars.[52] As we have seen, schooling the young had been prioritised in the re-foundation charter of 1547; by 1550 the hospital had acquired the Charnel in the cathedral close for the use of the school, and the civic authorities continued to regard education as a means of social reformation.

The 1570–71 account roll provides evidence of extensive renovation and rebuilding on the estates at Hethel, at 'Master Coddes', at the Charnel (by then the Norwich grammar school) and at God's House itself. Maintenance of the hospital's assets, as apparent from the multiple entries for payments to shore up 'the reede whiche felle downe', to repair collapsed walls, and for fencing and clearing ditches, must have seemed an interminable drain on the resources, though a necessary and unavoidable part of any landlord's responsibilities. Sums expended on thatchers, carpenters, 'dawbers' (plasterers), masons, blacksmiths and glaziers, together with their servants, labourers and apprentices, constituted a major outgoing, and the accountant was careful to note daily rates of pay. As well as providing a valuable source of information about the building trades in the sixteenth century, the 1570–71 account roll supplements the surviving architectural evidence concerning the changed usage of the hospital. Payments made for building a new chimney with a 'maintree' (mantelpiece) 'in the new lodging hows',[53] which also contained 'new beddes for the poore people', may refer to the vertical partitions that were constructed to separate the parish church of St Helen from the infirmary hall and chancel. The wards at both ends were horizontally divided to become two-storey buildings and a new chimney was erected where the high altar had previously stood. Female residents were accommodated in the

[50] Lymbert's speech is recorded in D. Galloway, ed., *Records of Early English Drama: Norwich 1540–62* (Toronto, 1984), pp.266–71.

[51] Hudson and Tingey, *Records of Norwich*, vol. 2, pp.387–9.

[52] M. 8r.

[53] M. 11v.

former chancel and men dwelt in the infirmary. The act of housing women in what had been the sacred space of the chancel, hitherto the preserve of male priests and reserved for the celebration of the Mass, served conspicuously to reinforce the division between old and new orthodoxies.

Changes to the hospital layout and administration may have made it inconvenient or unsafe to store the records on site. The accountant recorded payments totalling £9 for work on a hospital treasury in the city guildhall. The purchase of keys and boxes (presumably wooden chests) indicate an increased need for security. Once the treasury was ready for use (3d having been paid 'for carrying charcoal thither which was brent theare to ayre the chamber and bookes with'), 'the loose wrytynges [were carried] owt of the oulde treasourye into the newe'. The 'old accomptes' may have been stored on 'all the shelves on th'one side of the treasourye' for ease of reference. Maintaining accurate records had been important for medieval hospitals and continued to be so for God's House.[54] As an important civic institution and a key part of the city's poor relief scheme, it was vital that the hospital should be competently managed and that accurate accounts should be promptly rendered each year.

The 1570–71 roll shows that God's House was on a sufficiently firm financial footing to undertake major expansion and renovation whilst continuing to provide care for the resident poor. Arrears had been brought under control and the hospital was in the process of consolidating disparate holdings and acquiring more properties to support its charitable work.

Conclusion

Of all the charitable institutions in Norwich that fell within the post-Dissolution poor relief scheme, God's House received the highest and most sustained level of civic support. In the late 1540s, plans to acquire the hospital had been set in motion and substantial sums expended to meet the costs. By the time that the 1570–71 account roll was drawn up, the authorities had established an integrated system of poor relief based around existing parish structures and incorporating the more successful medieval hospitals and *leprosaria*. The genuinely needy were cared for at God's House and some of the former leper houses, while St Paul's was transformed into a Bridewell; and efforts to curtail damage caused by the apparently feckless poor, both to themselves and to the Commonwealth, became more repressive. Within this wider scheme, God's House was the pre-eminent charitable establishment in the city. By 1571, Bishop Walter Suffield's hospital was simultaneously a bulwark against the threat posed to the Commonwealth by the disaffected poor and a showpiece for civic policy.[55]

[54] The importance of maintaining accurate records is discussed in C. Rawcliffe, 'Passports to Paradise: How English Medieval Hospitals Kept their Archives', *Archives*, 27, 2002, pp. 2–22.

[55] The city's policy regarding the poor has been described as mingling 'medical, moral and environmental concerns with alarms about law and order in a sweeping indictment of a city in distress': P. Griffiths, 'Inhabitants' in Rawcliffe and Wilson, *Norwich since 1550*, pp.63–88.

The Account Rolls

The account rolls of the Great Hospital constitute a unique source of documentary evidence for the hospital and the wider social, religious and economic life of the city.[56] The sixteenth-century accounts are part of a much longer run held by the Norfolk Record Office which covers the early fourteenth to the twentieth century. As the complexity of the hospital's financial arrangements increased, the account rolls grew correspondingly in size: the 1549–50 roll is 31cm×34cm, but by 1570–71 the dimensions had grown to 34cm×58cm and the roll comprised a greater number of membranes. Another difference is that the 1549–50 roll is written on paper, while the 1570–71 roll is on parchment. The two rolls cast valuable light upon the financial health of the hospital and provide a fascinating insight into the management of the city's most prestigious institution. However, one cannot apply modern standards of profit and loss accountancy to a system whose primary aim was to ensure that the hospital was being properly and honestly run. It has been observed, with regard to later medieval practice, that although 'the basis of the account [changed] from an estimate of the liability of the accounting official to an estimate of yearly profit and loss' the need to keep a check on employees still came first.[57]

Both the 1549–50 and 1570–71 rolls follow a standard format which had changed little from the Middle Ages.[58] Each account covers the year running from the feast of the Nativity of St John the Baptist (24 June) to the same feast twelve months later. Charges (or receipts) preceded discharges (or outgoings), but the receiver or collector first noted any arrearages (or uncollected receipts carried over from the previous year) which, in most cases, were added to the current charge. The extent of the personal liability of the receiver can be seen in the arrears section at the start of the 1570–71 account, where the new receiver, Thomas Corye the younger, notes 'the seyd accomptaunt is not to be chardged with tharrearages ... for that this is his fyrst accompt'. Such a task was a serious undertaking; the failure of Nicholas Graves successfully to manage the finances of Hugh atte Fenne's almshouse in Herringby resulted in his prosecution for debt in the court of Chancery.[59]

A list of the year's rents and any supplementary income, such as gifts or legacies, which were known as 'foreign (i.e. extraneous) receipts', then followed. Income derived from leasing out properties or land was entered under two separate headings by 1570–71; rents from the city of Norwich were noted first and then receipts from holdings in Norfolk, Suffolk and Essex, which

---

[56] NRO, NCR 24a, Great Hospital account rolls. For a discussion of hospital archives see Rawcliffe, 'Passports to Paradise'.

[57] C.D. Ross and T.B. Pugh, 'Materials for the Study of Baronial Incomes in Fifteenth Century England', *Economic History Review*, 2nd Series 6 (1953), pp.185–94.

[58] The system of accounting is described in detail in Rawcliffe, *Medicine for the Soul*, pp.66–70.

[59] TNA, C1/421/48.

yielded a greater income. The section marked 'foreign receipts' is the most varied and in many ways the most interesting part of the charge, as it lists major financial transactions, such as sums borrowed from the city, which were usually intended to fund the purchase of more property or land. The acquisition of additional holdings reflected longer-term investment by the corporation, whose members sensibly decided not to rely on *ad-hoc* legacies and gifts to increase regular income, especially in a period of inflation.

In the discharge (or outgoings) section of the accounts the receiver first noted payments made 'by charter' on behalf of the city authorities, that is in accordance with the indenture tripartite refounding the hospital in 1547. Entries in this section record the number and wages of hospital staff, as well as expenditure on the diet and board of the residents and their nurses. Regular outgoings, such as pensions, annuities, rewards, legal costs and other day-to-day expenses then followed. The less lucrative aspects of owning land and property are revealed by continuous and often substantial payments for the maintenance of buildings at various sites. At the other extreme, purchases costing a few pennies reflect the *minutiae* of daily life within the hospital and the overriding concern with the accountant's honesty. Allowances made to him for additional payments or, more usually, for unpaid rents which he simply could not collect, also had to be considered. Miscellaneous payments were separated from persistently overdue rents, which were generally grouped at the very end under the separate heading of 'remayneth'.

Finally, the account was scrutinised for any signs of creative accounting. One can still see strokes and dots in the margin denoting how figures recorded on parchment in Roman numerals were actually expressed in counters on the auditor's chequer-board. If all was in order, the account was signed by the surveyors (the city officials charged with overseeing the management of the hospital) as being a true and accurate record. Following the takeover of the hospital by the city, the accounts were written in English rather than in Latin as they had been previously. Latin would not have been understood by some of the auditors and surveyors who verified the accounts and were generally merchants or artisans. The switch was more than a practical solution to a linguistic problem; it marked a new Protestant regime, which is nowhere more obvious than in the change of the hospital's name from its Catholic invocation of 'St Giles' to the pragmatic 'God's House', or the 'House of the Poor People on Holme Street'. Caring for the body, both of the individual and of the wider commonwealth, now took precedence over care of the soul.

Acknowledgements

I am grateful to the Norfolk Record Office for permission to reproduce the material here and to the staff at the NRO who answered numerous queries. Many colleagues deserve thanks for their support during the long process of producing this edition, especially Steve Cherry, Christopher Harper-Bill,

Peregrine Horden and David King. Carole Rawcliffe commented on the text and offered many helpful suggestions and clarifications. Elizabeth and Paul Rutledge guided the edition from start to finish and made useful points along the way, for which I am grateful. I would also like to thank Phillip Judge, for the use of his parish map, and Isla Fay, for discussion about our joint interests.

Editorial note

Within the transcription, the symbols * * indicate words which have been inserted and < > words which have been deleted. [*italics*] indicates editorial remark within the text and /*italics*/ a marginal entry or annotation. Roman numerals have been converted into Arabic.

The Account Rolls
1549–50 and 1570–71

ACCOUNT ROLL 1549–50[1]

[*m. 1r*] Thaccompt of Thomas Kyng collectour of all and singuler rentes revenues and proufightes of the hooll possessions of the late hospitall of St Gyles nowe called Goddes House or the house of the poore peopull in Holmestrete within the Cittie of Norwich[2] with thappurtenances to the same bilonging or apperteigning aswell within the seide Cittie as the countye of Norfolk and elleswhere. And also of all manere of forreyn receiptes groweng to the same for one hooll yere that is to saye from the feast of the Nativitie of St John Baptist [24 June 1549] in the thredde yere of the reign of our sovereign Lorde King Edwarde the syxte by the grace of God of Englande Fraunce and Irelande defendour of the feyth and in earth of the Church of Englande and Irelande cheif and supreme head, untill the same feaste of Saint John from thens next ensuing in the fourte yere of our seide sovereign Lorde the King his Maiesties reign

The scite of the place with the church there[3]

Of my lorde Shaxton for a quartour ferme of the seyte of thospitall
with the yerdes groundes and medews with the precynte of the same
<for a quartour> of [*sic*] endid at Michaelmas within the tyme of this
accompte 33s 4d. And of Master Necton alderman for a nother
quartour ferme of the same *viz* from Our Lady thannunciacion
untyll Mydsomer upon the determynacion of this accompte 33s 4d.
And as concerning thother half yere the seide place was destitute
of a fermour by reason of the comoycion and brynnyng of the
houses there from Mychaelmas unto Our Lady so charged this yere   66s 8d

Of John Fyssher clerke for the tythe offering and other proufightes
groweng and coming of the rectory of St Ellen churche there within
the scyte of the same place for the hooll yere within this accompt for
that the hooll strete whiche belong to the same is brente by the
rebelles in the comoycion tyme therefore charged here   *nihil*

Woodsale there this yere within the scyte of the seide place and tymber   20d

[*Total*]   68s 4d

---

[1] NRO, NCR 24a, Great Hospital account rolls.
[2] Holmstreet was the present Bishopgate. For the location of the Great Hospital within Norwich see Figure 2.
[3] The headings and the section totals have been brought in from the margins without comment.

[*m. 1v blank*]

[*m. 2r*] **Holmstrete**

Of Richarde Thorrolde and Thomas Hamond and John Sharborn
for thole yeare ferme of the first tenement all next unto the place   12s

Of Robert Towe John Blewet and the seide John Sharborn for thole
yere ferme of the nexte tenement towardes Bisshoppgates   10s

Of William Eche and Robert Heyman for the hooll yere ferme of the
thredd tenement adioyning   10s

Of John Dukker for the ferme of one voyde grounde lately buylded
being 4 tenementes <graunted> brent by the rebelles graunted to
him at 26s 8d by yere for the terme of three quartours *viz* from
Mychaelmas unto Mydsomer uppon the determynacion of this
accompte the some of   20s

Of Master Cotton and Sir John Fyssher for the voyde groundes next
adioyning late buylded a tenement and brent by the rebelles with
an osyeryerde for the hole yere ended at Michaelmas   13s 4d

Of Master Codde alderman Thomas Whalle Thomas Pecke and
Thomas Bemonde for the voyde groundes next adioyning <to the
ryver> fromthens to the ryver syde late buylded and brente by the
rebelles *viz* seven tenementes two meeses with three houses by
the ryver side and one medow thereunto adioyning graunted to them
at 60s by yere for the terme of one quartour ended at
Mydsomer uppon the determynacion of this accompte   15s

                                               [*Total*]   £4 4d

St Vedastes[4]

Of Thomas Burman for one hooll yere ferme of a meese called
Skypwythes Place ended at Michaelmas last   28s

Of Master Henry Fuller alderman for a close theare by for the
holl yere ferme thereof   20s

Of Robert Emmes for hole yeres ferme of a nother close there   16s 8d

Of John Walpoole for the hooll yere ferme of a litell grounde late
in the tenure of John Fellow   6s 8d

Of Felyx Puttok alderman for the hoolle yere ferme of a litell
ground lieng in the same parisshe late William Myngaye   3s 4d

Of Alexander Mather for the hooll yere ferme of a close there
late John Fellowe   6s 8d

    [4] For the Norwich parishes see Figure 1.

Of Master Augusten Stywarde alderman for a close and other grounde there by the hooll yere		20s
Of Adryan Mace for an osyeryerde there		1d
	[*Total*]	£5 17d

[*m. 2v blank*]

[*m. 3r*] **St Augustene**

Of Master Thomas Codde alderman for the hooll yere ferme of the place called the Lathes with thappurtenances with certen landes in Catton and by Norwich payeable at Our Lady and Mychaelmas		£4 15s
Of William White for one hooll yere ferme of a tenement with a garden there		8s
	[*Total*]	£5 3s

St Peters of Mancrofte

Redditus assise

Of the churchewardens there for rente by yere	12d
Of the chambleyn of the cittie of Norwiche for rentes by yere	13s 4d
Of Thomas Conye for rente	4d
[*End of assise rent but no total given*]	

Of the seide Thomas Coney for ferme of a tenemente whiche he holdethe by yere		12d
Of John Bengeamyn for a nothere tenement there		6s 8d
	[*Total*]	22s 4d

St Crouches

Of Master Robert Rug alderman for the hooll yere ferme of a garden there by yere		5s
Of John Beverley for the ferme of a nother garden late John Melton by yere		20d
	[*Total*]	6s 8d

St Stephenes

Redditus assise

Of Henry Holden for rent of a tenement in the same parisshe by yere	13d
Of Margaret Grene now Thomas Larwoode for rente of a tenement by yere	4s
Of Richard Hedde for rent of a tenement there by yere	12d
[*Total*]	6s 1d

All Seinctes

Redditus assise

Of John White scolemaster now Michaell Clerke for rente of a
tenement in the same parisshe [*by*] yere   1d
Of John Awsten for rente by yere   12d
                                                    [*Total*]   13d

St Martenes at the Pallacegate

Of the Lady Calthorpp for the hooll yere ferme of the scholehouse
with thappurtenances and a tenement   10s 8d

Of William Brigges for the first tenement by yere   8s

Of John Leche for the seconde tenement by yere   6s 8d

Of the Lady Calthorpp for the 3rd tenement by yere   7s

The 4th tenement is in lease with the scholehouse   *nihil*

Of Walter Spycer for the 5th tenement by yere   4s

Of Margaret Hulle for the 6th tenement by yere   4s

Of John Bartylmewe for the 7th tenement by yere   8s

                                                    [*Total*]   58s 4d

[*m. 3v blank*]

[*m. 4r*] **St Simon and Jude**

Redditus assise

Of John Revell the yonger for rente there by yere   51d
Of Alexander Mather for rente   4d
Of the seide Alexander for rente   4d
[*End of assise rent but no total given*]

Of John Ling for a garden there by yere   3s 4d

Of Nicholas Norgate for a tenement by yere   10s

                                                    [*Total*]   14s 2d

St Andrew

Of Thomas Marsham alderman for the hooll yere ferme of a parcell
of grounde late voyde and by him nowe buylded in the same parisshe   20d

St Martenes in Coslany

Redditus assise

Of Thomas Hering for rente of a tenement there by yere	4d
Of John Bungay for two tenementes lieng nexte rente by yere	6d
Of Gylbert Martens for a tenement nexte by yere	52d
Of Robert Harrolde for his tenement	52d
Of Bryan Taylour for two tenementes there by yere	6d
Of John Bungay for two tenementes there by the yere	12d
[*End of assise rent but no total given*]	

Of John Bungay for ferme of a close at Michaelmas	3s 4d
Of Robert Grene for a nother close there	5s 1d
Of Master Bryan Taylour for ferme of a close at Michaelmas there	10s 4d
Of Thomas Drury for a tenement late Thomas Bull	<8s> 9s
Of Hewe Albon adioyning thereto by yere	<8s> 9s
Of Nicholas Chylde for a nother tenement there	6s 8d
[*Total*]	46s 3d

St Peters at Southgate

Of Edmund Browne for the hooll yeres ferme of a tenement there by yere	8s

St Edwardes

Of William Stephenson for a voyde grounde late a tenement buylded and brente by the rebelles in Connesford late in ferme for 8s by yere now graunted to Leonarde Sotherton for thole yere endid at Mydsomer last	4s

St Johns Sepulcre

Of Edmunde Tooly bocher for one half yere ferme of a close sometyme Bisshoppe Goldewelles[5] lande dewe at Midsomer upon the determynacion of this accompt	8s 4d

[*m. 4v blank*]

[*m. 5r*] St Bartilmew

Of Agnes Cannerde wedowe for one half yere ferme of a close sometyme Bisshopp Goldewelles landes at Mydsomer	11s 8d

---

[5] Bishop Goldwell: bishop of Norwich 1472–99.

St Michaelles

Of John Fyssher bocher for the half yere ferme of a close sometyme
Bisshopp Goldewelles landes at Mydsomer   16s 8d

Redditus assise.

   Of Henry Harpour bocher for rente of a tenement by yere   2s

                                            [*Total*]   18s 8d

St Margaretes at Fibrig gates

Of Thomas Wolman for a tenement gyven to this house by [*the*]
Masters Scholehouse lieng by the northe syde of St Margaret chappell
for the hooll yere at Mydsomer   12d

All Sainctes in Fybrigg

Of Robert Sucklyn for the ferme of the parisshe churche yerde of
All Sainctes in Fybrig graunted to him for the yerely ferme of 6s 8d   *nihil quia*
nothing charged here for that his terme begyn at Mydsomer   *primus annus*

St Saviours and St Botulphs

Of Richarde Wheteley for the hooll yere ferme of a meese and groundes
late gyven to this house by Master Woode alderman decessed   40s

Of Roberte Reignoldes for the hooll yere ferme of a tenement and
grounde late gyven by the seide Master Woode at Mydsomer   <1> 25s <8d>

Of Thomas Chamber for the hooll yere ferme of a tenement and
grounde gyven also by him dewe at Midsomer   26s 8d

Of Thomas Burman for thole yere ferme of an orcheyerde to the
seide tenement adioyening <for> at Mydsomere   33s 4d

                                  [*No total given*]

St Clementes in Consford

Of Thomas Howell for ferme of the parishe churche and churche
yerde of <the> St Clemente graunted to him for 20s by yere he
bering reparacions nothing charged here for his terme begyn at   *nihil quia*
Mydsomer   *primus annus*

[*m. 5v*] **Summa totalis** of all the rentes fermes and possessions within
the cittie of Norwich this yere   £33 9s 8d

/ *Burman 13s 4d/* [6]

   [6] This is presumably related to the Thomas Burman entry under St Saviour's, above.

NORFOLK

[*m. 6r*] Swanington

Of Thomas Mego fermour of a meese with thappurtenances in Swannyngton with all pastures feadinges medews landes arrrabyll marisshes allercarres lieng in Swannyngton Heverlande [*Haveringland*] and other townes adioyning late in the tenure of Richarde Elyson payeable at Our Lady and Michaelmas within this accompt   58s 4d

Sprouston

Of John Corbet esquyer for certen landes pastures feadinges groves arable lande moredoles[7] with thappurtenances in Sprouston by yere graunted to him and his heyres at Michaelmas   12s 4d

Catton

Of certen landes lieng in Catton nowe graunted with the Lathes in the cittie in the parisshe of St Austen to ferme therefore they be charged here   *nihil*

Newton

Of Robert Osbern of Kyrby Bedon gente for a pece of marisshe grounde lieng in Newton in a mersshe there by the Glotton for ferme of the same by yere   18d

Carrowe

Of Master Doctour Manfeld for a rede mersh nighe unto Carrowe place called Paradyse for the yerely ferme therof at Michaelmas   12d

Horsted

Of Robert Clerke gent for ferme of an acre of lande in the same towne by yere   6d

Lympenhowe

Of Ser John Clere knight for the yerelye ferme of a marysshe in Lympenhowe late in the tenure of James Underwoode   5s

Redeham

Of the Bisshopp of Norwich for a certen annuytie going oute of the mannour of Redeham yerely payeable at Michaelmas   26s 8d

---

[7] Portions of wet common.

[*m. 6v blank*]

[*m. 7r*] **The manour of Cringleford**

Of the fre and coppieholders for their rentes of the mannour there
payeable at St Hyllary as particulerly apperithe in the rentall
thereof made by the yere   £10 15s 3½d

Of thexecutours of Sir Richarde Gressham of London knight for
the yerely ferme of the mannour there called Heylesdon with
thappurtenances payeable at Our Lady and Michaelmas within
the tyme of this accompte   £5 13s 4d

Of Robert Akers for the yerely ferme of the water mylne with the
myllehouse and other house adioyning to the same with the fysshing
in the mylne dame and with fysshing in the waters perteyning to the
mannours of Cringleford with the hookewoode[8] in the mylle dame
growing together with a close and an acre of lande payeable at
Michaelmas Cristmas Our Lady and Mydsomer even porcions   100s

Of Edwarde Ostery clerke for the hooll yere ferme of the rectory
there with all tythes alterages and all other comodyties and of the
prestes chamber garden and churchyerde at Mychaelmas   3s 4d

                                    [*Total of rents*]   £26 11s 11½d

Woodesale there   *nihil hoc anno*
Perquisites of courte   6s

                                             [*Total*]   £26 17s 11½d

Costessey and Ryngland

Rentes

Of the heyres of Robert Grey for a 3 roode of lands parcell of
2 acres in one pece late John Gothe   9½d

Of [*blank*] for certen landes late Humfrey Smalpece   2s 2d

Of [*blank*] for certen landes late the seide Smalpece before Roger Pettite   12d

Of [*blank*] for certen landes late the forseide Smalpece before Thomas Neve   2d

Of [*blank*] Laverok for rente of 3 roodes of lande called St Mary
roodes late the foreseide Smalpece before John Stokes   1½d

Of Richard Aldriche for ferme of a close late in ferme of Avelyn
Newman for 4s 8d by yere and now letten to him for   2s 8d

                                    [*Total of rents*]   £10 16s 11d

---

[8] For 'hookwoode' and other unfamiliar terms see General glossary.

Wodesale there   *nihil hoc anno*

Tythe conyes[9]   *nihil hoc anno*

                                    [*Total*]   £10 16s 11d

[*m. 7v blank*]

[*m. 8r*] **Trowce Rokeltes**

Of Master William Rogers alderman for the hooll yeres ferme of the
mannour there called Rockeltes with all landes tenementes liberties
faldercourse rentes servyces belonging to the same in Trowse and
Byskeley with 3 hylles of feding called Blakes Hylles with the
swannesmarke called Blakes swan marke[10] with all proufightes to
the same payeable at Lammas Hallowmas Candlemas and Crochemas   £4 5s

Trowse Blakes

Of Robert Howlyns for the hooll yere ferme of all that meese or place
called Blakes with houses inclose medews fedinges pastures and
with all other arrabyll landes in Trowse and Byskeley at 4 termes
viz Michaelmas Cristmas Our Lady Mydsomer   £4 3s 4d

Horsforth

Of John Gybbes for certen landes and tenementes medewes
feadinges pasture woodes and underwoode lieing in the feldes of
Horsforth and Horsham St Feyth payeable at Michaelmas   21s 9½d

Cowteshale

Of Walter Basepoole for the hooll yere ferme of 63 acres and
3 roodes of lande with thappurtenances lieng in Colteshale and
other townes adioyning payeable at Candelmas   26s 8d

Salhouse cum Wroxham

Of Hugh Spendelove for the yerely ferme of a meese or place in
Salhouse with certen inclose thereunto adioyning 2 fysshinges called
Holdes and other fysshinges and certen landes in Salhouse one close
called Stormes with an osyeryerde and of one tenement with
9 acres lande in Wroxham payeable at Candelmas and Crochemas   68s

Of Thomas Moyne for 2 acres of lande   15d

Of Henry Pyg for 2 acres in 2 peces and 3 roodes lieng in 2 peeces by yere   12d

---

[9] Rabbits payable as tithe.
[10] Land called 'Blackes Hilles' and a 'marke of the swannys called ... by the name of Blakes
Swane Marke' together with the swans bearing the mark was purchased in 1498: Rawcliffe,
Medicine for the Soul, p.93.

Of Thomas Eche for certen landes	2s 2d
Of the same Thomas for other landes	12d
Of William House for landes and fysshinges there by the yere	3s
Of Robert Chapman for certen landes	3s 3d
Of Thomas Langman for certen landes	9d
Of the same Thomas for other landes	12d
Of Richarde Lawes for certen landes	18d
Wodesale or tymber	*nihil hoc anno*
[*Total*]	£4 2s 11d

[*m. 8v blank*]

[*m. 9r*] Calthorpe Erpingham Wolterton Wikmere

The rentes of certen landes in Calthorpp Bannyngham Erpingham and other townes by yere	3s 10½d
Of John Bonde for a tenement and houses there and 15 acres of lande by yere	18s
Of Robert Whalle for 3 acres of medewe at called [*sic*] Skarrowe Medewe by yere	3s
Of Alane Colmere for the herbage of the Myllecarre <called>	
Of William Tubbing for the hooll yere ferme of the tythe cornes of Calthorpp and the berne payeable at Candelmas Hallowmas and Crouchemas by the yere	£5
Of Master Moore of Wolterton for ferme of twenty acres of land and 2 peces with a pitell	13s 4d
The same Thomas[11] 3 combes of [*sic*] *2 busehelles* of maulte and he to have for the same allowed him and the bringing thereof home yerely at 20d the combe	3 combe & 2 bushells malte
Memorandum this barley is solde the bailyf this yere at 2s the combe he payeng Master Moore so in this charge	14d
Of Henry Harwarde gent for a yarde called Rydlingford there by the yere	10d
Of Master Lownour for 2 peces of lande cont[*aining*] an acre for ferme by the yere	12d
Of Thomas Langdon gente for an halfe acre of pasture the ferme by yere	6d

---

[11] Possibly Master Moore, as there is no previous Thomas in this section.

Of Robert Kyttes for ferme of half acre 2 peces   6d

Of James Lubbok for ferm of eighte acres of lande lieng in Wikmere by yere   4s

Of the same James for the seide grounde pryced at 2s the combe *summa* 8 combes
barley and so graunted yerely to the bailif by the surveyours   16s

Of Thomas Gylbert for ferme of 4 acres and [a] half in Erpingham by the yere 5s

Of Joachim Smetten for 4 acres and [a] half in the same towne by yere   5s

[*Total*]   £8 18s 7½d

Woodesale there   *nihil*

Item when the vycar dye he shall pay his best horse oxe or cowe
for a haryette [*heriot*]

Hardeley

Redditus assise

Of William Drake gente	20s
The same William	2d
Robert Bunne	4s 7d
John Quayntrell	2s 8d
John Skerming	4s
The seide William Drake for lande late John Penteney	4d

Of the seide William Drake for the ferme of all the tythe cornes and
rectory there payeable at Lammas and Candelmas by yere   66s 8d

[*Total*]   £4 18s 5d

Wodesale this yere   *nihil hoc anno*

[*m.9v blank*]

[*m. 10r*] **The manour of Mundham and Sething**

Of the free and coppye holders there for the rentes of ther landes as
apperith particulerly by the rentall thereof made by the yere   £4 7s 11½d

Of William Sponer for the hooll yere ferme of the tythe bernes
and cornes of the benefyce of Sething payeable at Lammes   £8 13s 4d

Of rentes of 2 capons there yerley pryce   8d

Of the fre and coppie holders for there rentes of assyse of ther
landes as apperith perticulerly in the rentall thereof made   £9 14s <11> 7d

Of the wife of John Woodyarde for the hooll yere ferme of the
tythe berne and cornes belonging to the rectory of Mundham
payeable at Lammas Cristmas and Our Ladye   £10

	[*Total of rents*] £32 16s 6½d
Woodesale there	*nihil hoc anno*
Perquisite of the courtes of Sething and Mundham	26s 7d
	[*Total*] £33 18s 1½d

The manour of Hethill and Carleton

Of the free and coppye holders of the mannours there for thole yere rentes of assise of their landes as perticulerly appere by rentalles	£11 4s 8d
Of rentes there also by yere 2 capons price	8d
Woodesale this yere	*nihil hoc anno*
Perquisites of courtes	6d
	[*Total*] £11 5s 10d

Southwalsham

Of John Kytbalde for the hooll yere ferme of the rectory berne with all the tythe cornes belonging to the same payeable at Cristmas Our Lady and Mydsomer	<£11> £12

Birlingham Beighton and Lingwoode

Of Nicholas Howlet for 21 acres and halfe of lande lieng in Southbirlingham in 6 peces	12s 6d
Of William Reignoldes and Roger Reignoldes for ten acres and halfe in nyne peces in Birlingham Lingwoode and Beighton by yere	6s 10d
Of Thomas Leman for 6 acres lieng in 2 peces in Birlingham by yere	3s 7d
Of John Reignoldes for 5 acres of landes with thappurtenances in Birlingham and Lingwoode	2s 11d
	[*Total*] 25s 10d

[*m. 10v blank*]

[*m. 11r*] **Rollesbye**

Of John Ufford for rente of a tenemente late Jollyes by yere	18 <£> d
Of Henry Norwiche for the hooll yere ferme of <the> all the meese or place ther with landes medews fedinges pastures closures hethgrounds in Rollesby and other townes adioyninge payeable at Candelmas and Crochemas the some of	£6
Woodsale there this year	*nihil*
	[*Total*] £6 18d

Reppes and Bastwik

Of William Woode for the hooll yere ferme of tythe berne and
tythe cornes there with thalterages and glebes of the benefyces of
Reppes with the chappell of Bastwik payeable at Candelmas and
Crouchemas £10

Fobbing in Essex

Of John Shaxburgh gent and Roberte Brown of Hadley in Essex for
the hoolle yere ferme of 2 marysshes called Fangewik and Bolif late
in the ferme of William Hale payeable at Michaelmas and Mydsomer £13 6s 8d

Tweighte [*Suffolk*]

Of Edwarde Reve of Twaighte for a certen annuitie there by yere 53s 4d

Summa totalis of all the rentes fermes revenues of the seide house
within Norfolk Suffolk and Essex as before it doethe appere £162 8s 3d

[*m. 11v blank*]

[*m. 12r*] **The forreyn receiptes** this year with casualities
[*irregular income*]

Of Robert Reignoldes chamberleyn for the pryce of a lytell house
within the scyte of the hospitall standing by the water syde solde to
hym by Master Marsham and Master Mather surveyours with
thadvyce of Master Codde mayour and others besides the thake
tyle uppon the same the some of 50s

Of Master Thomas Marsham alderman surveyour for 8 thousande
thak tyle receyved by him there in the seide place at 6s 8d the
thousand 53s 4d

Of Thomas Grey and John Bengeamyn for the pryce of the long
entrye and twoo other crosse houses with the same and the tyle uppon
them solde by the seide surveyours and others for the some of £7

Of Thomas Morley alderman for the quere with the pavemente in
the same and all other thinges there solde to him by the seide
surveyours the some £25

Of Master Marsham alderman for 8 loodes of breke and brekes endes
receyved by him out of the place and brente groundes to the water
syde by his owne declaracion pryced at 20d the loode 13s 4d

Of him for certen olde tymber whiche was ther pryced nowe at this
accompte 3s 4d

Of Christopher Soham for the pryce of the parysshe churche of
All Sainctes in Fybrig with all the leade tymber 3 belles glasse
iron stoon and all thinges therin solde to him by the seide surveyours
in the hooll for the some of   £10

Memorandum a rente of 6s 8d yerely for the church yerde   *nihil hic quia*
                                                                                                         primus annus

And also a peyer of challeis [*chalices*] remayning in one Boxforthes
handes whiche Master Bacon promysede to be delyvered at all
tymes, being broughte before Master Rug mayour by the seid
Boxforth Catby and dyvers other of the parissheoners the same peir
of challeis cont[*aining*] in weight tenne ounces priced at 5s thounce
summa 50s whereof delivered to the parissheoners aswell of a debt
2s 8d as also in rewarde to them by Master Mayour order 8d
summa 3s 4d. So there in charge nowe   46s 8d

[*m. 12v blank*]

[*m. 13r*] Of Leonarde Sotherton and John Reede for the pryce of
the north ale of the parisshe churche of St Clementes in Conessford
with all the leade there, and two belles solde to them by the seide
surveyours for the some of   £27 2s 6d

Of Master Marsham for dyvers thinges solde by him there as
appereth perticulerly by a byll thereof made the some of   £4 7s 2d

Of Master Codde alderman and Master Mather for all the marbyll
stones and other pavementes within the seide churche and quere
reserving the ale and the vestrye solde to them for the some of   30s

Memorandum remayning the handes of Master Codde a peir of
chales too handbelles and certen other thinges which belonged to
the seide churche

Memorandum a rente reserved to this house for the seide   *nihil hic quia*
churche and churche yerde of 20s by yere   *primus annus*

Memorandum for coopes vestmentes and other superfluous
ornamentes now perteyning to the churche of St Awdry[12] and they
of righte ought to belong to the hospitall

Of him for a stooll or a pewe solde out of St Awdryes churche the
some of   5s

Of Thomas Marsham alderman for the parysshe churche called
St Crowches with all the leade tymber three belles glasse iron stoon
and all other things within the same churche or perteyning ther

---

[12] Audrey or Awdry was the late medieval version of the Anglo-Saxon Etheldreda. St Etheldreda's
parish church was in King Street in Norwich.

unto excepte the churche yerde as doth appere by his accompte
therof made the some of £62

Of the mayour shreves citesens and comynaltye for a certen ayde
graunted by them at their commen assemble to thuse of this house
in releif of the same and ar [*sic*] to dyscharge the debte of the same
to the seide cittie the some £80 5s

Of John Fyssher clerke for certen money by him receyved of dyvers
persons aswell of the cittie as otherwhere gyven into the releif
of the pore, as appereth perticulerly by his bill thereof – 22s 6d.
And of the churche boxe by him also – 24s. Of the pryce of a
popple 12s <a storing barrall 20d> solde to John Mate, and a
storing barrell – 20d. Over and besides twoo barrells of bere
6 gallons of ale 5 busshelles of whete and one busshell of meslym
33 loves of bredde 7 salted fysshes and three cheses gyven also to
the releif of the poore as doth appere perticulerly by his booke 48s <8d> 10d

[*m. 13v*] Of the chamberlyn of the cittie for the yerely proufightes
of the landes whiche were sometyme Bisshoppe Goldewelles by the
terme of [*blank*] yeres, in arrerages £14 13s 4d

Of Sir Robert Dowe of a gifte from him self to the releif of the
poore house this yere 20s

Summa of the forreyn receiptes this yere as bifore apperith £282 18s 6d

Summa of the whole charge of all the posessions of this house
aswel within the cittie, the countye of Norfolke, as elleswhere,
with the forreyn receptes in this accompte conteyned is £478 16s 5d

Wherof

[*m. 14r*] *Unde super* [*whence*]

Allowed to thaccomputaunt *viz*

For thannuytie of Tweighte not levyed this yere	53s 4d
For certen rentes in Cossey and Ringlande not levyed	4s 3d
For certen rentes in Calthorppe and Erpingham not levyed	3s 10½d
For certen rentes in Rollesbye	18d
For certen rente in Newton	18d
For certen ferme in Hardeley	4d
For certen rente in Mundham	2d
For St Crowches parisshe churche in thandes of Thomas Marsham alderman	£40

For the landes of Bisshopp Goldewell before charged and not levyed
for dyvers consideracions £14 13s 4d

[*Total*] £57 18s 3½d

And so remayneth to be accompted for the some of   [*no total given*]

Whereof payed *viz*

Reparacions

The King – To the Kinges maiestie for his rente   £9

The curate – To Sir John Fyssher his stypende   £6 13s 4d

The visitour – To Sir Robert Dowe his stypende   £6

The scholemaster – To Walter Haws scholemaster for his stypend by yere   £10

The ussher – To Richard Toly ussher for his stypende from
Crochemas untill Midsomer at this accompte   20s

[*Total*]   £32 13s 4d

The dyettes of 40 poore folkes with officers and kepers

To Doctor Shaxton from Mydsomer to Lammas 5 weekes 3 dayes   £8 9s 7d

The 20 dayes nexte ensuing the poore was kepte by Sir John
Fyssher with the almes of goode peopull by him collected to
the valewe of   <47s 8d> 48s 10d

To Sir John Fyssher from the 21st day of August to Mychaelmas   £9 10s 6d

From Mychaelmas to Christmas   £19 19s 11d

From Cristemas to Our Lady in Lent   £27 <1s> 11s 3½d

From Our Lady in Lente to Mydsomer uppon the determynacion
of this accompte this yere   £23 2s 8½d

[*Total*]   £91 2s 9¾d

[*m. 14v*] Necessaries for the poore *viz*

For a bestedde there this yere   12d

For shoes boughte for the poore   8s 9d

For 5 shetes to bery the pore in   8s 5d

For 5 yerdes of canvas for twoo table clothes this yere   3s 9d

For twoo boken tubbes to boke and wasshe with and candell bromes
and threde   5s 11d

[*Total*]   27s 10d

Woode and fewel *viz*

To Thomas Mego of Swanington for caryeng of woode	43s 10d
To diverse personnes for woode for felling lopping caryeng and ryving the same and their bourde as apperith by Ser John Fyssher his book this yere	35s 6d
[*Total*]	79s 4d
To my lorde Shaxton for kepers and officers wages and borde as by his bill appere for 5 weekes 3 dayes *summa*	33s 2d

Keperes wages *viz*

To Ellen a keper there	10s
To Avelyn a keper	33s 4d
To Elizabeth Cooke	10s
To Margaret Chapman	8s 4d
To Alice Norgate	29s 8d
[*Total*]	£4 11s 4d

Offyceres wages and dyettes

To John Fyssher <caytour> for wages	8s 4d
To Thomas King <rent gatherer> his stypende	60s
To John Butler 16s 8d and other in that office 29s 8d	46s 4d
To Margaret Thorolde the coquies for wages this yere	19s 4d
The dyette of the rent gatherer 60s and for certen allowances to him by his patent 33s 4d the rest of thofficers *nihil hoc anno*	£4 13s 4d
[*Total*]	£11 17s 4d

The baylives of Hundreddes

To the bailif of Humlyerde hundred for certen rentes there	17s 10d
To the balif of Loddon hundrede for certen rente there	3s 8d
To the bailif of the hundred of Blofeld and Walsham for rente	2d
To the balif of the hundred of Erpingham for certen lete fee	2d
[*Total*]	21s 10d

Proxies and sinages \<rentes resolute\> *viz*

The churche of Calthorpp	6s 6d
The churche of Cringleforde	6s
The churche of Hardeley	9s 5½d
The churche of Sething	9s 7½d
The churche of Mundham *Petri*[13]	8s 4d
The churche of Mundham Ethel[14]	5s 6d
The churche of Southwalsham	\<7s 7½d\> 9s 7½d
The churche of Repps in Bastwick	9s 11½d
The churche of Costessey	9s 11½d
Arrerages of singage	4s 1d
[*Total*]	79s 1½d

[*m. 16r*] **Penciones *viz***

To Doctour Shaxton	£23 6s 8d
To Sir Richarde Thacker at Mundham	66s 8d
To Sir Michaell at Seething	40s
To the vicar of Calthorpp	40s
To Christchurch [*the cathedral*] from Cringleforde	33s 4d
[*Total*]	£33 6s 8d

Fees and annuities *viz*

To Master Pykerell audytour	23s 4d
To Master Corbet stewerde	20s
To Master Crooke	20s
To Master Myngaye	20s
To Master Taylour	10s
To Master Peter Reede	10s
[*Total*]	£5 3s 4d

Barbour and surgeon

To Thomas Reignoldes surgeon to the poore this yere	66s 8d
To Belton barbour to the poore	13s 4d
[*Total*]	£4

---

[13] The church of St Peter.
[14] The church of St Ethelbert.

Rentes resolute *viz*

To the cathedrall churche		£4 6s 8d
The mannour of Wroxham		10s 2d
The mannour of Cosseye		7s
The mannour of Loddon		2s 11d
The mannour of Sething		20½d
Master John Barney rente		10s 2d
John Ormesby of Lingwoode		2s 2d
The chamberleyn of the cittie		4½d
The bishopp of Norwich		13s 4d
	[*Total*]	£6 14s 6d

Costes of the courtes

At Cringleford manour		3s 8d
At Mundham and Sething		5s
At Hethill and Carleton		3s
	[*Total*]	11s 8d

Rewards *viz*

To Master Myldemayes clerke		8d
To John Sycke in rewarde		20d
	[*Total*]	2s 4d

To Sir John Fyssher for reeding masons woorke glasing nayles lyme sande strawe lokkes keyes and other thinges as apperith by his billes therof — 24s 9¾d

To Master Marsham for fencing brent <h> grondes in Holmestrete to the gates *15s 8d*, with a dorstall *2s 4d*, the westgate in thospitall medewes *2s 2d*, leding the chauncell *6s 4d*, the systers yerde a chymney and entrey into the chauncell and other places *£5 4s 8d*. At St Awdryes *10s 10d*, a wyndo there *8d*, certen stoone *15s*. At Cosseye *19s 6d*. At Reppes *7s*. At Hethill fencing the woode *18d*, as doth appere perticulerly by his bookes thereof — £8 16s 8d

To Master Marsham for 10 loodes of clay *9s 2d*, to Cringleford bourde there occupied *25s*, carieng of it *10d*, workmanshipp 2 men 7 dayes *5s 10d*, ramyng the ground *4s*, a lok on the systers dore *6d*, 400 large naylies for the myle [*mill*] *3s 4d*. And for <certen> all [*ale*] breweng vesselles in thospitall to Mylis the cowper made newely there *£4 11s* — £6 19s 8d

[*m. 16v*] To Master Necton alderman for certen reparacions doon
by him within the scyte of the seide poore house as perticulerly
dothe appere by his accompte and booke there uppon made and
perused uppon the determynacion of this accompte, and sommed
with thande of Thomas Marsham alderman surveyour the some of   £16 8s 1½d

[*Total*]   £33 9s 3¾d

Money payed before hande towardes the charges of this house the yere next ensuing

For woode and fewell *viz*

To Master Necton before hande towardes the provyson of fewell for
the poore and house graunted to him by the surveyours for the yere
nowe nexte ensuing   £13 6s 8d

For the dyettes of the poore

To the seide Master Necton before hande to and for the dyettes
and expenses of the poore for the quartour *viz* from Mydsomer uppon
the determynacion of this accompt untill Michaelmas next ensuing   £20

[*Total*]   £33 6s 8d

Sum of payementes   £325 18s 10½d

Forreyne payementes this yere *viz*

To the chamberlayne
Imprimis to Robert Reynebalde for his paynes taking for this house
abought the landes and making bookes thereof   50s

Master Morleye
To Master Morley alderman for the dyscharge of twenty poundes
whiche he lente to the cittie for this house in the price of the quere
solde to him for £25 this yere   £20

Master Codde
To Master Thomas Codde alderman towardes the dyscharge of the
debte of this house dewe to him as in former accomptes it doth
appere in the price of the forsede quere solde to Master Morley
for £25 the some of   £5

Christ church
To the cathedrall churche payed by Master Marsham of All Saintes
in Fybrig and St Awdries in Consforde this yere the some of   £27 3s 4d

To the cathedrall churche for the parisshe churche <of> called
St Crowches also this yere   £22

The Cittie

To Master Thomas Codde alderman for a certen ayde graunted to this house by the mayour shreves and comynaltie of the citie to dyscharge the debte of this house to the same as by the Chamberlyn accompt appereith £80 5s

[*m. 17r*] To Sir John Fyssher for certen allowances conteyned in his billes this yere 50s 8d

Summa totalis of all the deduccions and payementes beforesade in this accompte allowed
Allow £485 7s 10½d whiche some of allowance dothe excede the charge as hereafter appereth

Surplus

And so the seide accomptaunt is in surplussage and hathe payed more thenne his charge dothe extende unto this yere as in thaccompte here fully and playnely apperith to the some of £6 <1> 11s 5½d

And allowed to hym for that he is overecharged *viz* uppon Master Marsham in Holmestrete 15s

And likewyse overecharged uppon Master Woodes house 6s 8d

And of Master Reedes fyne at Cringleford 4s

And for Reignoldes of Burlingham 10d

And for Leman there overecharged 1d

Item to this accomptaunt for his costes and expenses with the surveyours in and about the perusing of thaccomptes of this howse, fyve dayes payed by him 8d every daye *summa* 3s 4d

[*Total*] £8 <9s 4½d> 16½d

Examinatur per nos
[*Signed:*] *Per me* Thomas Marsham, by me John Alldryche, Alexander Mather, Thomas Sotherton, Johannem Pykarell

ACCOUNT ROLL 1570–71[15]

God's Hows

[*m. 1r*] Thaccompt of Thomas Corye the younger collectour and receyvour of all and singuler rentes revenues and proufittes of all the whoall possessyons of the late hospitall of Sainct Gyles nowe called Goddes Hows or the Hows of the Poore People in Holme

---

[15] NRO, NCR, 24a, Great Hospital account rolls.

Streete within the cittie of Norwiche with all and singuler the profittes
to the same belongyng and apperteynyng as well within the seid
cittie as in the countye of Norfolk and else wheare and also of all
maner of forreyne receyptes cummyng and growyng to the same
for one whoall yere that is to saye from the feast of the Natyvytee of
St John Baptist *anno domini* 1570 beeyng in the twelth yere of the
raigne of our sovereyne Ladye Elizabeth by the grace of God
Quene of Englond Fraunce and Irelond defender of the faith etc.
to and untill the feast of the Natyvytee of St John Baptist then next
insuyng *anno domini* 1571 and in the thirtenth yere of the raigne
of our seid sovereyne Ladye Quene Elizabeth.

Arrerages

The seyd accomptaunt is not to be chardged with tharrerages
remayneng in the title of *unde supra* upon the foote of the last yeeres
accompt as parcell of the chardge of this accompte for that this is his
fyrst accompt neverthelesse hee dooth here chardge himselfe with
certeyn summes of money beeyng parcell of the same arrerages
remayneng *in supra* [*see above*] upon certeyn persons upon the foote
of the last accompt and by hym receyved within the tyme of thys
accompt *viz* of Thomas Gawdye sergeaunt at the lawe for part of
the ferme of the mannour of Seethyng £8 3s 5d of John Thoirbon
for the half yeres ferme of the landes in Hethill purchased of
Crosseman £9 and of Robert Quene for part of the ferme of the
howse late Master Coddes in Conesforde 10s in all as in the foote
of the last yeres accompt emong others particulerly dooth and may
appere   £18 13s 5d

The scyte of the place

Of William Olyver for the ferme of the scyte of the hows or place
with the medowes ortyardes gardeynes groundes howses bernes and
stables within the precynct of the same which are graunted to the
seid William Olyver withowt eny ferme to be paide for the same
and therfor here in chardge   *nihil*

Holmestrete

Of the ferme of the first tenement next the place letten to John Myles
from yere to yere after the rate of 13s 4d by yere and here chardged
for the whoall yere endyd at the feast of the Natyvytee of St John
Baptist *anno domini* 1571 upon thend of this accompt   13s 4d

Of Wylliam Joyster for the ferme of the next tenement therunto
adioyneng letten to hym from yere to yere after the rate of 12s by

yere and here chardged for one whoall yere endyd at the feast of
the Invencion of the Holy Crosse called Crouchemas within the
tyme of this accompt   12s

Of Wylliam Garrarde for the ferme of the next tenement (beeyng
the last of the three tenementes under one roof) letten to hym from
yere to yere after the rate of 12s by yere and here chardged for
the whoall yere endid at the feast of the Natyvytee of St John Baptist
in the end of this accompt   12s

Of Robert Gyrdler for the whoall yeres ferme of a grounde in the
same street which was letten to John Ducker for 21 yeeres determyned
at Mychaellmas *anno* 1570 and houlden now by the seyde Robert
Gyrdler at will and here chardged for the yere endid at the feast of
the Natyvytee of St John Baptist in thend of this accompt   16s 8d

Of John Sucklyng alderman for the whoall yeres ferme of a ground
next adioyneng with an ozyeryard lyeng at the north ende therof
whiche was letten to one Hugh Harryson by indenture from the feast
of St Michaell tharchaungell *anno* 1543 and in the 35th yere of the
raigne of King Henry VIII for 60 yeres this beeyng the 27th yere of
his terme and he to paye yerely therfor at Mychaellmas only   13s 4d

Of the same John Sucklyng for the whoall yeres ferme of a certeyne
ground next to the aforeseid grounde letten to the seid John by
indenture from the feast of St Mychaell tharchaungell *anno* 1564 and
in the 6th yere of the raigne of our sovereyne Lady Quene
Elizabeth duryng 21 yeres this beeyng the 6th yere of his terme
and he to paye yerely therfor at Our Lady and Mychaellmas by
even porcions   20s

Of Thomas Peck alderman for the whoall yeres ferme of a ground
in Holmestrete whiche was letten to Master Thomas Whall alderman
by indenture from the feast of St Mychaell the Archaungell *anno*
1562 and in the 4th yere of the raigne of our sovereyne Lady Quene
Elizabeth for 21 yeres this beeyng the 8th yere of his terme and he
to paye yerely at Mychaellmas only   3s 4d

[*m. 1v*] Of Thomas Bemonde alderman for the whoall yeres ferme
of a ground lately brent in Holmestrete letten to hym by indenture
from the feast of the Natyvyte of St John Baptist *anno* 1547 and in the
fyrst yere of the raigne of Kyng Edward VI for 60 yeres this beeyng
the 24th yere of his terme and he to pay yerely at Christmas and
Midsoomer by even porcions   5s

Of Thomas Peck alderman for the whoall yeres ferme of a ground
lately builded and all the long rowe of howses by the water syde

with the medow belongyng to the same letten to hym by indenture
from the feast of the Natyvytee of St John Baptist *anno* 1552 and in
the 6th yere of the raigne of Kyng Edward VI for 60 yeres this beyng
the 19th yere of his terme and he to paye yerely at 4 severall termes
in the yere   40s

[*Total*]   £7 5s 8d

St Vedastes

Of Richard Bate for the whoall yeres ferme of a messuage called
Skipwithes Place letten to hym by indenture from the feast of St
Michaell tharchaungell *anno* 1565 and in the 7th yere of the raigne of
our sovereyne Lady Quene Elizabeth for 21 yeres this beeyng the
5th yere of his terme and he to paye yerely by even porcions   40s

Of John Sotherton the younger for the whoall yeres ferme of a
medowe or closse lyeng in St Vedastes and letten to hym by
indenture from the feaste of St Mychaell tharchaungell *anno* 1552
and in the 6th yere of the raigne of Kyng Edward VI for 40 yeres
this beeyng the 18th yere of his terme and he to paye yerely at the
Annunciacion of Our Lady and Mychaellmas by even porcions   20s

Of Anne Fletcher widowe for the whoall yeres ferme of a little
parcell of grounde which John Walpole somtyme hadd in St Vedastes
and late in thoccupacion of Richard Fletcher alderman payeng
yerely therfor at Mychaellmas   10s

Of Margarett Puttock wedowe for the whoall yeres ferme of a
ground in St Vedastes whiche was letten to William Myngaye by
indenture from the feaste of St Michaell tharchaungell *anno* 1543
and in the 35th yere of the raigne of Kyng Henry VIII for 99 yeres
this beeyng the 27th yere of his term and he to pay therfor yerely
at Mychaellmas only   3s 4d

Of Elizabeth Myngaye wedowe for the whoall yeres ferme of a
ground in St Vedastes letten to [*blank*] by indenture for terme
of [*blank*]   6s 8d

Of William Stewarde for the whoall yeres ferme of a hows with
a closse and a medowe in St Vedastes as yett holden at will
payeng yerely at Mychaellmas and Our Lady by even porcions   20s

Of Fraunchys Allen for the whoall yeres ferme of an ozyer ground
in St Vedastes whiche is letten to hym by indenture from the feast
of St Mychaell tharchaungell *anno* 1566 and in the 8th yere of the
raigne of our sovereyne Lady Quene Elizabeth for 21 yeres this
beeyng the 4th yere of his terme and he to paye yerely at Our Lady
and Michaellmas by even porcions   66s 8d

Of Ellyse Bate alderman for the ferme aswell of his ould closse in
St Vedastes as of the closse there next adioyneng late in the tenure of
Anne Fletcher widowe now unyted together and letten to seid Ellyse
by indenture from the feast of Saint Mychaell tharchaungell *anno* 1570
and in the 12th yere of the raigne of our sovereyne Lady Quene
Elizabeth for 21 yeres payeng yerely for the same closes together at
Our Lady and Michaellmas by even porcions 30s and here chardged
for his ould closse for one whoall yere endid at the Annunciacion of
Our Lady *anno* 1571 20s and for Mistress Fletchers closse for halfe a
yere endid at the Annuncyacion of Our Lady *anno* 1571 5s over
and besides 10s above chardged upon Anne Fletcher wedowe for the
whoall yeres ferme of her seid closse endid at Michaellmas *anno* 1571
and so here receyved   25s

Of John Aldriche alderman for the whoall yeres ferme of twoo
tenementes and a closse in St Vedastes purchased of Robert
Raynbold and now letten to the same John by indenture from
the feast of St Mychaell tharchaungell *anno* 1567 and in the 9th yere
of the raygne of our sovereyne Lady Quene Elizabeth for 21 yeres
this beeyng the thredd yere of his terme and he to paye yerely at
Our Lady and Mychaellmas by even porcions   60s

Of Thomas Petwys for the whoall yeres ferme of a closse in
St Vedastes which Thomas Codd late alderman did geve emong
other howses and groundes to the mayntenaunce of the poore
people in Goddes Hows in Holmestrette and letten to the same
Thomas Petwys by indenture from the feast of St Michaell
tharchaungell *anno* 1566 and in the 8th yere of the raigne of Quene
Elizabeth for 21 yeres this beeyng the 4th yere of his terme and he
to pay yerely at Our Lady and Mychaellmas by even porcions   30s

[*Total*]   £14 20d

[*m.2r*] St Peters Permontergate

Of Robert Grene gent for the whoall yeres ferme of a capitall
messuage with the gardeynes ortyardes and groundes whiche the seid
Master Codd dwelt in and which he gave emong other groundes to
the use of the poore people in Goddes Hows which seid messuage
and other premisses wer houlden by a leas made to John Throkmerton
and nowe yelded upp by the seid Robert Grene and so houlden
at will payeng therfor at Michaellmas and Our Ladye   £9

St Benettes

Of John Clarke for the whoall yeres ferme of a certeyne ground
with taynters for a sherman whiche the seid Master Codd did lyke
wise gyve to the seid use of the poore and now letten to the same John

by indenture from the feast of St John Baptist *anno* 1566 and in the 8th yere of the raigne of our sovereyne Lady Quene Elizabeth for 21 yeres this beeyng the 5th yere of his terme and he to paye therfor yerely at Christmas and Midsoomer by even porcions   20s

Saynct Augustene

Of John Reade alderman for the ferme of the scyte of the place called the Lathes with the dovehows and yarde in the parrisshe of St Augusten and letten to hym by indenture from the feast of St Michaell tharchaungell *anno* 1554 and in the first and second yeres of Kyng Philipp and Quene Marye for 21 yeres this beeyng the 16th yere of his terme and he to paye yerely at Our Ladye and Mychaellmas   40s

Of Christopher Soham for the whoall yeres ferme of a closse beeyng parcell of Gildencroft and letten to hym by indenture from the feast of St Michaell tharchaungell *anno* 1554 and in the first and second yeres of Kyng Philipp and Quene Mary for 20 yeres this beeyng the 16th yere of his terme and he to paye yerely therfor at Our Lady and Mychaellmas by even porcions   35s 7d

Of Thomas Larkson for the whoall yeres ferme of a closse beeyng parcell of Gyldencroft letten by indenture from the feast of St Mychaell tharchaungell *anno* 1554 and in the first and second yeres of Kyng Philipp and Quene Mary for 21 yeres this beeyng the 16th yere of his terme and he to paye yerely at Our Lady and Mychaellmas by even porcions   35s 7d

Of John Reade alderman for the whoall yeres ferme of a closse beeyng parcell of Gyldencroft and letten to Henry Grenwood by indenture from the feast of St Michaell tharchaungell *anno* 1554 and in the fyrst and second yeres of Kyng Philipp and Quene Mary for 21 yeres this beeyng the 16th yere of his terme and he to paye yerely at Our Lady and Mychaellmas by even porcions   22s 3d

Of Mistress Mychell widowe for the whoall yeres ferme of a ground parcell of Gyldencroft which was letten to John Bougaye by indenture from the feast of St Michaell tharchaungell *anno* 1552 and in the 6th yere of the raigne of Kyng Edward VI for 21 yeres this beeyng the 18th yere of his terme and to paye yerely therfor at Our Lady and Mychaellmas by even porcions   20s

Of William Olyver for the whoall yeres ferme of 54 acres of arryable land lyeng in diverse peeces in the fieldes of Norwiche Heylesdon and Catton belongyng to the place called the Lathes in St Augustens letten to hym at will from yere to yere and to paye at 4 severall termes in the yere   60s

Of John Mason for the ferme of 24 acres of land lyeng in dyverse peecys in Catton and Sprowston which wer letten to John Stallor by indenture from the feast of St Michaell tharchaungell *anno* 1552 and in the 6th yere of the raigne of Kyng Edward VI for 21 yeres this beeyng the 18th yere of his terme and he to pay yerely therfor at Our Lady and Mychaellmas by even porcions   28s

Of William Syer for the whoall yeres ferme of a messuage and a tenement with a little gardeyne therunto belongyng in the parisshe of St Mary Unbrent which wer letten to John Staller by indenture from the feast of thannuncyacion of Our Lady *anno* 1557 and in the thredd and 4th yeres of King Philipp and Quene Mary for 21 yeres this becyng the 14th yere of his terme and he to pay yerely therfor at Michaelmas and Our Ladye   8s 8d

Of John Staller for the whoall yeres rent of a hows next the townewalles which he builded lately and payeth yerely therfor at Michaellmas   1d

[*m. 2v*] Of [*blank*] Parker widowe for the whoall yeres ferme of a barne at a place called the Lathes in St Augustens letten to Thomas Parker alderman deceassed by indenture from the feast of the Natyvytee of St John Baptist *anno* 1561 and in the thred yere of the raigne of our sovereyne Lady Quene Elizabeth for 21 yeres this beeyng the 10th yere of his terme and he to paye yerely therfor at Chrystmas and Midsoomer by even porcions   6s

Of Roger Clarke tyler for the whoall yeres ferme of one of those tenementes which the parson of St Clementes gave to the use of the poore and letten to hym from yere to yere he payeng yerely therfor at 4 severall termes in the yere   10s

Of Robert Tryll for the whoall yeres ferme of one other of the tenementes in the same parrisshe which seid parson did give to the use of the seid poore in thospitall and letten to hym from yere to yere he payeng therfor yerely at 4 termes in the yere   12s

Of Robert Thacker for one other of those tenementes in the seyd parrisshe which the seid parson of St Clementes gave to the use aboveseyd and letten to hym from yere to yere he payeng yerely therfor at 4 tymes in the yere   10s

Of Mother Margarett for the whoall yeres ferme of the 4th tenement in the same parrysshe which the seid parson did gyve to the use aforeseid and letten to her from yere to yere shee payeng yerely therfor at 4 termes in the yere   6s

[*Total*]   £14 14s 2d

St Peters of Mancroft

Rent assyse

Of the churchewardeyns thear for rent by yere	12d
Of the chamberleyne of the cittie for rent by yere	13s 4d
Of Geoffrye Kytmaye for rent of a tenement somtyme Master Conyes	4d
[*Total of assise rents*]	14s 8d

Of Thomas Hooke for the whoall yeres ferme of a tenement in the parysshe of St Peter of Mancroft which was letten to Thomas Conye by indenture from the feast of St Michaell tharchaungell *anno* 1538 and in the 30th yere of Kyng Henry VIII for 99 yeres this beeyng the 32nd yere of his terme payeng yerely at Michaelmas only — 12d

Of John Bygett for the whoall yeres ferm of a tenement in the parrysshe of St Peter Mancroft letten by indenture as it is supposed and payeth yerely at Michaellmas — 6s 8d

Of William Wyer for the whoalle yeres ferm of the capitall mesuage in the parrisshe of St Peter of Mancroft called the Lambe letten to Thomas Cork late alderman of Norwiche by indenture from the feaste of Annuncyacion of Our Lady *anno* 1551 and in the 5th yere of the raigne of Kyng Edward VI for 40 yeres this beyng the 20th yere of his terme and to paye yerely therfor at Michaellmas and Our Lady by even porcions — 50s

[*Total*] 72s 4d

Saynct Crowches

Of William Rugg gent for the whoall yeres ferm of a gardeyne grounde in the late parisshe of St Crowche letten to Robert Rugg late alderman deceassd by indenture from the feast of St Michaell tharchaungell *anno* 1531 and in the 23rd yere of the raigne of Kyng Henry VIII for 80 yeres this beeyng the 39th yere of his terme and to paye yerely at Mychaellmas only — 5s

Of George Drurye the younger for the whoall yeres ferme of a parcell of ground in the same parisshe letten to John Beverley in fee ferme payeng yerely therfor at Mychaellmas only — 20d

[*Total*] 6s 8d

Saynct Stephans

Rent assyse

Of John Gygges for rent of a tenement late Henry Pettyngale payable at Michaellmas	13d
Of Thomas Larwoode for rent of a tenement late Margarett Grene payable at Michaellmas	4s

Of Thomas Steward for rent of a tenement late Richard
    Hedd alderman paieable at Michaellmas   12d
                                 [*Total of assise rents*]   6s 1d

[*m. 3r*] Of Robert Sucklyng alderman for the whoall yeres ferme of
a certeyne closse lyeng withowt St Stephans gates which was
purchased of Henry Crooke late cittezen and alderman of Norwiche
and letten to Richard Hedd late alderman deceassed for 21 yeres from
Michaellmas *anno* 1565 and in the 7th yere of the raigne of our
sovereyne Lady Quene Elizabeth this beeyng the 5th yere of his
terme and he to paye yerely at Our Lady and Mychaellmas by even
porcions   40s
                                      [*Total*]   46s 1d

All Sainctes

Rent assise
    Of John Lowe for rent of a tenement late Mychaell Clarke yerely
        at Michaellmas   1d
    Of Robert Tooke for rent of a tenement late John Austen yerely
        at Mychaellmas   12d
                                   [*Total*]   13d

St Martyns at the pallace gate

Rent assise Of William Blenerhayssett gent for rent of twoo tenementes
late letten to dame Jane Calthropp and now sould to the same
William by deede he to paye in rent yerely at Mychaellmas only 4d   4d

Of the same William for the whoall yeres ferme of a certeyne
grounde in St Martyns called the Schoolehows Yarde letten to hym
by indenture from Michaellmas *anno* 1567 and in the 9th yere of
the raigne of our sovereyne Lady Quene Elizabeth for 68 yeres this
beeyng the thredd yere of his terme and he to paye yerely at
Michaellmas   6s 8d

Of John Kyng for the whoall yeres ferme of a tenement next
adioyneng which was letten to William Brygg by indenture from
the feast of the Natyvyte of St John Baptist *anno* 1553 and in first
yere of the raygne of Quene Marye for 21 yeres this beeyng the
18th yere of his terme and he to paye yerely at Chrystmas and
Mydsoomer   8s

Of William Hales for the whoalle yeres ferme of a tenement next
Master Hasettes letten to hym by indenture as it is supposed for
the which he payeth yerely at Christemas and Midsoomer by even
porcions   6s 8d

Of John Flynt for the whoall yeres ferme of three tenementes
which be letten to hym by indenture from Mychaellmas *anno* 1564
and in the 6th yere of the raigne of our sovereyne Lady Quene
Elizabeth for 30 yeres this beeyng the 6th yere of his terme and he
to paye yerely at Our Lady and Mychaellmas by even porcions   10s

                                                    [*Total*]   31s 8d

Saynct Symon and Jude

Rent assise

  Of Elizabeth Myngaye wedowe for rent of a tenement theare
    payable at Mychaellmas only   4d
  Of the same Elizabeth for rent of one other tenement theare payable
    at the same feast   4d
  Of the seid Elizabeth for rent of an entrye theare payable at the
    seid feast   2d
                                         [*Total of assise rents*] 10d

Of John Lyng for the ferme of a gardeyn theare payable yerly at
Mychaellmas only   3s 4d

Of [*blank*] Norgate wedowe for the whoall yeres ferme of a curtylage
or tenement lyeng on the backside of the mesuage called the Maydes
Hedd letten to Master Nicholas Norgate alderman deceassed from
the feast of St Michaell tharchaungell *anno* 1556 and in the thredd
and 4th yeres of Kyng Philipp and Quene Marye for 40 yeres this
beeyng the 14th yere of his terme and he to paye yerely therfor
at Mychaellmas only   10s

                                                    [*Total*]   14s 2d

St Andrew

Of Thomas Payne for the whoall yeres ferme of a parcell of ground
in the parrysshe of St Andrew letten to fee ferme to Thomas
Marsham alderman of Norwiche deceassed by indenture and he
to paye yerely therfor at Michelmas   20d

[*m. 3v*] St Martyns at the Oke

Rent assise

  Of John Harryson for rent of a tenement late Cecylye Broome
    payable at Mychaellmas only   4d
  Of Agnes Mychell wedowe for rent to twoo tenementes
    lyeng next the same payable at the same feast   6d

Of Leonerde Reade for rent of a tenement somtym Gylbertons
and late Wylliam Asshewelles 3d
Of Robert Spencer for rent of a tenement somtym Rychard
Wylkeynnson late John Wylkyns 6d
Of Agnes Mychell wedowe for rent of an other tenement theare 12d
Of the same Agnes for rent of an other tenement somtyme
Robert Harward 3d

[*Total of assise rents*] 2s 10d

Of the seid Agnes for ferme of a closse whiche was letten to John
Bougaye from the feast of St Mychaell tharchaungell *anno* 1544
and in the 36th yere of the raygne of Kyng Henry VIII for 99
yeres this beeyng the 26th yere of her terme and to paye yerely
at Mychaellmas only 3s 4d

Of Rychard Fytt for the whoall yeres ferme of a parcell of ground
late in the ferme of Robert Grene mason payeng yerely at
Mychaellmas only 5s 1d

Of Anthony Marker for the whoall yeres ferme of a closse which
was letten to Bryan Tayllour and Anne his wyfe by indenture from
the feast of St Mychaell tharchaungell *anno* 1554 and in the first and
second yeres of Kyng Philipp and Quene Mary for 21 yeres this
beeyng the 16th yere of his terme and he to paye yerely at
Our Ladye and Mychaellmas 40s

Of Robert Kyng for the whoall yeres ferme of a tenement which
was letten to Nycholas Chylde by indenture from the feast of
St Mychaell tharchaungell *anno* 1553 and in the first yere of the
raygne of Quene Marye for 21 yeres this beeyng the 17th yere of
his terme and he to paye yerely at Christemas and Mydsoomer 6s 8d

Of Agnes Mychell wedowe for the whoall yeres ferme of twoo
tenementes somtym Thomas Drewry and Hugh Albon and letten to
John Bungaye by indenture from Mydsoomer *anno* 1555 and in the
first and second yeres of the raygnes of Kyng Phillip and Quene
Marye for 89 yeres this beeyng the 16th yere of hir terme and to
paye at Christmas and Mydsoomer by even porcions 14s

[*Total*] 71s 11d

St Peters at Southgate

Of Richard Palmer mason for the whoall yeres ferme of a tenement
late in the tenure of John Styngate letten to the seid Rychard by
indenture from the feast of thannuncyacion of Our Lady *anno* 1566
and in the 8th yere of the raygne of our sovereyne Lady Quene
Elizabeth for 21 yeres this beeyng the 5th yere of his terme and to
pay yerely at Mychaellmas and Our Lady 12s 4d

St Edward

Of John Sotherton the younger for the whoall yeres ferme of the
grounde late brent adioyneng to the comon stathe letten to Leonerd
Sotherton late alderman of Norwyche deceassed from the feaste of
St Mychaell tharchaungell *anno* 1554 and in the first and seconde
yeres of Kyng Philipp and Quene Mary for 21 yeres this beeyng the
16th yere of his terme and to paye therfor yerely at Mychaellmas only   4s

St John Sepulchre

Of Edmond Tolye butcher for the whoall yeres ferme of a closse
somtyme Goldwelles letten to hym by indenture as it is sayed to
pay yerly therfor at 4 termes in the yere   26s 8d

St Bartillmew in Berestreete

Of Nycholas Baker alderman for the whoall yeres ferme of a closse
next adioyneng somtyme Goldwelles letten to hym by indenture
from the feast of St Mychaell tharchaungell *anno* 1552 and in the
6th yere of the raygne of Kyng Edward VI this beeyng the
18th yere of his terme and to pay at 4 termes in the yere   30s

[*m. 4r*] St Michaelles in Berestrete

Rent assise Of Rychard Blofelde butcher in the ryght of his wyfe for
rent of a tenement theare   2s

Of Robert Sucklyng alderman for the whoall yeres ferme of a closse
somtyme Goldwelles whiche was letten to Edwarde Fletcher by
indenture from the feast of St Mychaell tharchaungell *anno* 1552 and
in the 6th yere of the raygne of Kyng Edward VI for 21 yeres this
beeyng the 18th yere of his terme and to paye therfor yerely at 4
severall termes in the yere   51s

[*Total*]   53s

St Katherine

Of John Pype for the whoall yeres ferme of twoo closes called
Saynct Katheryns close with the berne and dovehows therupon
buylded and letten by indenture from the feast of St Mychaell
tharchaungell *anno* 1553 and in the fyrst yere of the raygne of
Quene Marye for 21 yeres to Master Allane Perrye this beeyng the
17th yere of his terme and to paye yerely at Our Lady and
Mychaellmas by even porcions   40s

St Margarettes

Of John Cobb for rent of a tenement lyeng on the north syde of the
chappell yarde called Saynct Margarettes chappell in Fybrygg   12d

All Saynctes in Fybrygg

Of Robert Sucklyng alderman for the whoal yeres ferme of the
churcheyarde of All Saynctes in Fybrygg letten to hym by indenture
from the feast of the Natyvytee of St John Baptist *anno* 1550 and in
the 4th yere of Kyng Edward VI for 499 yeres this beeyng the 21st
yere of his terme and he to paye yerely at Mydsoomer only   6s 8d

St Savyors and St Botulphes

Of Thomas Peck alderman for the whoall yeres ferme of all those
howses tenementes and groundes in St Savyours which Edmond
Woode alderman gave to thospytall letten to the seid Thomas by
indenture from the feaste of the Annunciacion of Our Blessed Lady
anno 1561 and in the thredd yere of the raygne of our sovereyne
Lady Quene Elizabeth for 21 yeres this beyng the 10th yere of
his terme and to paye yerely at Our Lady and Mychaellmas   53s 4d

Of Nicholas Sotherton for the whoall yeres ferme of twoo
tenementes and the churcheyarde called St Mary Unbrent letten to
hym by indenture from the feast of thannuncyacion of Our Ladye
anno 1569 and in the 40th yere of the raigne of our sovereyne Ladye
Quene Elizabeth for 500 yeres this beeyng the second yere of hys
terme and to paye yerely therfor at Mychaellmas only   6s 8d

                                                    [*Total*]   60s

St Clement in Fybrygg

Of John Read alderman for the whoall yeres ferme of a pece of
ground beeyng parcell of the tenement late Cecylye Suffelde in the
parisshe of St Clement letten by indenture to the same John and
others from the feaste of St Mychaell tharchaungell *anno* 1568 and
in the 10th yere of the raigne of our sovereyne Lady Quene Elizabeth
for 500 yeres this beeyng the second yere of his terme and to paye
yerely therfor at Mychaellmas only   3s 4d

Of [*blank*] Bullock parson of St Clementes in Fybrygg for the whoall
yeres ferme of an other parcell of the tenement late the above named
Cecylye Suffelde letten to diverse of the parissheners there by
indenture from the feast of St Mychael tharchaungell *anno* 1569
and in the 11th yere of the raygne of our sovereyne Lady Quene
Elizabeth for 500 yeres this beeyng the first yere of his terme and
he to paye yerely therfor at Mychaellmas only   3s 4d

                                                    [*Total*]   6s 8d

St Georges at Tombland

Of Thomas Gooche late chamberleyne of this cittie for the whoalle yeres ferme of a parcell of the ground called the Starre with thappurtenances whiche was somtyme in the occupacion of John Derne payeng yerely therfor at Our Ladye and Mychaellmas by even porcions   20s

Tombland

Of Robert Grene sadeler for the whoall yeres ferme of a piece of an ould hows adioyneng to the charnell and parcell of the same letten to hym by indenture from the feast of Saynt Mychaell tharchaungell *anno* 1564 and in the 6th yere of the raygne of our sovereyne Lady Quene Elizabeth for 30 yeres this beeyng the 6th yere of his terme and he to paye yerely therfor at Our Ladye and Mychaellmas by even porcions   4s

[*m. 4v*] Heygham

Of Thomas Corye thelder for the whoall yeres ferme of twoo acres of land lyeng withowt St Gyles gates letten to hym by indenture from the feast of St Mychaell tharchaungell *anno* 1566 and in the 8th yere of the raygne of our sovereyne Lady Quene Elizabeth for 21 yeres this beeyng the 4th yere of his terme and to paye yerely therfor   5s 4d

Fybrygg

Of Robert Lyng for the wharfage in Fybrygstathe for the whoall yere endyd at the feast of the Natyvytee of St John Baptyst in the end of this accompte   6s 8d

Chapell of the Fyelde[16]

Of Thomas Gooche *late* chamberleyne for the whoalle yeres ferme of a parcell of ground in Chapell of Fyelde crofte which parcell is letten with the whoall croft and agreed that the chamberleyn should paye therfor yerely at Mychaellmas only   3s 4d

Summa of all the rentes and fermes aforeseyd within the cittye of
Norwych   £72 7s 9d

Swanyngton

Of Henry Ryches esquyer for the whoall yeres ferme of a messuage <a messuage> with thappurtenances lyeng in Swanyngton and other townes adioyneng letten by indenture to Thomas Mege from the

---

[16] Chapelfield in the parish of St Peter Mancroft, Norwich.

feast of St Mychaell tharchaungell in the thredd yere of the raygne
of Kyng Edward VI for 40 yeres this beeyng the 21st yere of his
terme and to paye yerely at Our Lady and Mychaellmas   60s

Sprowston

Of Myles Corbett Esquyre for the whoall yeres ferme of certeyn
landes pastures feedynges dooles and groves with their appurtenances
in Sprowston graunted to John Corbett esquyre and his heyers in fee
ferme payeng yerely therfor at Mychaellmas   12s 4d

Carrowe

Of Thomas Whall alderman for the whoall yeres ferme of a peece
of marissh ground in Carrowe called Paradyse letten to hym by
indenture from the feaste of St Mychaell tharchaungell *anno* 1562
and in the 4th yere of the raygne of our sovereyn Lady Quene
Elizabeth for 40 yeres this beeyng the 8th yere of his terme and he
to paye yerely therfor at Christemas only   2s

Newton

Of Robert Sucklyng alderman for the whoall yeres ferme of a peece
of marisshe grounde in Newton conteyneng by estymacion [*blank*]
acres somtyme in the ferme and occupacion of Andrew Dey payeng
therfor by yere 5s and nowe in the occupacion of the seid Robert
at wyll payeng therfor by yere   *nihil*

Horstedd

Of the occupyers of one acre of land lyeng in Horstedd which was
somtye in the occupacion of Robert Clarke and payed yerely at
Mychaellmas   6d

Lympenhoo

Of Thomas Flegg for the whoall yeres ferme of certeyne peecys of
marishe grounde lyeng in Lympenhoo and other townes letten to
John Gybbys late alderman by indenture from the feaste of
St Mychaell tharchaungell *anno* 1566 and in the 8th yere of the
raigne of our sovereyne Lady Quene Elizabeth for 21 yeres this
beeyng the 4th yere of his terme and he to pay yerely at Our Lady
and Mychaellmas by even porcions   2s 8d

Redeham

Of the Bysshopp of Norwiche for a certeyn annuytee goyng out of
the manour of Redeham payeable yerely at Mychaellmas only   26s 8d

[*m. 5r*] **Cryngleford**

Of the profittes of the mannour of Cryngleford with all the demeasne
landes fowldecorrse and lybertye of fouldage profittes of courtes
ryaltyes weafes strayes and all other commodytees and profittes
to the same apperteyneng and also the landes somtyme Richard
Woode with the watermyll fysshyng and tythe of the benefyce theare
with all profittes and commodytees to the same belongyng all which
premysses were letten to George Redmayn by indenture payeng yerely
for the same *our Lady and Michaellmas* £34 14s 8d. And nowe
by reason of thatteynder of the same George fallen into the Quenys
highnes handes[17] by reason wherof the seid ferme is unpayd for
this whoall yere and therfor here in chardge   *nihil*

But of Nycholas Pede fermour of the mannour of Heylesdon in
Cryngleforde with certeyn landes and medowes therunto belongyng
beeyng parcell of the graund leas above grauntid to George
Redmayne and by this accomptaunt receyved for one whoall
yere endid at thannuncyacion of Our Ladye within the tyme of this
accompte   113s 4d

And of Thomas Welde fermour of the watermylles theare beeyng also
parcell of the seid grande leas made to the same George and by this
accompaunt receyved for one whoall yere endyd at the feaste of the
Natyvytee of St John Baptyst upon the determynacion of this accompt

£6 13s 4d

[*Total*]   £12 6s 8d

Cossey and Rynglonde

Rent assise

Of the heyers of Robert Graye for thre roodes of lande parcell
of twoo acres in one pece somtyme Gooches   9½d
Of [*blank*] for certeyn landes late Humfrey Smallpeece in
Rynglonde   2s 2d
Of [*blank*] for certeyn landes late the seid Smallpece before that
Roger Petytt   12d
Of [*blank*] for certeyn
landes late the seyd Smallpece before that Thomas Neve   2d
Of [*blank*] Laverock for rent of three roodes late the seid
Smallpece before that John Stokes   1½d
[*Total of assise rent*]   4s 3d

[17] George Redman of Cringleford, gent, was executed for treason on 2 September 1570
(F. Blomefield, *A Topographical History of the County of Norfolk*, vol. iii, 1806, p.284) and his lands
confiscated.

Of John Aldryche alderman for the whoall yeres ferme of a closse
theare letten to hym by indenture from the feast of St Mychaell
tharchaungell *anno* 1556 and in the thredd and 4th yeres of Kyng
Philipp and Quene Mary for 40 yeres this beeyng the 14th yere of his
terme and to paye yerely therfor at Michaellmas · · · · · · 2s 8d

Of William Raye and Randoll Smyth for the whoall yeres ferme of
the rectorye with all the howses therupon builded and all the tythe
cornes to the same belongyng and also certeyne glebe landes letten
to Alyce Graye wedow deceassed by indenture from the feaste of
thannuncyacion of Our Lady *anno* 1561 and in the thredd yere of the
raygne of our sovereyne Ladye Quene Elizabeth for 21 yeres payeng
yerely therfor at Christemas and Our Ladye this beeyng the
10th yere of their terme · · · · · · £9 3s 4d

[*Total*]   £9 10s 3d

Trowes Rockhilles

Of John Myngaye gent for the whoall yeres ferme of the mannour
called Rockhilles with all the landes tenementes lybertyes and
fowldcoursses rentes and servyces in Trowes and Byxley with the
feedyng of the hylles called the Blackehylles and a swan marke
whiche wer letten to William Rogers alderman deceassed from the
feast of All Saynctes *anno* 1537 and in the 29th yere of the raigne of
Kyng Henry VIII for 99 yeres this beeyng the 33rd yere of his
terme and to paye yerely at Lammas Hallowmas Candilmas and
Crowchemas · · · · · · £4 5s

[*m. 5v*] Trowes Blakes

Of Wylliam Howlyns for the whoall yeres ferme of all the messuage
or place called Blakes with the incloses medowes pastures and
feedynges and the aryable land in Trowes Newton and Byxley letten
to the seid William by indenture from the feast of St Mychaell
tharchaungell *anno* 1566 and in the 8th yere of the raygne of our
sovereyne Lady Quene Elizabeth for 40 yeres this beeyng the 4th yere
of his terme and to paye yerely at Christemas Our Lady Mydsoomer
and Mychaellmas · · · · · · £4 13s 4d

Horsforde

Of Anne Fletcher wedowe for the whoall yeres ferm of certyne
landes and tenementes fedynges and pastures lyeng in Horsforde
which wer letten to John Gybbys by indenture from the feast of
St Mychaell tharchaungell *anno* 1544 and in the 46th yere of the

raygne of Kyng Henry VIII 99 yeres this beeyng the 26th of her
terme and to paye yerely at Mychaelmas only   21s 9½d

Horsham St Feyth

Of the pryce of 200 astle and 200 fagottes which are due owt of
St Feythes woode by composycion from the late Pryour of
St Fathes to the late Master of the hospytall which wood this yere
is assigned to William Olyver keeper of the poore payeng   20s

Coltesale

Of Walter Baspoole for the whoall yeres ferme of 63 acres and
3 roodes of land in Coltesale letten to hym for one yere endyd at
Mychaellmas in the tyme of this accompt payeng therfor   26s 8d

Salhowse

Of Hugh Spendlowe for the whoall yeres ferme of all that messuage
in Salhowse with twoo fysshynges called Houldes and other waters
and also all the land aswell marrysshe as arryable and pasture
groundes lyeng in the towne and fyeldes of Salhows and Wroxham
and also one tenement and 9 acres of land and pasture lyeng in the
seid townes in diverse peeces from the feaste of St Mychaell the
Archaungell *anno* 1549 and in the thred yere of the raygne of King
Edward VI for 34 yeres this beeyng the 21st yere of his terme and to
paye yerely at Candyllmas and Crowchemas by even porcions   £4 2s 11d

Calthorpp

Rent assyse

    Of William Dyxe esquyre for the rent of certeyn tenementes and
        yardes lyeng in the towne of Wykmer whiche wer somtye in the
        tenure of James Lubbock payend yerely therfor at Mychaellmas
        only   13½d
    Of the rentes of certeyn landes lyeng in Calthorpe Barnyngham
        Erpyngham and other townes adioyneng   2s 10d

              [End of assise rents but no total given]

Of Richard Gubberd for the whoall yeres ferme of a tenement and
40 acres of land and a medowe called Carre medow conteyneng
10 acres and one yarde called Redlyngforde lyeng in Calthorpe fyve
peeces lyeng in Erpyngham letten to hym by indenture from the
feast of St Mychaell tharchaungell *anno* 1562 and in the 4th yere of
the raygne of our sovereyne Lady Quene Elizabeth for 21 yeres this
beeyng the 8th yere of his terme and to paye at Our Lady and
Mychaellmas   16s 8d

Of William Dyxe esquyre for the whoall yeres ferme of three peecyes
of land contenyneng 7 acres lyeng in the towne of Wykemer whiche
were letten to James Lubbock by indenture payeng yerely therfor
at Mychaellmas only   4s

Of the same William Dyxe for the whoall yeres ferme of three peecys
of land which payeth yerely 8 coombes barly so letten to the seid
James Lubbock by indenture and payable yerely at Mychaellmas
for which barly this accomptuant payeth 2s for every coombe as
other receyvours of these possessyons have payd   16s

Of Henrye Tylney for the whoall yeres ferme of the tythe berne and
tythe corne in Calthorpp letten to Wylliam Tubbyng by indenture
from Lammas *anno* 1565 and in the 7th yere of the raigne of our
sovereyne Lady Quene Elizabeth for 21 yeres this beeyng the
5th yere of his terme and to paye yerely at Hallowmas Candillmas
and Crouchmas   100s

Memorandum when the vycar shall dye he shall paye his best oxe
hors or cowe for a heryott but this yere none sutche receyved and
therfor here in chardge   *nihil*

                                                                   [*Total*]   £9 10s 7½d

[*m. 6r*] Mundham Seething and Hyardley

Of Thomas Gawdye sergeaunt at the lawe for the whoalle yeres
ferme of the mannour of Mundham Sethyng and Hardley letten
to William Myngaye late cittezen and alderman deceassed by
indenture from the feast of thannuncyacion of Our Lady *anno* 1562
and in the 4th yere of the raygne of our sovereyne Lady Quene
Elizabeth for 21 yeres this beeyng the 9th yere of his terme and to
paye yerely at Mychaellmas and Our Lady by even porcions   £16 6s 11d

Of Gabryell Poynt clerke for the whoall yeres ferme of the tythe
berne and tythe corne in Hardley letten to Thomas Lupton clerk by
indenture from the feast of thannuncyacion of Our Ladye *anno* 1567
and in the 9th yere of the raigne of our sovereyne Lady Quene
Elizabeth for 21 yeres this beeying the 4th yere of his terme and to
paye yerely at Lammas and Our Lady by even porcions   110s

Of Thomas Woodyarde for the whoall yeres ferme of the tythe
berne and tythe corne in Sethyng letten to hym by indenture from
Lammas *anno* 1557 and in the 4th and 5th yeres of Kyng Philipp and
Quene Marye for 21 yeres this beeyng the 13th yere of his terme and
to paye yerely at Mychaellmas and Our Ladye   £8 13s 4d

Of Richard Osborne for the whoall yeres ferme of the tythe berne
and tythe corne in Mundham letten to hym by indenture from the
feast of St Peter thadvincula *anno* 1558 and in the 5th and 6th yeres
of Kyng Philipp and Quene Marye for 21 yeres this beyng the
12th yere of his terme and to paye yerely at Christemas Our Ladye
and Lamas   £10

                                                [*Total*]   £40 10s 3d

Hethyll and Carleton

Rent Assisse

Of the free and copyehoulders in Hethill with 12s for the woode
    called Hyghokes   £6 7s ½d
This summe is abated for that thospitall purchased their owne
    copie hold of 29s 4d of yerely rente which lands wer purchased
    of Crosseman
Of the free and copyehoulders in Carleton as by the rentall maye
    appere   £4 15d
Of the rent of twoo capons theare   8d

                        [*Total of assise rent*]   £10 8s 11½d

Of [*blank*] Thurbon £9 and John Broome £9 for the whoall yeres
ferme of all that tenement with the landes therto belongyng late
Crossemans whiche wer letten to the seid Thurbon and here
chardged for one whoall yere endyd at thannuncyacion of Our
Ladye in the tyme of this accompt   £18

Woodesale theare this yere   *nihil*

Perquesites of courtes this yere which 43s wer of Henry Benselyn for
the fyne of a mesuage and 16 acres of land and 5 acres of medowe in
Carleton and a pyghtell called Inghams yarde all which he bought of
Robert Carter and Elizabeth his wyfe and with 12s received of
Thomas Skelton for a fyne of the revercion of those landes which
John Ellwyn sould unto hym and with 8s of Christopher Chapman
for a fyne of three acres of land and one acre of medow purchased
of Henry Benslyn with 2s 6d received of William Dabb for a fyne of
an acre and a roode of lande which did discend to him by
enheritaunce and with 9d of amercement   66s 3d

                                                [*Total*]   £31 15s 2½d

Southwalsham

Of William Ferrour alderman and Thomas Ferrour for the whoall
yeres ferme of the tythe berne and tythe corne that belongeth to the
parsonage of St Marye in Southwalsham which was letten by

indenture from Lammas 1556 for 15 yeres this beeyng the last
yere of his terme and to paye yerely at Christemas Our Lady and
Midsoomer   £12

Burlyngham

Of Nycholas Howlett for the ferme of 20 acres of lande in
Southbyrlyngham in 6 peecys letten to hym by indenture   12s 6d

Of Anthony Raynoldes for the ferme of [*blank*] acres of lande lyeng
in Burlyngham over and besydes [*blank*] acres which wer evycted from
hym as concealyd landes letten to hym by indenture   18d

Of Thomas Leman for the whoall yeres ferme of [*blank*] acres of
land lyeng in Burlyngham letten to hym by indenture   3s 6d

Of John Raynoldes for ferme of one acre of land lyeng in
Burlyngham over and bysydes 4 acres whiche he hadd lyeng in
Lyngwoode whiche wer evycted from hym as concealed landes
letten to hym and to Anthony Raynoldes by indenture   7s

                                                    [*Total*]   18s 1d

[*m. 6v*] Rollesbye

Rent Assyse Of John Ufford for rent of a tenement late Jolles by yere   18d

Of Thomas Norwiche for the halfe yeres ferme of a mesuage in
Rollesbye with all the landes medowes feedynges pastures incloses
heath groundes and other their appurtenaunces letten to hym by
indenture payend yerely therfor at our Ladye and Mychaellmas by
even porcions and here chardged for halfe a yere endyd at
thannuncyacion of Our Lady within the tyme of this accompt by
vertue of his new leas   60s

                                                    [*Total*]   £3 18d

Reppes and Bastwyck

Of Robert Phylyppes for the ferme of the tythe berne in Reppes and
the chapell of Bastwyck with all the glebe landes belongyng to them
and the tythes coommyng and growyng within eyther of the seid
townes letten to Sir William Barrett clerke by indenture from the
feast of thinvencion of tholy Crosse *anno* 1559 and in the fyrst yere
of the raygne of our sovereyne Lady Quene Elizabeth for 21 yeres
this beeyng the 12th yere of his terme and to paye yerely at
Hallowmas and Crowchemas   £8

Fobbyng [*Essex*]

Of John Drywoode Gent for the ferme of twoo marrisshes called
Vangewyke and Bolyf in Vange and Fobbyng in the countye of Essex
grauntid to hym by indenture payeng yerely at Our Lady and
Mychaellmas $£13 6s 8d

Twayte [*Suffolk*]

Of Edward Reve of Twayte in the countie of Suffolk for a certeyne
annuytee graunted owt of his landes to this hows as in fourmer
accomptes appereth by yere 53s 4d

Shropham

Of this accomptaunt for the remanyneth of £20 which he this yere
receyved of John Wenne by vertue of a leas made to hym of the
mannour of Shropham from the feast of St Mychaell tharchaungell
anno 1563 and in the 5th yere of the raygne of our sovereyne Lady
Quene Elizabeth for 21 yeres this beeyng the 7th yere of his terme
over and besydes £8 parcell of the same ferme payed by the seid
accomptaunt to Thomas Gooche late chamberleyne of the seid cittie
for the redeemyng of the toll and custome at the gates and brydges in
the seid cyttye and over and besydes £10 residue of the seid ferme
likewise by hym payed to the schoolemayster at Aylesham for his
yerely stypende and so here in chardge but 40s

Summa of all the rentes and fermes of the revenues and
possessyons in Norfolk Suffolk and Essex £167 10s 5½d

Foreyne Receiptes

The seyd accomptaunt chardgeth hymself with certeyn summes of
monye by hym receyved within the tyme of this accompt as of
forreyn receiptes *viz.* Of Thomas Norwiche of Rollesby by the
handes of Master John Aldryche mayour the 7th of October *anno*
1570 in part of payment of £46 13s 4d whiche the seid Thomas
should paye for a fyne of his leas of the landes in Rollesbye £16
13s 4d. Of Master Thomas Pettwys for money delyvered to hym to
preseante the sute in Essex and for other thinges whiche money
was not by hym expendid but agreed upon at the last accompt of
the seid hospytall to be payed to this accomptaunt and so by this
accomptaunt receyved £10. Of Richard Godbye for 3 fadom of
reede and other shruff which remayned at the cooveryng of the
walles about the closse late Master Coddes in Coonesforde 20d.
Of William Olyver for 100 wyllow faggottes and woode which was
made at Master Aldriches closse in St Vedastes 6s. Of Thomas

Peck alderman for a legacye given by Sir Richard Southwell knyght which was allotted to the seid hospytall 18s. Of the same Thomas as money by hym receyved of Thomas Whall alderman for the legacye of [blank] Beane of Erpyngham given to the seyd hospytall *3s 4d*. Of John Aldwiche mayour as money owt of the common hamper in the councell chamber which was toward the dischardge of the paymentes for Christemas quarter for that the receiptes woold not countervale the paymentes of that quarter £17 10s. Of the seyd mayour for money taken owt of Master Tyrryes hamper the last daye of January *anno* 1570 which was toward the payment of £33 6s 8d payed to Master Drywood £30. Of the treasourours of this cittie by thandes of John Aldwyche the younger toward the payment of the purchase of Chosyll Mannour in Wymondham £41 4s 9d. Of the same treasourours by thandes of Peter Peterson chaymberleyne toward the same purchase £18 12s 1d. Of Master Thomas Gooche *the seid treasourours by thandes of* late chamberleyne toward the seid purchase £34 13s 2d. Of Hugh Spendlove for certeyne woode soulde hym at Salhows by the surveyours £15. And of [blank] Gysborowe wedowe for the whoalle yeres ferme of her chamber in the hospytall 4s in all.

Summa of all the forreyn receiptes   £185 7s 4d

[m. 7r] And here note that the seid summes of money borrowed owt of the treasourye doo amount unto the summe of £94 10s and there was also borrowed owt of the same treasourye before this accomptaunt tooke his chardge £60 which was toward the purchase of Crossemans landes in Hethill which two summes do amount unto £154 10s. In consideracion wherof the hospytall must paye yerely owt of the mannour of Chosyll to the chamberleyne of the seyd cittie £8 at Mychaellmas and thannuncyacion of Our Lady by even porcions and when the hospytall doo paye unto the treasourours of the seid cittie thaforeseid summe of £154 10s then the seid yerely rent of £8 to the chamberleyn to ceasse and no more to be payed.

Summa totalis of the whoall chardge of thys accompt aswell of the arrerages as of the rentes fermes and forreyne receyptes   £442 18s 11½d

[Payments]

Fyrst allowed to thys accomptaunt for money by hym payed to Wylliam Beynbrygg *£6* and Richard Sharpe *£4* clerkes for mynystryng to the poore people in Goddes Hows and to the prysoners in the Guildehall for their stypendes for one wholle

yere endyd at the feast of the Natyvytee of St John Baptist upon
thend and determynacion of this accompte £10

Item to Master Stephan Lymbert chief master and teacher of
grammer at the common school for his stypend and wages for one
whoall yere endyd at the feast of the Natyvytee of St John Baptyst
upon the end of this accompte £20

Item to Adam Plombe ussher of the same schoole for hys stypend
and wages for one whoalle yere endyd at the same feaste £13 6s 8d

Item allowed more to this accomptaunt for monye by hym payed to
William Olyver for the dyettes of the 40 poore people and for the
wages and dyettes of the kepers for three quarters of a yere *viz* for
Mychaellmas Christemas and Our Ladye after the rate of
£26 13s 4d for every quarter £80

By chartour

Item allowed more to this accomptaunt for mony by him payed to the
seid William Olyver aswell for the dyettes of the 40 poore people and
their kepers for one quarter *viz* from Our Lady to Midsoomer
£26 13s 4d as also £20 payed hym for provysyion for woode and
it is to be noted that he the seyd William Olyver hadd at his first
entrye into the hows these two summes payed hym beforehand and
so hath it still payed hym yerely so that whensoever he shall leave
of from kepyng the same poore people although he shall kepe them
the whoall yere yett he is to be allowed but three quarters for that
he receyved for one quarter and for the woode before the yere
begynneth which summes this accomptaunt hath payed this yere
as it hath been payed in fourmer yeres *videlicet* £46 13s 4d

[*m. 7v*] Item more allowed to Thomas Corye receyvour of all the
rentes revenues and possessyons belongyng to Goddes Hows for his
fee for one whoall yere endyd at Mydsoomer in thend of this accompte £7

Item more allowed for monye by hym payed to the Quenys Maiesties
receyvour for rent reserved owt of the whoall possessyons of this
hows payable at Mychallmas only within the tyme of thys accompte
with 4d for thacquittance £9 4d

Item to the Baylyf of Humbleyerd hundred for rent leete fee and sute
to the shreves turne for the Mannours of Hethill Carleton and others
thys yere 10s

[*Total of payments so far*] £186 10s 4d

Barbour and Surgeon

Item to Robert Wrethham and Jamys Fyssher surgeons to the poore
people in Goddes Hows for their stypend for one whoall yere *viz* the
seid Robert for halfe a yere endyd at Christemas *anno* 1570 and the
seid James for halfe a yere endid at Mydsoomer in the ende of this
accompte   66s 8s

Item to the same Robert and Jamys barbours to the seyd poore
people for their stypend for one whoall yere *viz* the seid Robert
for halfe a yere endid at Christemas aforeseid 6s 8d and the seid
James for halfe a yere endid at Mydsoomer upon thend of this
accompt 6s 8d in all   13s 4d

                                                        [*Total*]   £4

Rentes resolute

Item payed to the deane and chapiter of the cathedrall churche of t
holy Trynytee in Norwiche for the whoalle yeres rent of the
hospytall medowe   20s

Item to Thomas Blowe baylyf to the duke of Norfolk for rent due to
the mannour of Wroxham thys yere with 6d for a rent henne   10s 8d

Item to Thomas Themylthorpe baylyf to the bisshopp of Norwiche
for rent due to the mannour of Hoveton Saynct Johns thys yere   8d

Item to the baylyf of Costessey mannour for rent of landes and sute
of court thear this yere   7s

Item to Master Barney for rent of certeyn landes in Burlyngham in
the tenure of Nycholas Howlett 5s 4½d Thomas Leman 18d and
Anthony Raynoldes 13d whiche is due and yerely to be payed to
his mannour of Strumpeshawe in all   7s 11½d

Item to John Debney baylyf to the deane and chapiter of
Christechurche for the rent of two churches *viz* All Saynctes and
Saynct Awdrye [*St Etheldreda*]   4d

Item to Thomas Holl gent baylyf to the bisshopp of Norwiche for
rent of certeyn tenementes due to the mannour of Heygham
Conventualles   13s 4d

Item to the chamberleyne of the cittie for rent of assyse for diverse
tenementes   4½d

Item to Rauf Shelton esquyre for the rent of those 4 tenementes in
St Augustyns parrisshe which the parson of St Clementes dyd gyve to
Goddes Hows   14d

Item to the baylyf of the mannour of Carleton for rent due to the
same mannour   2s

Item to the lord of the mannour of Horsford for rent due and payde
owt of those landes which Anne Fletcher late the wyfe of Rychard
Fletcher alderman deceassed hath   5s

Item to the deane and chapiter of Christechurche for the ferme of
a tenement late the tenure of Thomas Codd alderman deceased and
nere the hows which he gave to thospytall   10s

Item to the chamberleyn of the cyttye for rent due and goyng owt
of certeyne groundes and tenementes in St Peters Permontergate   2s

                                                                     [*Total*]   £4 6d

[*m. 8r*] Payementes

Proxie and Sinage

Item to the bysshopp of Norwyche and the archedeacon of Norfolk
for proxye and synage due unto them *viz* for Seethyng synage 2s
proxye 7s 7½d Cossey synage 2s 4d proxye 7s 7½d in all   19s 7d

Item to the archedeacon of Norfolk for proxye and synage *viz* for
Calthorp synage 18d for proxye 5s and for Southwalsham 7s 7½d
in all   13s 1½d

                                                                     [*Total*]   33s 8½d

Annuytee

Item payed to Thomas Crooke for his whoall yeres annuytee due
unto hym at the feaste of St Mychaell the Archaungell within
the tyme of thys accompt   20s

Pencions

Item payed to Robert Hawgh for the whoall yeres pencion of
Bysshopp Goldwell due to the deane and chapiter of Christechurche
for the whoall yere endyd at the feast of St Mychaell tharchaungell
in the tyme of this accompt   66s 8d

Item payed for the pencion goyng owt of the churche somtyme called
St Helens due to the deane and chapiter of Christechurch due for
the whoall yere endyd at Mychaellmas within the tyme of this accompt   13s 4d

Item to Sir Thomas Mychelson curate at Mundham for his whoall
yeres pencion   66s 8d

Item to the seid Thomas curate at Seethyng for hys whoall yeres
pencion   40s

Item payed to Sir Wylliam Browne vycar of Calthorpe for his
whoall yeres pencion   *nihil* not payed

Item to the master and fellowes of Corpus Christi Colledge in
Cambrydge toward the exhybycion and fyndyng of three schollers
in the same colledge accordyng to a certeyn covenant of indenture
made betwyn Mathew[18] now archebysshopp of Canterbury and the
mayour shrevis cittezens and cominaltie of this cittie and here payed
for one whoall yere endyd at the feast of the Annuncyacion of
Our Lady in the tyme of this accompt   £8

Item payed to Master Thomas Aldwyche archedeacon of Sudburye
for preachyng 4 sermons *viz* one at Thetford one at Wymondham
one at Saynt Clementes and one at the common place 30s and
to the mayour shrevis and certeyn other persons by vertue of
the indenture aboveseyd 10s in all   40s

                                        [*Total*]   £19 6s 8d

Landes purchased and dettes payed

Item payed to Henry Grenewood alderman the thred daye of
Marche *anno* 1570 for the purchase of a lyttle pece of ground withowt
St Gyles gates   13s 4d

Item to William Knyght alias Kett the 24th daye of June *anno* 1571
for the fyrst payment of £9 *20* for the purchase of the mannour
of Chosyll in Wymondham   £40

Item to Thomas Blowe bailif to the duke of Norfolk his grace of his
mannour of Wroxham the 7th daye of October *anno* 1570 for the
fyne of 25 acres and 1 roode of copyhold land in Salhows and
Wroxham houlden of the same duke   40s

Item to John Drywood for his ferme of the marsshes in Essex by
hym before payed for two yeeres and a halfe endid at thannunciacion
of Our Lady *anno* 1570 *as by the former accomptes doo apere* and
by an assemblye agreed to be repayed unto hym and so payed by this
accomptaunt   £33 6s 8d

Item to Master Anthony Marker for a surplusage of monye due unto
hym upon the determynacion of his last accompt and by this
accomptaunt payed by vertue of a warrant from the surveyours   £6 18s 5½d

                        [*Total for pensions and lands*] £102 18s 5½d

---

[18] Matthew Parker (1504–1575) was born in Norwich and became Archbishop of Canterbury
in 1559.

[*m. 8v*] **Expenses of courtes and surveyes**

Item payed to John Debney the 15th daye of December for keepyng
the courte at Hethyll   6s 8d

Item to John Broome for the chargdes and expenses of the same
courte wheare wer Master John Sotherton John Debney Thomas
Hogges and this accomptaunt   3s 8d

Item to the same John the 20th of Marche *anno* 1570 for the
dynners of Master John Sotherton John Brereton John Goodwyn[19]
John Debney Thomas Hogges this accomptaunt and certeyne of the
tenantes to the nomber of 14 persons at the first meetyng for the
survey at Hethyll   6s 7d

Item to the seid John for the suppers of John Goodwyn the same
daye and this accomptaunt and their dynners and suppers the next
daye tarryeng theare abowt the same surveye   2 s

Item to Henry Benselyn the 22nd of the same month for the dynners
of John Brereton John Goodwyn John Debney Thomas Hogges this
accomptaunt and the tenantes beyng at Carleton for the survey thear   4s

Item to the same Henry the 14th and 15th of May *anno* 1571 for
2 dynners and one supper of John Goodwyn this accomptaunt and
7 of the tenantes beeyng at Carleton at the treadyng owt of the
landes thear[20]   6s

Item to John Broome the 18th of May for 2 dynners and 2 suppers
of John Godwyn this accomptaunt and 6 of the tenantes at the
treadyng owt of the landes at Hethill   11s 3d

Item for the chardges and expenses of this accomptaunt for 8 dayes
aswell in rydyng from Norwich to Essex and from thence to
London as from London into Essex ageyn and so from thence to
Norwich at 2s each daye in all   16s

                                                   [*Total*]   56s 2d

Rewardes

Item in reward given to John Toftes for carryeng letters from Master
John Aldriche late mayour to Master Drywoodes in Essex   6s 8d

---

[19] The John Godwin listed as a surveyor in Norfolk, and who later became Surveyour of Lands
to Elizabeth I in 1595–96 was probably the John Goodwyn mentioned above: P. Eden, 'Land Surveyours in Norfolk 1550–1850 Part II', *Norfolk Archaeology* 36 ii (1975), pp.119–148. I am grateful
to Paul Rutledge for this reference.
[20] Establishing boundaries.

Item in reward gyven to one Master Dale a councell in London for his advyse when John Brereton and this accomptaunt did reenter the marisshes in Essex   6s

Item to a poore woman for carrying letters from John Brereton from Brentwood to Master Drywoodes hows concernyng the same reentrye   6s

Item in rewarde given to a man which did rowe John Brereton and this accomptaunt to the marisshes in Essex (thone beeyng almost a myle dystant from thother) and for other his paynes abowt the same busynes   2s

Item to Master Baspoles servaunt when Master Peck and Master Sotheron ridd to Coltesale for the lettyng of the landes theare   4d

Item to Father Ruft for goyng with John Goodwyn and this accomptaunt abowt the fyeldes in Hethill in the tyme of the surveye   8d

Item to John Toftes for carryeng £4 to Bennett Colledge [*Corpus Christi, Cambridge*] for the halfe yere endid at Mychaelmas   4d

Item to John Mondford carpenter aswell for his horsehyer as for his halfe dayes woorke in rydyng to see the berne at Hethyll   12d

Item to Geffrye Cobbes swoordbearer for sealyng aswell thone part of Kettes indenture as the letters of attourney wherby thestate was taken   4s

Item to Master Thomas Pettwys for monye by hym gyven to Master Kyndlemershe secretary to therle of Leicester for makyng the erles letters for the lycence for sale of the landes in Swanyngton as by his bill appereth   6s

[*m. 9r*] Item to the same Thomas for monye by hym gyven to one of the clerkes of the chauncerye for drawyng the same lycence as by his byll appereth   3s 4d

Item to Master Richard Davye councellour for pennyng the bookes betwin William Kett and the mayour shrevis etc. for the purchase of Chosyll Mannour in Wymondham   5s

Item gyven and delt in allmes at the parryshe of St Peter Permontergate on St Thomas daye before Christemas in remembraunce of Thomas Codde late cyttezen and alderman of Norwiche deceassed accordyng to a certeyn order made and agreed upon by Master Mayour and the aldermen   37s 6d

Item allowed to this accomptaunt for wrighting and engrossyng this accompt and for parchement for the same as fourmer accomptes hath been allowed   20s

Item to Master John Aldwryche alderman for money by hym gyven
to [*blank*] for drawyng the booke of the landes in Swanyngton
sold to Master Bychers   2s 6d

Item to the same John for monye by hym gyven to William Kett for
byndyng the bergayne[21] of the purchase of Chosyll Mannour in
Wymondham   3s 4d

Item to Charles Brethutt for makyng a hundred woode at Master
Aldwriches closse in Connesford   12d

Item to Edmond Smyth barbour for forcyng certeyne Egyptyans
at Master Aldriches commandment[22]   6d

                                                            [*Total*]   100s 8d

Writinges and horsehyre

Item to this accomptaunt for diverse and sondrye wrightinges by
hym made from the feast of the Natyvytee of St John Baptist
anno 1570 untill the feast of the Natyvytee of St John Baptist *anno*
1571 as by a byll therof signed with the handes of the surveyours
partyculerly dooth appere   25s 2d

Item to the same accomptaunt for monye by hym diverse tymes
payed for horshyre in rydyng abowt the affayers of the hospytall
within the tyme of this accompt as by his seid bill signed with the
seid surveyours handes particulerly dooth appere   14s 10d

                                                            [*Total*]   40s

Reparacions at

Hethill

Item to a dawber for dawbyng certeyn walles at Hethill abowt the
howses late purchased of Crosseman as by Thomas Thurbons bill
signed with thandes of Master Thomas Peck and John Brereton
surveyours maye appere   6s

Item for settyng twoo studdes   4d

Item for clay, sand and lyme with the carryage therof   4s

Item for takyng upp of bryck   12d

Item for hengles for 3 gates and dores and hookes for the same   3s

Item for 6 weekes woorke of a man in fencing and dytchyng abowt
the groundes at 4s the weke   24s

---

[21] To secure the contract. If enrolled, an agreement to sell coupled with payment (bargain and
sale) could itself act as a conveyance.

[22] See Introduction, p.12.

Item to Father Rust for fencyng the woode	12s
Item to a mason for 4 dayes woorke	2s 6d
Item to his twoo men for lyke tyme	2s 6d
Item for their boordes	4s
Item for 2 rackes for the stables	12d
Item for 2 bunches of lath	2s 4d
Item for 2 ladders	2s 10d
Item for carryeng the seid lath and ladders	2d
Item to Isaack Preston for 11 loades of straw	31s 10d
Item for twoo newe faldergates	9s
[m. 9v] Item for carryage therof	7s 4d
Item to John Broome for 5 loades of strawe	20s
Item to [blank] Corpe for strawe	5s
Item to Isaack Parsons for russhes	2s
Item for carryeng the same	4d
Item for carryeng claye	4s
Item for hempe	12d
Item to Corpe, John Broome and Thomas Thurbon for carryeng the tymber whiche was sawen into boordes	4s
Item for rede	2s 4d
Item for lyme	21d
Item to [blank] Rust for carryage therof	18d
Item for nayles	6d
Item to a thacher for 40 dayes woorkes	20s
Item to his server for lyke tyme	13s 4d
Item for their boord at 3d eche day eyther of them	20s
Item to twoo dawbers eche of them 20 dayes at eyther of them 5½d eche daye	18s 4d
Item for their boordes all the same tyme	13s 4d
Item to a carpenter for 16 dayes woorke	8s
Item for his boorde	5s 4d
Item to a labourer for 4 dayes	16d
Item for his boorde	16d
Item to Olyver Hardyng for fellyng hewyng and sawyng 12 hundred and a halfe of boorde and planck at 2s 2d eche hundred	27s 1d

Item to [blank] Corpe for a loade of sand	12d
Item for carryeng boordes	8d
Item for bryckes	52s 2d
Item to a mason and his man either of the twoo dayes	2s 6d
Item for their boordes	2s 6d
Item to Thomas Manbye carpenter for one wekes woorke in hangyng gates and amendyng the backhows at the seid hows late Crossemans as by John Broomes bill fermour theare signed with thandes of Master William Farrour and Master Thomas Peck and John Brereton surveyours maye appere	52s
Item for his boorde	2s 6d
Item to Robert Clarke carpenter and his twoo men for a weekes woorke in groundselyng and settyng upp the bakehows and for dores	7s
Item for their boorde	7s 6d
Item to Henry Hamont carpenter and his twoo men for a weekes woorke in settyng upp the kyll and plauncheryng the stable	7s
Item for their boorde	7s 6d
Item to Henry Munson mason and his man 11 dayes in pynnyng the stable and other places and for pavyng the hall wheare it was decayed	9s 2d
Item for their borde	8s
Item to Gerard Goldspynne for 7 dayes thacking the bakehows and cartehows	2s 4d
Item for his boorde	2s 6d
Item to a server	20d
Item for his boorde	2s 6d
Item to the person [parson] of Hethill for 2 loades of strawe	8s
Item to Carter for a loade of strawe	4s
Item to Smythe for a loade of strawe and somwhat more	4s 6d
Item for a thowsand and a halfe of bryck	12s
Item for the carryage therof	4s
Item for hookes and hengles for the great gate in the court yarde	2s
[m. 10r] Item for hengles and hookes for 8 dores	3s
Item for 2 hundred nayles for dores	16d
Item for a hundred smaller nayles	6d
Item for 2 hundred braddes for the kylle	14d
Item to Havers for hedgyng and dytchyng 27 roddes ageynst the moore	4s

Item to a man for 3 dayes diking agenyst the stable dore	12d
Item for his boorde	15d
Item to Havers for hedgyng 134 roddes abowt the woode at 1½d for eche rodd	16s 8d
Item to Pryour for makyng 2 fallgates and for his boorde	20d
Item for hengles and hookes for the same gate	8d
Item to Rust for dawbyng the bakehows and swynes coates [*pig sties*] by the greate[23]	5s
Item to hym for gatheryng and carryeng stones to pynne the howses with	2s
Item to hym for a loade of sande	12d
Item to Corpe for a loade of sand	12d
Item to Rust for settyng the pale over the yarde	2s 2d
Item to hym for hedgyng and dychyng 122 roddes downe the moore at 2½d eche rodd	15s
Item to Rychard Calfe for halfe a chalder of lyme and for carryage therof from Norwiche to Hethill aforeseyd	3s 4d
Item to hym for a fadom and a halfe of rede with the lyke carryage therof	9d
Item for 2 coombes of lyme	16d
[*Total*]	£22 12s 4d

Master Coddes closse

Item to Thomas Jakes the 5th of August *anno* 1570 for 6 dayes woorke at the wall abowt Master Coddes closse in Coonesford at 10d eche daye	5s
Item to hym for Richard Hedley his servaunt for lyke tyme at 6d eche daye	3s
Item to John Reade his labourer for like tyme at 8d eche daye	4s
Item to Thomas Jakes the 12th of August for himselfe and his seid servant eyther of them 6 dayes at 10d eche daye for hymselfe and 6d eche daye for his servant in all	8s
Item to John Reade labourer for like tyme	4s
Item to Thomas Jakes the 19th of August for hymselfe 5 dayes and his seid servant 6 days at their fourmer rates eyther of them in all	7s 2d
Item to John Reade labourer for 6 dayes then endyd at his fourmer rate	4s
Item to Robert Blythe the same daye for 2 loades of sande spent theare	20d

---

[23] Work undertaken 'by the greate' was completed for a fixed price, that is, not for a daily rate.

Item to Thomas Jakes the second daye of September for himselfe
and his servant eyther of them 3 dayes at their former rates   4s

Item to John Reade labourer for lyke tyme   2s

Item to Henry Hunt for a piece of tymber for a stulpe and 2 bracys
for the closse gate theare   2s 8d

Item to Nycholas Surryes for 3 penye and 4 peny nayles to amend
the gate which [is] theare   2d

Item to William Brend smyth for a staple and a hespe for the same gate   3d

Item to John Colson carpender for one dayes worke of twoo of his
servantes in cutting the post and bracys and for settyng the same in
the ground and amendyng the gate   20d

Item to the seid John for a sparre to make the nether ledge of the
same gate with   6d

Item to Thomas Jakes the 9th of September for himselfe and his seid
servant eyther of them 6 dayes at their fourmer rates   8s

Item to John Reade labourer for lyke tyme   4s

Item to Rychard Nyxon the seid daye for 9 chalder and a halfe of
lyme spent theare at 4s eche chalder in all   38s

Item to hym for 15 loades and a halfe of stone spent theare   15s 6d

[m. 10v] Item to the seid Richard Nyxon for 4 loades of sand   3s

Item to hym for carryeng 2 hundred bryckes from the hospytall to
the same walle   4d

Item to George Hall the 11th of September 1570 for halfe a hundred
rede to rygg the wall with   15s

Item to Thomas Jakes the 16th of September for hymselfe and his
seid servant eyther of them 6 dayes at their fourmer rates   8s

Item to John Reade labourer for lyke tyme   4s

Item to Thomas Jakes and his seid servant the 18th of the same
month eyther of them one daye at their fourmer rates   16d

Item to John Reade labourer for one daye   8d

Item to Richard Nixon the same daye 16 coombes of lyme   8s

Item to hym for a loade of sand   9d

Item to Robert Blythe the 21st of September for carryeng 2 loades
of stone from the hospitall to the seid wall   20d

Item to hym for 2 loades of claye spent theare   2s

Item to hym for 2 loades of sand spent theare   20d

Item to hym for carryeng 2 loades of reede from the common

stathe thyther	16d
Item to John Quayntrell dawber the last of September for 5 dayes at 10d the day	4s 2d
Item to William Marche and Edmond Frost labourers for the like tyme eyther of them at 8d eche daye	6s 8d
Item to Thomas Howell for a stond to cary water with	8d
Item to John Quayntrell the 7th daye of October for 5 dayes at 10d eche daye	4s 2d
Item to William Marche labourer for like tyme at 8d eche daye	3s 4d
Item to Edmond Frost labourer for 4 dayes then endid at the lyke rate	2s 8d
Item to John Quayntrell the 13th daye of October for 5 dayes at his fourmer rate	4s 2d
Item to William Marche and Edmond Frost labourers for the lyke tyme at their former rate	6s 8d
Item to Edmond Thurketyll the 14th of October for 32 fadom of reede at 2d the fadom	5s 4d
Item to Nycholas Taillour for a quarter of a hundred reede spent theare	9s 8d
Item to William Olyver for carryeng 3 loades of stone from thospitall to the seid closse	2s 6d
Item to hym for a loade of strawe to treade into the claye[24] for the wall theare	3s 4d
Item to hym for carryeng a loade of rede from Taillours in St Georges of Colgate to the seid closse	10d
Item to John Mason the 18th of November for 15 loades of claye occupyed theare	15s
Item to Richard Pallmer mason and John Colson carpenter for shoryng the corner hows at Master Coddes	14d
Item to William Grenes wyfe for slytt of her stopp and rope when the masons and dawbers fetched their water theare	16d
Item to William Grene the 7th of February 1570 for coldring stone one daye when the wall fell downe theare	8d
Item to John Davye labourer the same daye for the lyke	8d
Item to John Taillour labourer for 2 dayes woorke in makyng upp the old morter and for byndyng upp the reede whiche fell downe theare	12d
Item to Fraunces Allen for 100 wicker to bynde upp the same reede with	4d

---

[24] Treading in the clay – fibrous material such as straw, hair or clay was mixed into the mortar (clay) to help it adhere.

Item to Thomas Jakes the 7th of April *anno* 1571 for himselfe
2 dayes and a halfe and for Richard Hedley his servant 3 dayes
himself at 10d and his servant at 6d eche daye   3s 7d

[*m. 11r*] Item to John Hedley mason for 3 dayes then endyd at 10d
eche daye   2s 6d

Item to Symon Powell and Hugh Jones labourers eyther of them
3 dayes eyther of them at 8d eche daye   4s

Item to Thomas Jakes the 11th of Aprill *anno* 1571 for hymselfe and
his seid servant eyther of them 2 dayes at their fourmer rates   2s 8d

Item to John Hedley for the lyke tyme at 10d eche daye   20d

Item to Symon Powell and Hugh Jones for lyke tyme at their
fourmer rates   2s 8d

Item to Richard Nixon the 21st of Apryll for 9 coombes of lyme   5s 3d

Item to hym for a loade of sande   9d

Item to John Quayntrell dawber for 3 dayes endid the 23rd of June
in amendyng the clayework which fell downe when the wall fell   2s 6d

Item to William Marche labourer for like tyme   2s

Item to Robert Blythe for a loade of claye   12d

Item to Edmond Overton for 3 burthens of straw   6d

Item to George Hall for 2 fadom of reede   6d

Item to Grenes wyfe for water spent thear   2d

Item to William Olyver for carryeng a loade of stone from the
hospytall to Coonesforde   10d

                                                      [*Total*]   £13 6s 3d

The Charnell

Item to William Bynham the 17th of October *anno* 1570 for hymselfe
and his servant eyther of them 2 dayes hymselfe at 10d and his servant
at 9d eyther daye in stoppyng part of the wyndowes at the charnell   3s 2d

Item to Peter Staller labourer for 2 dayes at 8d eche daye   16d

Item to Thomas Freston smyth for 48 pound of yron bought of
hym by Master John Sotherton for a harthyron for the schollers at
the charnell at 2d eche pounde   8s

Item to Master Thomas Pettwys for monye by hym payed to Bryan
Skelton for a locke and a keye to the charnell dore   16d

Item to Robert Tolye for 2 coombes of lyme spent theare   12d

Item to Master Gooche chamberleyn for 100 bryckes occupyed
abowt the wyndowes thear   14d

Item to Pettyngale the 7th of June *anno* 1571 for byrche[25] for the schollers — 1d

Item to Richard Palmers servant the mason for amendyng a hole over the schoolehows dore — 2d

Item to Thomas Lathe glasyer for amendyng dyverse wyndowes in the schole hows and for takyng downe certeyne glasse theare as by his bill particulerly dooth appere — 8s

Item to William Pynchym the 18th of June *anno* 1571 for byrche for the schollers — 6d

Item to Master Robert Sucklyng alderman for *di.*100 [*50*] pavyng tyle spent in the schoolehows — 3s

[*Total*] — 27s 9d

The hospitall

Item to William Bynham mason for 4 dayes woorke *di.* [*4½ days*] of himselfe endid the 5th of August *anno* 1570 in amendyng the great owtward wall at the hospytall at 10d eche daye — 3s 9d

Item to Robert Lowthe his apprentice 6 dayes thear at 9d eche daye — 4s 6d

Item to Peter Staller labourer for 4 dayes and a halfe then endyd at 8d eche daye — 3s

Item to Robert Hargrave mason workyng theare 6 dayes endid the 5th of August at 10d eche daye — 5s

[*m. 11v*] Item to Henry Lee his labourer for lyke tyme then endyd at 8d eche daye — 4s

Item to William Hargrave his servant for lyke tyme then endyd at the lyke rate — 4s

Item to William Bynham mason the 12th of August *anno* 1570 for himselfe 3 dayes then endid at 10d eche daye and his servant 6 dayes then endid at 9d eche daye in all — 7s

Item to Robert Hargrave mason for himselfe 6 dayes then endid at 10d eche daye and his servant 5 daies then endid at 8d eche daye in all — 8s 4d

Item to Peter Staller fo [*sic*] labourer for 3 dayes then endyd at 8d eche daye — 2s

Item to Henry Lee labourer for 5 dayes then endid at the lyke rate — 3s 4d

Item to Robert Hargrave mason the 16th of August for himselfe 3 dayes then endid at 10d and his seid servant for like tyme at 8d eche day — 4s 6d

---

[25] Perhaps the scholars were particularly intractable because a further 6d was paid for additional birches eleven days later.

Item to Henry Lee labourer for lyke tyme then endyd at 8d eche daye   2s

Item to William Bynham the 19th of the same month for himselfe
4 daies *di.* [*4½ days*] at 10d eche daye and his seid servant
3 dayes *di.* [*3½ days*] at 9d eche daye   6s 4½d

Item to Peter Staller labourer for 4 *di.* dayes [*4½ days*] then endid
at 8d eche daye   3s

Item to Nycholas Surryes smyth for 2 jemowes 2 staples and a hespe
for the well dore in the wasshyng hows   5d

Item to Godfrey Skepmaker for 2 skeppes to carrye coulder[26] with   4d

Item to John Cryspe for a ladder of 19 staves   18d

Item to William Bynham the 26th of August for himselfe 5 dayes
and his seid servant lyke tyme at their fourmer rates   7s 11d

Item to Peter Staller and Rychard Foster labourers for like tyme
at 8d eche daye eyther of them in all   6s 8d

Item to Nycholas Surryes the 28th of August for 100 *di.* [*150*] of
3 penye nayles and lath nayles spent abowt the dore in the
wasshing hows and amending the beddes   11d

Item to John Byrche carpenter for a maintree for the new chymney
in the new lodgyng hows   5s

Item to Rauf Clementes for packthredd for the mason occupyed
abowt the same chymney   1d

Item to John Quayntrell dawber for 5 daies woorke endid the
26th of August in cooveryng part of the greate walle theare at 10d
eche daye   4s 2d

Item to William Marche and Thomas Aldriche labourers for lyke
tyme eyther of them at 8d eche daye in all   6s 8d

Item to Edmond Pallyng for 10 fadome of rede spent theare   3s 4d

Item to William Bynham the second of September for himselfe and
his seid servant eyther of them 6 dayes at their fourmer rates of 10d
and 9d   9s 6d

Item to Peter Staller labourer for like tyme at 8d eche daye   4s

Item to Richard Foster labourer for 5 daies then endid at the lyke rate   3s 4d

Item for an erthen pott to sett in the wasshing hows   3d

Item to William Bynham the 9th of September for hymselfe and his
servant eyther of them 6 dayes at their fourmer rates of 10d amd 9d   9s 6d

Item to Peter Staller and Rycharde Foster labourers for lyke time
eyther of them at 8d eche daye   8s

---

[26] Coulder: either stone chippings or chaff that was used to bind mortar.

Item to William Blewett Smyth the 15th of September for ankers[27]
layed in the mens chamber wayeng together 16 pound and a halfe
at 2d eche pounde   2s 9d

Item to hym for a staple of yron and for 100 3 peny nayles for the
pore folkes newe bedes   7d

Item to Robert Reason carpenter for one dayes woorke and a halfe
of his servant in taking downe thold plauncher over thold wasshyng
and for amendyyng certeyn stooles and other thinges theare at 10d
the daye   15d

Item to William Bynham the 16th of September for himselfe and his
servant ether of them 6 dayes in makyng upp the new chymney in the
newe lodging at their fourmer rates of 10d and 9d   9s 6d

[m. 12r] Item to Peter Staller labourer for lyke tyme at his fourmer
rate of 8d eche daye   4s

Item to Henry Lee labourer for 5 dayes then endid at the lyke rate   3s 4d

Item to Robert Reason the 22nd of September for 5 dayes woorke
of his servant in makyng a dore a dorestall wyndowes and other
thinges in the new wasshynghows at 10d eche daye   4s 2d

Item to William Blewett smyth the same daye for 2 little anckers of
yron layed into the ladyng adjoyneng upon the servants chamber
wayeng together 9 pound   18d

Item to William Bynham the 23rd of September for himselfe and his
servant eyther of them 5 dayes at their fourmer rates of 10d and 9d   7s 11d

Item to Peter Staller for like tyme at 8d the day   3s 4d

Item to Henry Lee labourer for 4 dayes then endyd at the same rate   2s 8d

Item to Robert Reason carpenter for 6 dayes woorke of his servant
endid the last of September in makyng new beddes for the poore
people at 10d eche daye   5s

Item to John Quayntrell dawber the 23rd of September for 2 dayes
woorke at 10d the daye   20d

Item to William Marche labourer for lyke tyme at 8d eyther daye   16d

Item to William Grene labourer for 1 daye   8d

Item to William Bynham for himselfe 1 daye 10d and his servant
2 dayes endid the 26th of September at 9d eyther daye   2s 4d

Item to Peter Staller labourer for 2 dayes then endid at 8d eyther daye 16d

Item to Robert Toyle lymeburner the 28th of September for
7 chalder and 6 coombes of lyme spent theare at 4s eche chalder   31s

---

[27] OED defines an anker as a piece of metal acting as a point of support, but its use in the con-
struction of the men's chamber is uncertain.

Item to Robert Reason carpenter *the 5th of October* for 4 daies
woorke of his servant in makyng and fynysshyng the new beddes
in the new lodgyng   3s 4d

Item to Alyce the wyfe of John Shypley the 5th of October for 22
coombes of lyme   11s

Item to William Olyver for 6 loades of sand spent theare   4s

Item to Allen of Ranworth for a quarter of a hundred reede spent
theare abowt ryggyng the walles   7s 3d

Item to John Mason the 18th of November 1570 for 5 loades of claye
for the same ryggyng   5s

Item to hym for a loade of sande   10d

Item to Thomas Manne glasyer for settyng 3 panes and 2 poyntes[28]
of new glasse in the newe lodgyng at the hospytall conteyneng in all
12 foote at 5d eche foote   5s

Item for settyng diverse pieces of glasse in thother wyndows theare
to the same Thomas   12d

Item to hym for amendyng 2 great panes in the churche wyndowes
theare   3s

Item to Master Thomas Peck alderman the 7th of December for
sparres lath and naylles spent at thospytall and at Hethill as by his
byll maye appere   13s 2d

Item to Henry Shypdham the 22nd of January for carryeng hydes
and a back[29] of lether for shooes for the poore folkes theare   5s

[m. 12v] Item to John Robynson the 24th of Marche 1570 for makyng
2 dozen and a halfe of shoes of the same lether at 3s eche dozen   7s 6d

Item to Margarette Bond at Master Peckes commandement for
kepyng Alice Dyngle and Roger Stapleforde   3s 4d

Item to William Olyver for money due to hym for diverse thinges as
by his bill may appere whiche was to be payed in the last accompt
but by warrant sett over to me to paye as by the same warrant under
the surveyours handes maye appere   £4 9s 2d

Item to Alice Shypley for 14 chalder and 2 coombes of lyme and
8 loades of stone which should likewise have been payed in the last
accompt but sett over to me to paye by warrant as by the same maye
appere   65s

Item to John Hewer bladesmyth for a shodd shoovel to make graves with   8d

---

[28] Perhaps glass at the top of an arch, in contrast to the 'panes' in the main lights below. I am
grateful to Dr David King for suggesting the distinction.

[29] Thick, well-tanned hide.

Item to John Byrche carpenter for one dayes woorke of hymselfe
and 6 men in removyng 6 great dormondes from the bisshoppes
pallace to the hospytall yarde   6s

Item to the same John for his tryces occupyed abowt the same   12d

Item to a labourer for makyng a hole in the pallace wall to gett out
the dormondes at [sic]   8d

Item to Richard Fytt for carryeng the same dormondes from the
pallace to thospitall yarde upon his carte   5s

Item to John Byrche carpenter for makyng 3 new beddsteddes theare
at thappoyntment of Master Aldriche then mayour   8s

Item to William Blewett carpenter for 300 3 peny nayles spent
abowt makyng beddes   18d

                                    [Total]   £23 3s 1½d

The hospitall treasourye

Item to Nycholas Surryes for a little keye to the owtward dore next
the guildehall porche   4d

Item to the same Nicholas for a keye to the owtward dore of the
hospitall treasourye in the guildehall   6d

Item to hym for 200 lath nayles and tackes to amend the boxes
with theare   6d

Item to John Ballyston for 100 and 8 ynches of halfe ynche boorde
for the boxes   6s 4d

Item to Richard Spurlyng for 2 sparres either of them 13 foote long
occupyed theare   12d

Item to hym for 5 coople of quarters for seeling every of them
2 foote long   2s

Item to hym for a coople of quarters 3 foote long   6d

Item to hym for 2 greate pieces for the sydes and feete wheron the
boxes stode   12d

Item to John Byrche the 21st of October 1570 for 100 4 foote of
ynche boorde for staunches   8s

Item to hym for 100 halfe ynche boorde for seelyng boorde for the
same treasourye   6s

Item to Byborne Flanders *joyner* the 21st of October for 3 dayes
woorke and a halfe theare at 12d eche daye   3s 6d

Item to John Wake joyner for 2 dayes woorke then endid   2s

Item to John Cork the same daye for a pound of candle for them
to woorke wyth   3d

[*m. 13r*] Item to Nycholas Surreys smyth for 400 little nayles spent
abowt the boxes and new boordes   12d

Item to John Wake joynour for one dayes woorke 24th of October
anno 1570   12d

Item to Byborne Flannders the 27th of the same month for 4 dayes
woorke and a halfe   4s 6d

Item to John Byrche the last of October for halfe a hundred and
5 foote of ynche boordes for staunches   4s 4d

Item to John Cork the same daye for a pounde of candle   3d

Item to John Wys joynour the 27th of October for hymselfe and his
servant eyther of them 2 dayes eyther of them at 12d eche daye   4s

Item to John Adamson for tournyng 3 postes for the benches feete   4d

Item to John Wys the second daye of November for 2 hundred halfe
 ynche boorde   13s 4d

Item to hym the same daye for a hundredd and 12 foote of ynche
boorde for staunches   11s

Item to the same John the 4th of November for hymselfe and his
servant eyther of them 4 daies *di.* [*4½ days*]   9s

Item to Byborne Flannders for 5 dayes woorke then endyd   5s

Item to Nicholas Surryes for nayles   2d

Item to Byborne Flannders the 11th of November for 4 dayes worke
then endyd   4s

Item to John Wys the 10th of the same moneth for 2 daies worke
and a halfe of his servant   2s 6d

Item to John Cork the 11th of the same moneth for 2 poundes of candle   6d

Item to Byborne Flannders the 18th of November for 6 dayes
woorke theare   6s

Item to John Wys the same daye for Robert Robynson his servant
for the lyke tyme   6s

Item to John Byrche the 20th of November for a hundred halfe
ynche boorde   6s 4d

Item to Nicholas Dunnock for a pound of glewe to joyne certeyne
of the seelyng together   4d

Item to Byborne Flanders the 25th of November for 6 dayes
woorke then endyd   6s

Item to John Wys the same daye for himselfe 3 dayes and his servant
4 dayes then endid   7s

Item to Byborne Flannders the seconde daye of December for
5 dayes woorke   5s

Item to John Wys the same daye for himselfe 2 dayes and a halfe and his servant 5 dayes	7s 6d
Item to Nicholas Surreyes for 2 payer of buttes and 3 hengles for the boxes dores	8d
Item to Byborne Flannders the 6th of December for 3 dayes woorke then endyd	3s
Item to John Wys the same daye for 2 of his servants thone 2 dayes and a halfe and thother 3 dayes	5s 6d
Item to John Cork the 5th of December for a pound and certeyn odde candles	4d
Item to a poore woman for sweepyng aswell the seid treasourye as the assembly chamber ageynst an assemblye	4d
Item to Robert Syxe smyth for braddes and great nayles spent theare	10d
Item to John Byrche the 5th of December for a quarter of a hundred and 2 foote of ynche boorde spent theare	2s 2d
Item to hym for a quarter for a hundred of halfe ynche boorde to fynyshe the woorke with	18d
[m. 13v] Item to Harkins for carryeng the loose wrytynges owt of the oulde treasourye into the newe	2d
Item to Abraham Panworth for settyng in a quarrell of glasse into the treasourye wyndowe	1d
Item to Nicholas Surreyes smyth for 4 yron rynges to drawe owt the boxes with	4d
Item to John Wys joynour for a framed table and 2 joyned stooles for the same treasourye	10s 4d
Item to John James for sweepyng the same treasourye and for carryeng charcole thither which was brent theare to ayre the chamber and bookes with	3d
Item to Robert Lyng for 6 forrelles of parchement to bynde upp thold accomptes with	18d
Item to John Adamson joynour for all the shelves on thone syde of the treasourye and for a ladder of fyrre stondyng theare he fyndyng boorde	10s
Item to John Cork for small nayles spent theare	1d
Item to Nycholas Surryes smyth for 3d peny and 4 peny nayles occupyed abowt the same shelves	8d
[*Total*]	£8 14s 9d
Sum of all the payments aforeseyd	£398 10s 8½d
And so ys owyng	£44 8s 3d

Remayneth

In thandes of [*blank*] for the ferme of one acre of ground in Horstedd
somtyme in the tenure of Robert Clerke this yere unpayed   6d

In thandes of Thomas Townesend esquire for the rent of a certeyne
medowe called Sylver Medow this yere remayneng unpayed   12d

In the handes of the same Thomas for the rent of all those landes
whiche Hugh Hartley gent lately helde of the mannour of Hethill
which landes the seid Thomas holdeth untaken upp[30] therfor it was
commaunded to the bailif not to receyve the same rent untill order
be taken so that the same rent is behynde and unpayed (besydes £4 8s
dependyng *in supra* upon thend of the last accompt) for thys yere   29s 4d

In thandes of the seid Thomas Townesend for the rent of all those
landes whiche John Prettyman helde of the mannour of Hethill and
whiche the seid Thomas houldeth untaken upp therefor the bailif
was commaundid for this as for thother above so that the rent of
those landes is unpayed (besydes 107s 8d depending *in supra* upon
thend of the last accompt) for this yere   53s 10d

In the handes of diverse persons for rentes due owt of diverse townes
hereafter mencioned *viz* Tweyte 53s 4d Cossey and Rynglonde
4s 3d Calthorp Erpyngham and Barnyngham 2s 9d and Rollesbye
18d in all this yere beeyng behynde and unpayed   61s 10d

In the handes of thabove named Thomas Townesende aswell for
the rent of the landes late Sewalles for this yere 12½d as also for
sute fyne for the same yere used to be payed by Prettyman 4d in
all this yere   16½d

In thandes of John Drywoode for the whoall yeres ferme of the
two marrishes in Essex due at thannuncyacion of Our Lady 1571
and for that the same John cannot have the possessyion of the seid
marisshes therfor by the consent of the surveyours remayneth in his
handes   £13 6s 8d

In thandes of the accomptuant for money remayneng due upon
thend and determynacion of this accompte   £23 13s 8½d

*/Memorandum that the £28 6s 8d which before was repayed to Master Drywood
must be called for and answered with these summes in supra/*

[*m. 14r*] *Examinatur per nos*

[*Signed:*] Robert Suckling, Thomas Whall, Nycholas Sotherton, Thomas Stakys

---

[30] 'Untaken up' meant that Thomas had not been formally admitted tenant at the manor court.

Tripartite Refoundation Charter, 1547[1]

TRANSCRIBED BY CAROLE RAWCLIFFE

The Grant of the Hospitall of St Giles

This indenture trypartited *indented* made the eight day of March in the first yeare of the reigne of our Sovereigne Lord Edward the Sixt, by the grace of God of England, France and Ireland Kinge, defender of the faith and of the Church of England and Ireland in earth the supreme head, Betweene the same kinge, on the first party, and the right honorable prince Edward, duke of Sommerset, uncill and Counsellor to our said Sovereigne Lord, Governor of his gratious person and Lord protector of his highnes realmes and dominions, The reverend Father in God Thomas, Archbishoppe of Canturbury, Sir William Pawlett, Knight of the most honerable order of the garter, Lord St John and greate Master of the Kings most honerable howsehould, Sir John Russell, Knight of the same most honerable order of the garter, Lord Russell and Lord privy seale, Sir John Dudley, knight of the same most honerable order of the garter, Earle of Warwicke and great Chamberlyn of England, Sir Thomas Wryothesley, Knight of the same most honerable order of the garter, Earle of Southampton, the reverend father in God Cuthbert Tunstall, Bishoppe of Duresme, Sir Anthony Browne, Knight of the same most honorable order of the garter and Master of the Kings horse, Sir William Paget, Knight of the same most honorable order of the garter and cheife secretary to the Kings highnes, Sir Anthony Denny, Knight, Sir William Herbert, Knight, Sir Edward Mountague, Knight, cheife Justice of the Comon place, Thomas Bromeley, Knight, one of the Justices of the please before our Sovereigne Lord the Kinge to be houlden, Sir Edward North, Knight, Chanceller of the Kings Court of Th'augmentacions and revenewes of his highnes Crowne, Sir Edward Wootton, knight, and Nicholas Wootton, doctor of Lawe, executors in the last will and Testament of the most noble kinge of famous memory, Kinge Henery the eight, late disceased, of the second party, And the maior, sheriffes, cittizens and commonilty of the citty of Norwich, of the third party wittnesseth that, where the said late Kinge Henery the eight by his said last will and testament, amongest divers other thinges, willed that all such grantes and gifts as his highnes had made, given or promised to any which ben not yet perfected under his gratious signe, or any his highnes seales as they ought to be, and all such recompences for exchanges, sales or any other thinge or thinges as ought to have bene made by his highnes and ben not yet accomplished, should be perfected in every point towards all mannor of men for dis-

---

[1] NRO, NCR 17b, 'City Revenues and Letters' (*Liber Ruber Civitatis*), ff.80v-84v.

charginge of his gratious conscience, charginge his gratious executors and all the rest of his counsalors to see the same done, performed, finished and accomplished in every point, foreseinge that the said guiftes, promises and recompences should appeare to his said executors, or to the most part of them, to have ben made, granted, accorded and promised an any manner of wise.

And further, his Majesty willed that, for because the variety and nomber of things, affaires and matters are, or may be, such as his highnes, not knowinge the certeinty of them before, could not convenientely prescribe a certeyne order or rule unto his said counsellors for ther behavors and proceedings in this charge, which his grace hath and doth appoint unto them about his graces sonne duringe the tyme of his minority, his highnes therefore, for the speciall trust and confidence which his grace had in them, did, by the said last will and testament, will and grant full power and auctorite unto his said counsellors that they all, or the most part of them, beinge assembled together in councell, or, if any of them should fortune to dye, the more part of them as is aforesaid, should and might make, devise and ordeine what things soever they, or the most part of them, as is aforesaid, duringe the mynority of his highnes said sonne thinke meete, necessary or convenient for the benefitt, honor and surety, or the wele, proffitt or comodity of his said sonne, his realmes, dominions or subiectes, or the discharge of his conscience; and the same thinges devised, made or ordeyned by them, or the more part of them, as is aforesaid, should, or might lawfully doe, execute and accomplishe, or cause to be done, executed and accomplished, by ther discretions, or the discretions of the more part of them, as is aforesaid, [*f. 81r*] in as large and ample mannour as his highnes had, or did, expresse unto them by a more speciall comition under his great seale of England, every particuler cause that might chaunce or occurr duringe the tyme of his said sonnes minority, and the selfe same mannour of proceedinge which they should for the tyme thinke meet for to use and followe, willinge and charginge his said sonne and all other which should hereafter be councellors to his said sonne that they never charge, molest, troble nor disquiet his said councellors, nor any of them, for the devisinge or doinge, nor any other person or persons for the doinge of that they should devise, or the more part of them devise or doe assembled, as is aforesaid, as by the same last will and testament, amongst many other things, more at large doth and may appeare.

And forasmuch as it is manifest to the said Lord protector and other his coexecutors that the said last Kinge Henery the Eight did intend and was fully minded and resolved to have assured and taken into his hands and possession the late hospitall of St Gile within the citty of Norwich, and also all and singuler the mannours, landes, tenementes, hereditamentes, church lead, bells, timber, iron, glasse, tile, stone, ornamentes and all other possessions and things of the same late hospitall, and all other hereditamentes hereafter in this present indenture expressed and declared, for and to the intent and purpose to have given and granted the same to the maior, sheriffes, cittizens and commonilty of his said citty of Norwich and to their successors for ever, [and] to have clerely discharged and exonerated the same of all first fruites and tythes for the causes and consideracions hereafter in this present indenture spetified and conteyned.

And also further intended for the same causes and consideracions to have given and granted lycence to the said maior, sheriffes, cittizens and commonilty and their successours to have had, received and taken to them and their successours, aswell of his highnes, his heires and successours, as of any other person or persons, bodyes politike or corporall, mannours, lands, tenementes and hereditamentes to the cleare yearely value of two hundred poundes or under, aswell within the said citty of Norwich as else wher within the realme of England or other his graces dominions.

And, forasmuch also as the said late hospitall, mannours, landes, tenementes, hereditamentes and other things so purposed and minded to have bene given by the said late Kinge to the said maior, sheriffes, cittizens and commonilty and ther successours wer not assured and taken into the hands and possetion of the said late kinge, nor wer assured to the same maior, sheriffes, cittizens and commonilty and ther successours in the life tyme of the same late Kinge, ne none other of his said intentes accomplished or performed accordinge to his graces godly will and purpose in that behalfe, therefore the Kings highnes that nowe is, mindinge the accomplishment and performance of the will, premise, godly intent and purpose of his said most dere and intirely beloved father in that behalfe and to the intent the said maior, sheriffes and commonilty and ther successours should have and enioy the said late hospitall lands, rentes, hereditamentes and other things, accordinge to the will and intent of his said father, with the consent of the said Lord protector and other his coexecutors before rehersed, mindinge also, accordinge to ther most boundinge dutyes, the very true accomplishment and performacon of the said will and testament, hath not onely assumed and taken into his <said> hands the said late hospitall, with all the possessions and hereditamentes of the same, of the giftes, grantes and surrender of the master of the same late hospitall and other havinge interest in the same, but also his Majesty is contented and pleased that the said maior, sheriffes, cittizens and commonilty shall have to them and ther successours for ever the said late hospitall, and all and singuler the lands, tenementes, hereditamentes and other things hereafter in his indenture spetified and conteyned, in like mannour and forme and for the same intentes and purposes as the said late Kinge Henery the Eight intended, and as hereafter in this present indenture is expressed and declared; whereupon the said maior, sheriffes, cittizens and commonilty, yeildinge most humble thankes to the Kings Majesty, and prayinge dayly for the increase of his honer and continuance of his health, and for the soule of the said Kinge Henery the Eight, his gratious father, mindinge also the accomplishment of all and every the said Godly Acts and ordinances which the said late kinge intended to have prescribed, limited and appointed to have bene executed, performed and done by the said maior, sheriffes, [*f. 81v*] cittizens and commonilty and ther successours, and in this indenture hereafter expressed and conteyned, the same maior, sheriffes, cittizens and commonilty most humbly beschinge the Kings Majesty that it may please his highnes to give and grant unto the said maior, sheriffes, cittizens and commonilty the said late hospitall and all and singuler the lands, tenementes, hereditamentes and other things hereafter in this indenture spetified and conteyned, and that it may be ordained, promised, covenanted, granted and agreed betweene his highnes the said Lord protector and his said coexecutors and the said maior, sheriffes, cittizens and commonilty in manner and forme hereafter ensuinge.

In consideracion whereof, and for and in accomplishment of the said will and testament of the said late Kinge Henery the Eight, our said Sovereigne Lord the Kinge that now is, with the advise and consent of the said Lord protector and other his said coexecutors, is pleased and contented to promise and grant, and by theise presentes promiseth and granteth, and the said Lord protector and his said coexecutors covenaunten, and by theise presentes graunten, to and with the said maior, sheriffes, cittizens and commonilty and ther successours that the same our Sovereigne Lord the Kinge, by his graces letters pattents in due forme to be made under his great seale of England before the feast of the Nativity of St John the Baptist next ensuinge the date hereof, will and shall give and grant unto the said maior, sheriffes, cittizens and commonilty all that site, circuit, compasse and precinct of the said late hospitall of St Gile within the citty of Norwich in the parishe of St Ellen next the Bishoppe gate ther / *The Grant of the Hospitall of St Giles/*, and all the church of the same late hospitall and the said belles, timber, iron, glasse, tyle and stone of the same church and late hospitall, and all the ornamentes of the same church and late hospitall, and all plate, stuffe of howshould and other things to the same church and late hospitall, or to eyther of them, belonginge or apperteyninge, and also all and singuler howses, buildinges, gardens, meadowes, mannours, messuages, lands, tenementes and all other his graces possessions and hereditamentes within the site, circuit, compas or precinct of the said late hospitall, and also all and singuler his graces mannours, parsonages, messuages, mylles, howses, buildings, lands, tenementes, meadowes, feedings, pastures, woodes, underwoods, rentes, revercions, services, courts, leets, perquesites and proffittes of courtes and leetes, vewse of frankplege, advousions, tythes, <oblig> oblacions, pencions, porcions, wayves, strayes, wardes, marriages, releifes, hariots, escheates, warrens, fold courses, and all other his graces hereditamentes, with all and singuler ther appurtenaunces, aswell spirituall as temporall, of whatsoever kind or nature they bin of, or by whatsoever name or names the same bin knowne, reputed or taken, scituate, lyinge or beinge in the said citty of Norwich and in the countyes of Norfolk, Suffolk, Essex and citty of Norwich, or any of them, or else wher within the realme of England, to the said late hospitall of St Gile lately belonginge or apperteyninge, or which at the tyme of the disolucon of the said late hospitall wer knowen, reputed, taken, used, occupied or letten as part, parcell or member of the same late hospitall, or of any of the possessions thereof, and also all that the parishe <of> church of St Ellen in Holmestreet within the said citty of Norwich, and the rectory and parsonage of the same parishe church of St Ellen in Holmestreet aforesaid, or by whatsoever other name, or names, the same church is called or knowen, and the steple, bells, lead and site of the same church, and all the tithes, oblacions, obvencions and offerings of the inhabitants of the same parishe from henceforth for the tyme beinge, and all messuages, lands, tenementes, hereditamentes, pencions, porcions and other proffittes, revenewes, comodytyes and possessions, as well spirituall as temporall, of the same parishe church of St Ellen, or to the same rectory, parsonage or parishe church, or to the parson of the same in the right of the same church belonginge, or in [f. 82r] any wise apperteyninge, to have and to hold the said site of the said late hospitall and the said parsonage of St Ellen, and all and singuler the said mannours, messuages, lands, tenementes, tythes, oblacions and all other the premisses with all and singuler ther appurtenaunces to the said maior, sheriffes, cittizens and commonilty and ther successours for ever, to hould of our said sovereigne Lord the Kinge, his heires and successours in soccage by fealty onely and not in cheife, and yeildinge yearely unto our said sovereigne Lord the Kinge, his heires and successors nyne poundes of lawfull money of England to be paid yearely at the feast of St Michaell the Archangell in the Court of Augmentacions and revenuse of our said sovereigne Lord the Kinges Crowne for all mannur of other rentes, services and demands therefore to our said sovereigne Lord the Kinge, his heires or successours to be yelden, done or paid.

And alsoe our said sovereigne Lord the Kinge, for and in further accomplishment of his said fathers will and testament, is further pleased, and by the advise and concent of the of the said Lord protector and his said coexecutors is contented, and by theise presentes willeth, comandeth and ordeineth that the said late hospitall of St Gile shalbe from henceforth a place and howse for the releife of poore people, and shalbe called Gods howse, or the howse of the poore in Holmestreet within the Citty of Norwich, of the foundacon of Kinge Edward the sixt and Kinge Henery the eight, his most noble father / *The Title or name of the Hospitall of the foundacon of Edward the Sixth, King of England etc*/ and that the church ther shalbe the parishe church of St Ellen, as heretofore it hath bene used for divine service, with all mannur of sacramentes and sacramentalles to be from henceforth said, songe and ministred ther, aswell to the parishe of St Ellens parishe in Holmestreet aforesaid for the tyme beinge and to the inhabitants within the site of the said late hospitall for the

tyme beinge, as also to the poore people, officers and ministers from henceforth to be resident or commorant within the precinct of the said late hospitall, and that all howses, buildinges, ground and soyle within the said site of
the said late hospitall shall hereafter be called gods howse, or the howse of
the poore, as is aforesaid, and from henceforth shalbe accepted and taken to
be part and parcell of the said parishe and parishe church of St Ellen in
Holmestreet aforesaid, and of none other parishe, any thinge heretofore used
to the contrary hereof in any wise notwithstandinge.

And our said sovereigne Lord the Kinge is also further pleased and contented, and by the said advice and consent of the said Lord protector and his
said coexecutors further willeth and ordeineth, that ther shalbe from henceforth for ever in the said parishe church of St Ellen one preist suffitiently
learned to serve the cure ther /A Priest/, which shalbe called the curate, or
chapleyne, of the parishoners of St Ellens in Holmestreet next Bishopps gates
and to the poore of Gods howse, or the howse of the poore aforesaid, and
shall have for his yearely stipend or pencon six poundes thirteene shillings
fower pence, and a suffitient mantion howse for his habitacon within the site
and precinct of the said late hospitall.

And that ther shalbe for and in the same parishe church one other preist
suffitiently learned, which shalbe called the Visitor of the Guildhall in
Norwich aforesaid, who shall attend to visitt the prisoners of the Guildhall
aforesaid within the citty of Norwich, / The Visitor to Accompany such a goe to Exe-
cucon/ and from tyme to tyme to say and doe devine service and Masse in the
chappell of the said Guildhall, and to minister sacramentes to the prisoners
ther, as heretofore hath bene accustomed, and also shalbe confessor to the
said prisoners and accompany such as shall goe to execucon, and shalbe all-
wayes resident ther for the same purpose, and shall have for his yearely
stipend or pencion six pounds, and a suffitient mantion howse for his habitacon with in the said site and precinct of the said late hospitall.

And alsoe that ther shalbe from henceforth for ever at the said late hospitall
one scholemaster /one Scholemaster/ and one [f. 82v] usher under him, suffitiently learned in the Lattin tonge and meete and able for ther lerninge, discretion and other vertuous qualityes to teach and learne children the art or
scyence of grammer, which scholemaster and usher shalbe attendant ther for
the instruction and teachinge of the said children, ther by them to be
instructed and taught the said art and science of grammer from tyme to tyme
freely without any reward other then <they> ther Stipends and Salarys, and
shall have for ther salaryes or stipends yerely £16 13s 4d, that is to say to the
sholemaster for his yearely stipend tenne poundes, and the said usher for his
yearely stipend £6 13s 4d, and convenient mantion howses for ther habita-
cions and dwellinges within the said site of the said late hospitall.

And also our said Sovereigne Lord the Kinge is further pleased and contented, and by the said advise and consent of the said Lord protector and his
said coexecutors promiseth and granteth, and the said Lord protector and his
said coexecutors covenanten and granten by theise presentes, to and with the
said maior, sheriffes, cittizens and commonilty that the same our Sovereigne
Lord the Kinge shall by his graces said letters pattentes, in due form to be
made under his great seale of England, give and grant lycence to the said
curate or chaplin, and the said visitor, scholemaster and usher and every of
them [*that they*] may have, receive and take of the gift and grant of the said
maior, sheriffes, cittizens and commonilty and of their successours from tyme
to tyme severall gifts and grantes to be made in writinge under ther common
seale to the said chapline, visitor, scholmaster and usher and every of them
for the tyme beinge of their said severall stipendes and manciones, To have
and to hold the same stipendes and manciones to them and every of them so
longe and duringe such tyme as the same chaplin, visitor, schoolemaster and
usher shall demeane them selves well and to be of good and honest behavior
and conversacon, and shall dilligentely execute and doe their office */ To continue soe Long as the afore mencioned officers shall demeane themselves well/*.

And over this our said Sovereigne Lord the Kinge is further pleased and
contented, and by the said advice and concent of the said Lord protector and
his said coexecutors promiseth and granteth, and the said Lord protector and
his said coexecutors covenanten and granten, and by theise presentes to and
with the said maior, sheriffes, cittizens and commonilty and ther successours,
that the same maior and his successours, maiors of the said citty for the tyme
beinge, with the assent of the most number of the aldermen of the said citty
for the tyme beinge, shall from tyme to tyme have the nominacon and
appointment of the said chapline, visitour, scholemaster and usher, and of
every of them, and of all other the officeres and ministeres of the said late
hospitall, hereafter named, and of every of them */ The maior and maior part of
the aldermen to have the nominacon of the said officers and of all other officers and ministers
of the same/*.

And also that it shall and may be lawfull to the said maior of the said citty
for the tyme beinge and his successours, with the assent of the most number
of the aldermen of the said citty for the tyme beinge, to amove, expell and
put out from ther roomes and offices the said chaplin, visitor, scholemaster
and usher and every of them and ther successours, and the successours of
every of them, and all other ministers and officers which shalbe in the said
howse of the poore, and every of them and ther successours, and the successours of every of them, */ The maior and maior part of aldermen for good cause to dis-
place any officer or minister/* for any notable crime, offence or negligence to be
comitted by the said chapline, visitor, schoolmaster and usher, and other the
said officers and ministeres of the said late hospitall, or by any of them, or for

disobeyinge or not doinge and performinge of such good and reasonable rules, ordinances and preceptes as shalbe hereafter prescribed, assigned or appointed to them, or to any of them, by the said maior, sheriffes, cittizens and commonilty or ther successours to be done, executed or performed.

And the said maior, sheriffes, cittizens and commonilty, for them and their successours, covenanten and by theis presentes graunten to and with our said Sovereigne Lord the Kinge, the said Lord protector and his said coexecutors that they, the same maior and his successours, maiors of the said citty for the [f. 83r] tyme beinge, with the assent of the greater number of the aldermen of the said citty for the tyme beinge, shall within the space of two monthes next after any of the persons aforesaid shalbe amoved from any of their said roomes or offices, as is aforesaid, name, assigne and appoint one other able, meete and convenient person to the same roome, office and promocon from which any such person shalbe soe amoved, expelled or put out.

And also the said maior, sheriffes, cittizens and commonilty for them and ther successours covenanten and granten by theise presentes to and with our said Sovereigne Lord the Kinge, the said Lord protector and his said coexecutors that they, the same maior, sheriffes, cittizens and commonilty and ther successours, shall, within the space of six months next after the date hereof, / *To make graunts and assureances under the common seale to the said officers*/ make, or cause to be made, to the said chapline, visitor, schoolemaster and usher, and to every of them, severall and suffitient giftes, grantes and assurances by wrytinge under the comon seale of ther said severall stipends and mantions to be severally given and granted to them out of the possessions of the said late hospitall within the said citty, with suffitient clauses of distresse for the non payment of the same stipendes, to have and to hold the said stipendes to them and every of them so longe and duringe such tyme as they and every of them shall demeane themselves well and byn of honest and good conversacon and shall diligentely execute, performe and done ther said offices. And also that the same maior, sheriffes, cittizens and commonilty and ther successours shall from tyme to tyme make like grantes and assurances to every of the same officers within the space of one month next after any such officer shalbe named and appointed to any of the same offices.

And also the said maior, sheriffes, cittizens and commonilty, for them and ther successors, further covenanten and granten by theise presentes to and with our said Sovereigne Lord the Kinge, the said Lord protector and other his said coexecutors that they, the same maiors, sheriffes, cittizens and commonilty and ther successours, at their proper costes and charges, shall from and after the end of six months next after the date hereof provide, find and mayneteyne continually and for ever at the said site of the said late hospitall of St Gile, hereafter to be called Goddes howse, or the howse of the poore, suffitient and convenient lodginge, meate, drinke, beddinge, wood and all other thinges necessary for forty poore persons to be resident lyinge, abidinge and found from tyme to tyme in the said late hospitall, and fower women to make the beddes, washe and attend upon the same poore persons, and shall pay yearely to every of the same fower women thirty thre shillings and fower pence for ther wages and apparrell, The same fourty poore persons and every of them to be all waies removable from day to day, weeke to weeke, month to month and tyme to tyme, and other to be taken and received into their roomes and places, at and by the discretion of such person and persons as shalbe named and elected from tyme to tyme by the maior of the said citty for the tyme beinge, with the assent of the most part of the said aldermen for the tyme beinge, to omit, receive, take and remove in to and from the said Howse of the poore, or goddes howse, the said forty poore persons.

And also that they, the same mayor, sheriffes, cittizens and Commonilty and their successours, shall at ther like costes and charges continually and for ever provide and find at the said late hospitall to be called Goddes howse, or the howse of the poore, as is aforesaid, one convenient and suffitient person to be cater, or steward, of and for the provision of the poore ther /A Steward/, and shall give, pay and allowe unto him yearely one coate, or gowne, of the price of 10s for his livery, forty shillings for his wages and suffitient meate and drinke in the said howse, and also shall at their like costes and charges continually and forever provide and find ther one other suffitient and con-venient person to be the rent gatherer, /A Collector of the rents/ or collector of the rentes and revenues of such possessions as shalbe given to and for the sus-tentacon of the said poore persons and other the premisses, and shall give and allowe yearely unto him for his office 3 [blank]; [f. 83v] and also shall at their like costs and charges continually and for ever provide and find ther one other suffitient <person> and convenient person to be porter and butler of the said late hospitall, /A Porter and Butler/ and shall give, pay and allowe unto him yearely one coate, or gowne, of the price of tenn shillinges for his livery 13s 4d for his wages and suffitient meate and drinke in the said howse, and also shall at ther like costes and charges continually and for ever provide and find ther on other suffitient and convenient person to be baker and br[e]wer of the said late Hospitall, /A Baker and Brewer/ and shall give, pay and allowe unto him yearely one gowne, or coate, of the price of 10s for his livery, 13s 4d for his wages and suffitient meate and drinke in the said howse.

And our said Sovereigne Lord the Kinge, in consideracon of the great charges which the said maior, sheriffes, cittizens and commonilty and their successours shall susteyne and beare yearely for the cawses above remembred, is pleased and contented, and by the said advise and consent of the said Lord protector and his said coexecutors promiseth and granteth, and the said Lord protector covenanten and granten by theise presentes to and with the said

maior, sheriffes, cittizens and commonilty that the same our Sovereigne Lord
the Kinge, by his graces said letters patentes, shall give and grant to the same
maior, sheriffes, cittizens and commonilty lycence, full power and authority
to take and receive to them and their successours for ever to the use, sustentacon and mayntenance of the premisses by purchase, bargaine, sale, alien-
acon, gift, grant, legacy, bequest or otherwise, aswell of his highnes and of his
heires and successours, Kinges of this Realme, as of any other person or
persons, bodyes politique and corporate, mannours, parsonages, lands, tenementes, tythes, rentes, revercions or other revenues, possessions or hereditamentes to the yearely value of two hundred powndes or under, over and
above the mannours, lands, tenementes and hereditamentes abovesaid, aswell
within the citty of Norwich as els wher with in the realme of England or in
Wales or in any other the Kinge his dominions, although the same mannours,
parsonages, lands, tenementes, tythes, rentes, revercions, revenues, possessions
or hereditamentes be or shalbe houlden of the Kinge his Majesty, his heires
or successors in cheife or otherwise, the statute and statutes whereby it is provided and enacted that landes and tenementes should not be putt to mort-
mayne, or any other act or statute heretofore made or hadd to the contrary,
or any other lawe, custome, provision, matter or cause in any wise to the contrary notwithstandinge.

And the said mayor, sheriffes, cittizens and commonilty doe covenant,
promise and grant for them and ther successours to and with our said Sovereigne Lord the Kinge, his heires and successours that the hole yearely proffittes and revenues of the said mannours, lands, tenementes, tythes,
possessions, hereditamentes and other the premisses appointed to be given
and granted to the said maior, sheriffes, cittizens and commonilty and ther
successours, and which the same maior, sheriffes, cittizens and commonilty
shall buy and purchase, or that shalbe given to them by reason of the said
lycence, over and besides the findinge of the said chaplin, visitor, schoolemaster and usher and other necessary ministers and officers as are before
appointed to be found by the said maior, sheriffes, cittizens and commonilty,
and over and besides the maynteyninge of the necessary reparacions and
buildinges of the said late hospitall and of other the premisses, shall holly be
bestowed, employed and goe to the releife and sustentacon of the poore.

And our said Sovereigne Lord the Kinge is further pleased and contented,
and by the said advise and consent of the said Lord protector and his said
coexecutors promiseth and granteth, and the said Lord protector and his said
coexecutors covenanten and granten by theise presentes, to and with the said
maior, sheriffes, cittizens and commonilty that the same our Sovereigne Lord
the Kinge, by his graces said letters pattentes, shall accquitt [f. 84r] and discharge aswell the same maior, sheriffes, cittizens and commonilty and their
successours, as the said chapline, visitor, schoolemaster and usher, and other

the said officers and ministers of the said late hospitall, and every of them and their successours and the successours of every of them, and all and every their pencions, salaryes and stipends, as also the said mannours, parsonages, landes, tenementes and other the premisses to be given and granted to the same mayor, sheriffes, cittizens and commonilty and their successours by the Kinges highnes in forme aforesaid, and all other mannours, landes, tenementes and hereditamentes which the said maior, sheriffes, cittizens and commonilty or their successours by reason of the said licence or otherwise shall hereafter have by the gifte, grant, bequest, bargaine or sale of the Kinges highnes, his heires or successours, or of any other person to the use and intent aforesaid, of all and all manner of tenthes and first fruites, and of all and singuler somme and summes of money for and in the name of tenth, or yearely tenth part, or for, or in, the name of first fruites of the said late hospitall, mannours, parsonages landes, tenementes and other the premisses to be given and granted by our said Sovereigne Lord to the said maior, sheriffes, cittizens and commonilty and their successours by the said letters pattentes, or of any other mannours, landes, tenementes or hereditementes or [*sic*] which the same mayor, sheriffes, cittizens and commonilty or ther successours shall hereafter have and obteyne by guift, grant, will, legacy, bequest, bargaine or sale of any person, or persons, by vertue of the said licence to be granted in fourme aforesaid, due and payable, or to be due or paid, to our said Sovereigne Lord the Kinge, his heires or successours by the said maior, sheriffes, cittizens and commonilty or their successours, or by the said chapline, visitor, schoolemaster, usher and other the said officers and ministers of the said late hospitall, or by any of them, or by their successours, or by the successours of any of them, by reason of the act of parliament made and provided in the 26th yeare of the reigne of the said late Kinge Henery the eight for and concerninge the grantinge or payment of tenthes and first fruites to his highnes, his heires and successours, or by reason of any other act, provision or lawe made for the payment of first fruites and tenthes, and that aswell all and singuler the premisses, as also the said mannours, landes, tenementes and hereditamentes, and that the said maior, sheriffes, cittizens and commonilty and their successours, and the said chaplin, visitor, schoolemaster, usher and all the said officers and ministers of the said late hospitall, and every of them and ther successours, and the successours of every of them, shalbe by the said letters pattentets clerely and fully discharged, pardoned and acquitted of, and for, all and all manner of Intrusions comytted, or to be comitted, and of, and for, all manner of fines, forfatures, paynes and sommes of money lost, due or forfated, or to be lost, due or forfeted, to our Sovereigne Lord the Kinge, his heires or successours by, or for, the not findinge of suertyes for the true payment of the said first fruites, or by, or for, the non payment of the said first fruites and tenthes, or any parcell thereof, made in the said 26th yeare of the reigne of the said late Kinge, the same act, or any other statute, act, provision or lawe heretofore had or made to the contrary in any wise, notwithstandinge, and that the said letters pattents under the great seale of England shalbe unto the chancellor of the said Court of First Fruites and Tenthes, and to all other officers and ministers of the same court for the tyme beinge, a suffitient warrant and discharge for the exoneracon and allowance of the said first fruites and tenthes in manner and forme above written.

And over this our said Sovereigne Lord the Kinge is further pleased and contented, and by the said advise and consent of the said Lord protector and his said coexecutors promiseth and granteth, and the said Lord protector and his said coexecutors covenanten and granten, by theise presentes to and with the said maior, sheriffes, cittizens and commonilty and their successours that the said maior, sheriffes, cittizens and commonilty and their successours shall from henceforth be masters, rulers and governers of the said late hospitall oredeyned nowe for the poore, and that they and ther successours for the tyme beinge shall have the order, rule and governance of the same late hospitall, hereafter to be called Gods howse or the Howse of the poore as is aforesaid, and of the people ther, and shall have full power and authority to see and cause the rentes, revenues and profittes of the landes and possessions of the same late hospitall to be imployed and bestowed to the releife of the poore people ther and of other the charges above remembred, according [f. 84v] to the meaninge of the foundacon of the same, or otherwise as it shall please the Kinges Majesty for better orders to devise for the same.

And to the intent the said good and godly perpose may have good successe, to the honor and glory of God and to the aid, helpe and releife of the poore, the Kings Majesty is further pleased and contented, and for him, his heires and successours, by the said advise and consent of the said Lord protector and his said coexecutors, promiseth and granteth, and the said Lord protector and his said coexecutors covenanten and granten, by theise presentes to and with the said maior, sheriffes, cittizens and commonilty and their successours that our said sovereigne Lord Kinge, his heires and successours from tyme to tyme at all times hereafter shall do and suffer to be done at the proper costes and charges of the said maior, sheriffes, cittizens and commonilty and their successours all and every such act and actes, thinge and thinges, be it by letters pattents, confirmacon or otherwise, for the better or more profitt, assurance and makinge sure of the said mannours, parsonages, tythes, landes, tenementes and all and singuler the premisses appointed, or to be granted and made sure to the said maior, sheriffes, cittizens and commonilty and to their successours, and for the sure erecton, foundacon and establishment of all and singuler other the purposes and effectes afore expressed in fourme aforesaid, as by the learned councell of the said maior, sheriffes, cittizens and commonilty and ther successours from tyme to tyme shalbe devised or advised, and that the said maior, sheriffes, cittizens and commonilty, by vertue of these presentes, shall freely have the one part of this indenture sealed with the greate seale of England without any fine or fee, lyttell or great, to be paid for the same in the Hamper of the Chancery or else wher.

In consideracion whereof, the said maior, sheriffes, cittizens and commonilty for them and their successors covenanten and granten by theise presentes to and with our said Sovereigne Lord the Kinge and the said Lord protector and his said coexecutors that the same maior, sheriffes, cittizens and commonilty and ther successours shall yearely from tyme to tyme well and truly content and pay, or cause to be contented and paid, to our said Sovereigne Lord the Kinges bayliffes of the hundreds of Humlyerd Blowfeild and Loddon, in the said county of Norfolk, and to every of them to his Highnes use, all such rentes and sumes of moneyes as by the late master of the said late hospitall, or any of his predecessours, masters of the same hospitall, have bene used or accustomed to be paid to the same bayliffes of the said hundredes, or to any of them.

In wittnes whereof to the one part of these indentures remeyninge with the said maior, sheriffes, cittizens and commonilty the Kinges Majesty that now is hath caused his greate seale of England to be putt, and the Lord protector and other his coexecutors have putt to their seales; and to the second part of these indentures remeyninge with the said Lord protector and other his coexecutors the Kinges Majesty that now is hath caused his greate seale of England to be putt, and the said maior, sheriffes, cittizens and commonilty have also putt to ther comon seale; and to the third part of this indenture remeyninge with the Kinges Majesty that now is the said maior, sheriffes, cittizens and commonilty have put to their said comon seale the day and yeare first above written.

APPENDIX 2

Agreement between William Oliver, keeper of God's House, and the civic authorities, 1566[1]

1566 Indenture betwixt the surveyours of thospitall and the keper of the same

Thys wryghtyng indentyd made the last daye of Maye in the yere of our Lord God 1566, and in the eight yere of the raigne of our sovereyn ladie Elizabeth by the grace of God Quene of Inglond Fraunce and Irelond defender of the faith etc. betwyn Thomas Sotherton mayour of the cittie of Norwiche Thomas Whall and Thomas Parker alderman and surveyours of the hows of the poore, otherwise called Goddes hows in Holmestrete within the cittie of Norwiche on the one parte, and William Olyver of the same cittie bere brewer on the other parte, witnesseth that the seid mayour and surveyours for their part and lykewise the seid William Olyver for his part have covenanted for the kepyng of the forty pore people, which are to be kept in the seid hows of the pore, otherwise called Goddes hows, upon souche agreamentes and artycles as hereafter be declaryd.

In primis the seid mayour and surveyours covenant and agree that the beforenamyd William Olyver shall enter and take the chardge of keepyng and provydyng of meat and drynk for the forty pore people and their kepers at the feast of St John Baptist next insuyng the date herof, and he to have then payed £31 13s 4d at his entrye for one quarters dyettes of the same forty pore people and their kepars before hand payed, whiche (if he shall fortune to dye or otherwise to depart before thend of eny yere duryng all the tyme that he shalbe keper thear), he shalbe bound to leave and repay ageyn to the use of the hows at his goyng of.

Item the seid mayour and surveyours covenant and agree that the seid William Olyver shall have and receyve at that his entryng into the hows for provysyon of wood and cole for the forty pore people and their kepars, for the whole yere then next following, £20, and shall enter bond with suretye that if he shall fortune to departe this lyfe at eny tyme within one yere after his entrye, and so for every yere that he shall contynue keper thear, that he shall leave or cause to be left suffycyent wood or coale to serve the forty pore people from the tyme that he shall enter untill that tyme twelvemoneth, and so allweys shall have £20 payed hym before hand at Midsoomer for provysyon of wood and coale for the whole yere following.

[1] NRO, NCR 24b (36), Seven covenants between the governors and keepers of the hospital, 1556–1686.

Item it is further covenanted and agreed that the seid William Olyver shall have and receyve for the keepyng of the of the forty pore people for their dyettes and the dyettes and wages of their kepers and offycers £26 13s 4d every quarter, by covenant so made with hym in great so that he shall allweys have one quartere dyettes payed before hand, whiche he shall leave and repay ageyn to the use of the seid hows at his goyng owt.

Item it is allso covenanted and agreed that the seid William Olyver shall have the scyte of the hows with all the gardeyns medowes ortyardes and groundes (only two howses except), which shal be reserved for storehowses to lay in thynges necessary for reparacions withowt eny rent or ferme payeng.

Item it is allso covenanted and agreed that the seid William Olyver shall have the land withowt St Augustyns gates which Vincent Tesmond now hath, and to paye therfor 60s by yere *videlicet* every quarter of a yere 15s.

And the seid William Olyver for his part, covenaunteth to and with the seid mayour and surveyours, that he the seid William shall keepe the seid forty pore people in sycknes and in helth and four women keepers, accordyng to the foundacion, with meat drynk fyryng and wasshing meete and convenyent for allmes people, and that they shalbe fedd with no courser bread then whole wheat bread withowt either rye or barlye to be putt and myxed thereith.

And the seid William Olyver allso covenanteth for his part that he, his wyfe, and kepers shall well and gently use and intreate the seid forty pore people, and every of them at all tymes, withowt eny correccion or beatyng of them or eny of them, but in case they or eny of them will not be ordryd and rulyd, then he to complayne to the surveyours of their mysdemeanours, and allwes to keepe the full nomber of forty pore folke, and if eny shall fortune to dye or else depart the hows, then he to signifie their names so dead or departed from the hows, to the surveyours or one of them at the least within twoo dayes after they shalbe departed from the hows.

And the seid William Olyver further covenanteth that if he shall fortune to departe this lyfe at eny tyme before eny of the four quarters of the yere shalbe fully accomplisshed and ended, forsomocheas he shall allweys have the forty markes for a quarters paiement before hand, that he shalbe bound with good suretye to kepe the seid forty pore people and their four kepers duryng the tyme of the whole quarter, to the rate for so many weekes, as shalbe wantyng of the quarter.

And the seid William Olyver convenanteth to keepe a booke of all the names of the forty pore people which he shall receyve into the hows, with the day of their entryng into the hows, and the daye of their death, or otherwise departyng owt of the same hows, and allso shall save all souche apparell or sheetis as eny of the shall fortune to leave at the day of their death to help the rest with.

And the seid William shall allso kepe a booke of all souch legacyes and gyftes, either of bedding, shettis, shirtes and smockes, lynnen, and woollen, or monye as shall fortune to cum into his handes of the gyft of eny body towardes the relief of the pore people.

Allso the seid William Olyver shall save and preserve to the use of the seid hows, all souche beddyng, stuff and utensilles of hows as shalbe comytted and delyvered to the seid William Olyver by inventorye or otherwyse.

In witnes whereof to the one parte of these present wrightynges indented remayneng with the seid William Olyver, thaforeseid Thomas Sotherton mayour, Thomas Whall and Thomas Parker have sett their handes and seales, and to the other part of the same wrightynges indented remayneng with the seid Thomas Sotherton mayour, Thomas Whall and Thomas Parker, the seid William Olyver hath sett his hand and sealle gven at the seid cittie of Norwiche the daye and yere first above wrytton.

[*Witnessed by:*] William Olyver berebrewer, John Fayerclyf myllar, Titus Norrys glover, Thomas Sotherton mayour, Thomas Whall alderman, Thomas Parker alderman

Sealed and delyvered in the presence of Master Thomas Peck alderman and Thomas Corey the youngour

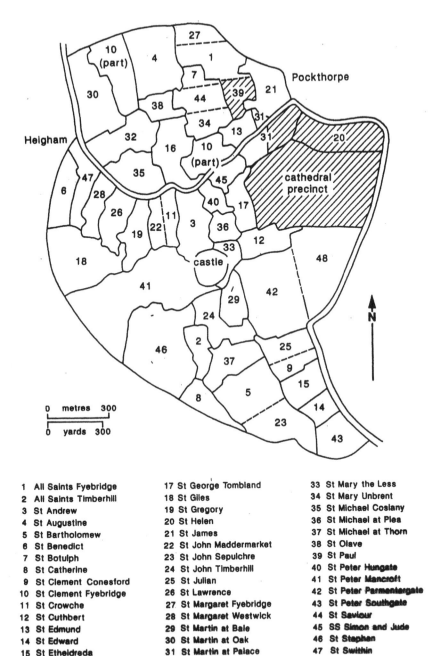

1 All Saints Fyebridge	17 St George Tombland	33 St Mary the Less
2 All Saints Timberhill	18 St Giles	34 St Mary Unbrent
3 St Andrew	19 St Gregory	35 St Michael Coslany
4 St Augustine	20 St Helen	36 St Michael at Plea
5 St Bartholomew	21 St James	37 St Michael at Thorn
6 St Benedict	22 St John Maddermarket	38 St Olave
7 St Botulph	23 St John Sepulchre	39 St Paul
8 St Catherine	24 St John Timberhill	40 St Peter Hungate
9 St Clement Conesford	25 St Julian	41 St Peter Mancroft
10 St Clement Fyebridge	26 St Lawrence	42 St Peter Parmentergate
11 St Crowche	27 St Margaret Fyebridge	43 St Peter Southgate
12 St Cuthbert	28 St Margaret Westwick	44 St Saviour
13 St Edmund	29 St Martin at Bale	45 SS Simon and Jude
14 St Edward	30 St Martin at Oak	46 St Stephen
15 St Etheldreda	31 St Martin at Palace	47 St Swithin
16 St George Colegate	32 St Mary Coslany	48 St Vedast

FIGURE 1: The parishes of late-medieval Norwich. The hatched area shows the liberty of the Dean and Chapter (Christchurch). (Phillip Judge)

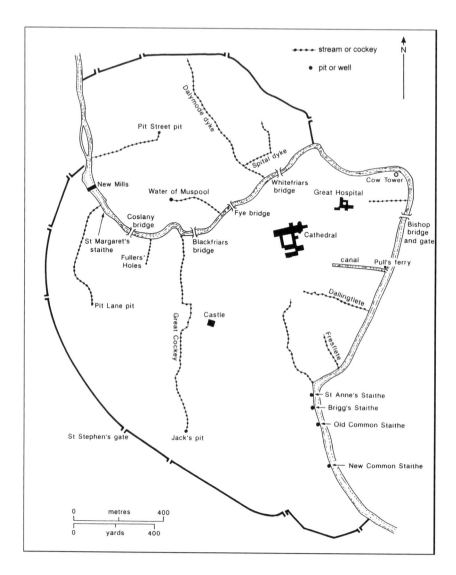

FIGURE 2: The river and cockeys of Norwich.
(Mike Evans, after Phillip Judge)

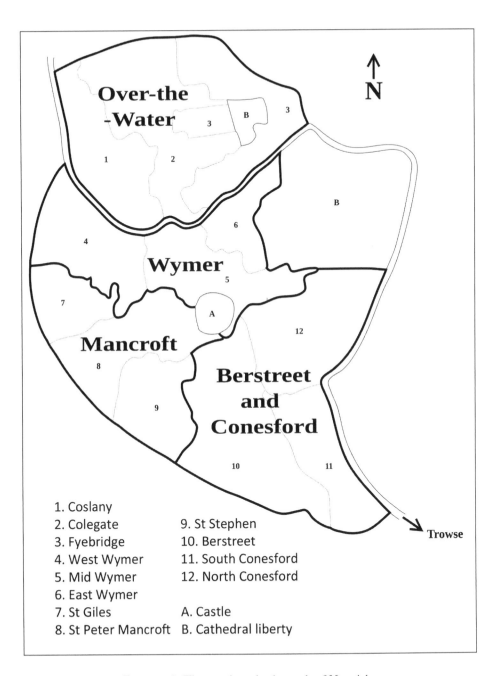

FIGURE 3: The wards and sub-wards of Norwich.
(Mike Evans)

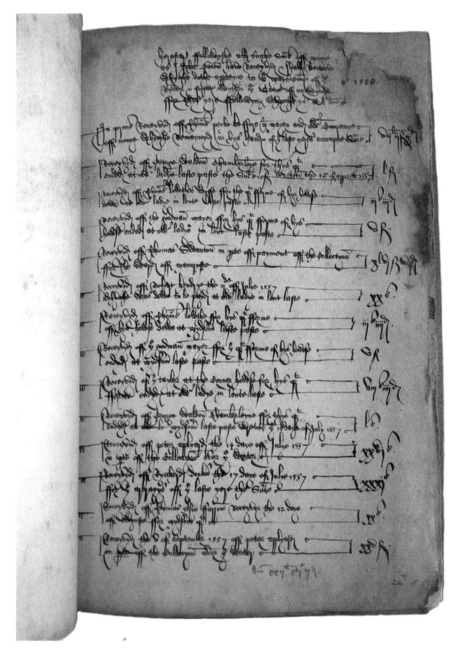

PLATE 2: The second page of the River and Street account for 1557–58
(NRO, NCR 19b, Account Book, 'River and Streets', 1556–1641, f. 2r),
showing part of the receipts.
(Photograph: Isla Fay)

The Norwich River and Street Accounts, 1557–61 and 1570–80

EDITED BY ISLA FAY

Introduction

The Norwich annual river and street accounts record the financial transactions of a committee founded by the city's government in 1552 for the purpose of improving sanitation in public areas.[1] The committee constituted one element in the ruling elite's post-Dissolution campaign to improve standards of health in the population. As a pageant staged a few years later in honour of the mayor of Norwich pointed out, civic magistrates had a duty 'to seeke [*to strive on behalf of*] the peoples heallthe'.[2] The removal of decaying or bad-smelling waste was seen to be a key factor in securing such a goal.

Medical writers identified the many dangers to human health commonly found in densely populated cities. According to Andrew Boorde (d. 1549), a physician who was briefly employed by Thomas Howard, 3rd duke of Norfolk, any waste product that was liable to 'infect, putryfye and corrupte [...] the ayre', including stagnant water, poorly drained ground and rotting carrion, risked causing 'many dyseases and infyrmytyes'. Boorde argued that people should not live too close to 'stynkynge dyches, gutters nor canelles [*kennels, watercourses*], nor corrupt dunghylles, nor synkes [*pits or conduits for waste-water or sewage*]' unless they were regularly purified and cleaned out.[3] Tudor parliaments responded to sanitary advice like this, as well as to economic imperatives, by passing legislation to improve the quality of the roads and watercourses across the country.[4] The Norwich river and street accounts provide evidence of how these mandates were interpreted in one of England's largest and wealthiest provincial cities.

---

[1] Norfolk Record Office (hereafter NRO), Norwich City Records (hereafter NCR) 19b, Account Book ('River and Street') 1556–1641. The series continues to 1835.

[2] D. Galloway, ed., *Records of Early English Drama: Norwich 1540–1642* (Toronto, 1984), p. 38 (1556). On the city's schemes, see the Great Hospital accounts above in this volume, and also M. Pelling, *The Common Lot: Sickness, Medical Occupations and the Urban Poor in Early Modern England* (London, 1998).

[3] Andrew Boorde, *A Compendyous Regyment or a Dyetary of Helth* (London, Robert Wyer, 1542), sigs. B[4]r–v. The text was dedicated to Thomas Howard, who was building a town house in Norwich at the time.

[4] See P. Slack, *From Reformation to Improvement: Public Welfare in Early Modern England* (Oxford, 1999), chapter one.

Initiatives for cleaning the river and streets: 1287 to 1580

Before 1552

At its inauguration, the river and streets committee was presented as a reform-
ing body. In fact, several of its powers were not new. Indeed, attempts to regulate standards of cleanliness in the river, streets and 'cockeys' (small natural
streams and watercourses, see *figure* 2) are evident in even the earliest surviving
records from Norwich.[5] Juries of local residents were encouraged to report
any individuals who committed environmental misdemeanours to the ruling
bailiffs at the local leet courts (that is, at hearings convened in each of the
city's four wards, see *figure* 3). In 1287/88, for example, John le Redepriest
was accused by the residents of the parish of St Peter Mancroft of blocking
one of the city's public watercourses with a sewer (*cloaca*).[6] Subsequent reports
drew attention to the dumping of putrid or stinking matter; for instance,
Roger Benjamin was fined 2*s.* in 1288/89 for the double offence of building
a muckheap in the highway, and for burying offal inside it.[7] In the wake of
the Black Death, such behaviour was cited in medical texts and government
edicts as a prime reason for the rapid spread of the plague.[8] In 1352, in the
hope of preventing a further outbreak, the Crown issued letters patent which
ordered Norwich's principal officers to compel unemployed men and women
under the age of sixty to provide man-power for cleansing and paving the
highways.[9]

Over the next one hundred and fifty years, the city's governing body
enforced a series of measures to fund improvements in the city's largest water-
course – the river Wensum.[10] The river was a vital asset to the city, providing
access to trading centres on the coast. It was also used to dispose of quantities
of industrial and manufacturing waste as well as human and animal ordure
(although the latter, in theory at least, was only dumped downstream of the

---

[5] The cockeys named in the accounts are listed in Appendix 1. On the question of whether
the cockeys ran with mostly dirty or clean water, see John Kirkpatrick, *The Streets and Lanes of
Medieval Norwich*, ed. W. Hudson (Norwich, 1889), pp. 99–100; and see M. Pelling 'Health and
Sanitation to 1750' in C. Rawcliffe and R. Wilson, eds, *Norwich since 1550* (London, 2004), pp.
129–31.

[6] W. Hudson, ed., *Leet Jurisdiction in the City of Norwich during the XIIIth and XIVth Centuries*, Selden
Society 5 (London, 1892), p. 9, and see pp. 3, 6.

[7] Hudson, *Leet Jurisdiction*, p. 23, and see pp. 24, 26, 30.

[8] C. Rawcliffe, *Urban Bodies: Communal Health in Late Medieval English Towns and Cities*
(Woodbridge, 2013), chapter three.

[9] *Calendar of Patent Rolls 1350–54*, pp. 283–4 (1352), echoing provisions in the Statute of
Labourers, 1351.

[10] W. Hudson and J.C. Tingey, eds, *The Records of the City of Norwich* (hereafter *RCN*, 2 vols,
Norwich, 1906–10), i, pp. 265 (1366), 267 (1367), 277 (1422), 288 (1496); ii, pp. cxxix-cxxx, 96–
8 (1467), 102 (1478 and 1479). The right of the ruling elite to raise rates for maintaining the river
was confirmed by letters patent in 1378: *Calendar of Patent Rolls 1377–81*, p. 121, and see *RCN*, ii,
pp. 318–19 (*c.* 1452).

city's defences). Additionally, it provided valuable resources: water, fish, and reeds for use in the building trade. A survey recorded in the minutes of the civic assembly in *c.* 1511 showed that, despite the regulations, the river continued to be misused in a number of ways. These included: blockages caused by trees and various structures erected by the residents;[11] pollution from textile manufacturing and the outflows of privies and gutters; diversion of the river into gardens and fish ponds; and the disposal or storage of large quantities of muck at the water's edge or on people's properties.[12]

The administration of Norwich was aware that conditions in the streets and cockeys inevitably impacted on the state of the river; waste material left in public spaces washed into the Wensum following every fall of rain. In 1517, therefore, an annual tax was collected from the inhabitants to fund the wages of a *canel-raker*, who was tasked with clearing the watercourses and street gutters. The civic assembly authorised the purchase of two carts to facilitate the cleaning,[13] and the initiative was supported by private funds. In 1518, for example, Elizabeth Thursby, a resident of St Andrew's parish (*figure* 1) left a sum of £10 in her will, amongst an extraordinary list of other charitable gifts, to continue the service in her neighbourhood.[14] The long-term future of the scheme was secured by alderman Robert Jannys in the following year. He gave three tenements situated near the market to the corporation, stipulating that the income from the rents should be ring-fenced for the collection and carting away of the 'filthye mater comyng from the makyng clean, foweng [*feying*: clearing] and sweeping of the ... stretes and cisterns'.[15]

A further stimulus to improve conditions came in 1532, when the central government at Westminster established a nationwide Commission of Sewers.[16] This empowered officials to investigate local problems in the country's waterways. The governors of Norwich responded by compelling residents either to clear reeds from the river themselves, or to fund workmen to do it.[17] Householders risked fines if they did not comply, whilst industrial polluters were required to meet extra charges. An unspecified number of temporary 'surveyors' was nominated by the city authorities to oversee the works.[18] Throughout the next decade, the Norwich chamberlains (the senior financial

---

[11] Namely, quays, tanners' staves for washing hides, and even a dam.

[12] NRO, NCR 16c/2, Assembly Minute Book 1510–50, f. 2r-v.

[13] *RCN*, ii, pp. 109 (1517), 110 (1518).

[14] NRO, NCC, Will Register Gylys, f. 97r.

[15] NRO, NCR 16d/2, Assembly Proceedings 1491–1553, f. 102r. Cisterns served to cleanse the water supply by sieving muck and preventing it from entering the river: Pelling, 'Health and Sanitation to 1750', p. 131; and see NRO, NCR 17b, City Revenues Book, f. 23r (1561) for a civic lease containing provisions regarding the cleaning of a cistern.

[16] 23 Henry VIII c. 5.

[17] *RCN*, ii, p. 115.

[18] NRO, NCR 18a/5, Chamberlains' Accounts (hereafter CA) 1531–37, f. 141r; NRO, NCR 16d/2, Assembly Proceedings 1491–1553, f. 165r. Norwich commonly appointed individual aldermen to supervise finite civic projects, for example, when assessing repairs to the city's defences: *RCN*, ii, p. 93 (1457).

officers) paid out regular sums towards clearing the river, streets and cockeys as part of their responsibility for maintaining the corporation's property and public spaces.[19]

However, early in the next decade, an unforeseeable event precipitated a crisis, when flash flooding in 1541 wrecked several cockeys and street surfaces. The chamberlains embarked on a programme of repairs, but there were insufficient resources to execute the task properly.[20] As a result, waste began to pile up in particular areas across the city.[21] In 1542/43, for example, it was reported that sixteen or seventeen cartloads of 'muck' had been deposited in a cockey next to the Three Bells inn.[22] Another heap of fifteen loads at Westwick gates was apparently preventing people from passing through.[23] The situation was bad even in the very centre of Norwich; when the corporation heard that the duke of Norfolk was planning a visit, it quickly ordered the removal of similar quantities of refuse from the market place.[24] With such an accumulation of putrefying material it can hardly have been surprising (at least to the medically-informed) when another outbreak of plague struck the city in 1544.[25]

Alert to a shortage of both civic funds and man-power to improve the situation, alderman Edmund Wood (d. 1548) made a generous bequest of 100 marks (£66 13s. 4d.) to the city's government, to help initiate a new strategy for cleaning the streets. He supplemented his gift with another £20 towards clearing the river. The city corporation responded by paying for the Wensum to be dredged,[26] and the mayor issued a general proclamation reminding the citizens of their obligation to sweep the streets on a weekly basis.[27] In May 1548, the civic assembly sanctioned the purchase of a further four carts which were used over the next six-month period to remove the accretion of 'filtie [sic] and vile mater in the stretes'.[28]

The city was only just beginning to reap the benefits of these combined activities when it suffered yet another disastrous set-back. In August 1549, fuelled by grievances arising from a combination of local economic, social and political tensions, many residents joined Kett's rebels in an uprising against

---

[19] See NRO, NCR 18a/5, CA 1531–37, *passim*; NRO, NCR 18a/6, CA 1534–47, *passim*. The chamberlain also rented out a city-owned 'muck boat' to a private contractor, who shipped waste out of the city. A lease of 1566 shows that the muck boat was a vessel with a freight of 2½ tons: NRO, NCR 22g/1, City Lease Book A, f. 40v.

[20] NRO, NCR 18a/7, CA 1541–49, ff. 64r, 111r, 163r.

[21] NRO, NCR 18a/7, CA 1541–49, f. 19br.

[22] Location unknown. See NRO, NCR 18a/7, CA 1541–49, f. 20r.

[23] NRO, NCR 18a/7, CA 1541–49, f. 59r.

[24] NRO, NCR 18a/7, CA 1541–49, f. 20r

[25] On the medical context, see A. Wear, *Knowledge and Practice in English Medicine, 1550–1680* (Cambridge, 2000), chapter 4.

[26] NRO, NCR 18/7, CA 1541–49, f. 301r. Twenty-two boatloads of material were removed. See also NRO, NCR 16a/4, Mayor's Court Book 1534–49, pp. 475–6.

[27] NRO, NCR 16a/5, Mayor's Court Book 1540–49, p. 514.

[28] NRO, NCR 16/2, Assembly Proceedings 1491–1553, f. 211r.

land enclosures. Battles in the streets of Norwich between the rebels and royal troops resulted in several city buildings and structures becoming seriously damaged, and men on both sides were killed.[29] The cockeys, streets and cisterns were also harmed during the violence, and a programme to repair them cost the city between £15 and £17 *per annum* over the next four years.[30]

A series of presentments at the leet courts a couple of years after the suppression of the uprising shows that the residents of Norwich continued to be concerned about the state of the environment. In the winter and spring of 1551, for example, scores of individuals were presented for having noisome gutters, for leaving muck in the highways, for encroaching on, or throwing muck into, the river, and for not maintaining proper paving outside their properties.[31] The chamberlains were also personally criticised for failing in their duty to clean several cockeys, and were forced to pay a fine in restitution.[32] A permanent solution to the problem of maintaining sanitary standards was required.

Foundation of the 1552 committee

On 28 March 1552, the civic assembly issued an ordinance which noted that the implementation of previous by-laws for the removal of sanitary nuisances had been hampered by a lack of funds. The streets apparently remained 'fowle and fylthye', while the river was becoming increasingly congested.[33] The assembly therefore appointed a body of twelve men (known collectively as 'the surveyors') to identify and to rectify problems, to tax the citizens to fund their works, and to enforce existing by-laws – if necessary, by arresting and imprisoning anyone who refused to comply with their orders. The accounts that comprise this edition are a record of the surveyors' financial activities.

According to the ordinance, the committee was required annually to replace half of its number, and to notify the civic assembly of the names of the new members by 24 February (St Mathias day). Each year, the committee was joined by one new alderman and five new common councillors. In the following year, these men took the places of the 'old' surveyors, and six 'new' officers joined them.[34]

The committee comprised:

- two **aldermen,** who were nominated from the council of the twenty-four aldermen, the most senior officials in the city's four wards (*figure 3*);

[29] A. Wood, 'Kett's Rebellion' in C. Rawcliffe and R. Wilson, eds, *Medieval Norwich* (London, 2004), pp. 277–99.

[30] NRO, NCR 18/7, CA 1551–67, ff. 15v, 32r, 69v, 96r.

[31] NRO, NCR 5c/3, Leets before the Sheriffs; NRO, NCR 5d/4, Sheriffs' Tourn.

[32] *RCN*, i, pp. 386–7.

[33] *RCN*, ii, pp. 127–31 (quote at p. 127). The ordinance utilised the powers of the Statute of Sewers instituted by two acts of parliament: 23 Henry VIII c. 5, and 3 & 4 Edward VI c. 8.

[34] For example, see the main text, f. 5r (1558–59).

- four **surveyors**, one for each ward, who determined the amount of money each eligible resident should pay according to a scale set out in the 1552 ordinance;
- four **collectors**, one for each ward, who were responsible for raising the sums specified by the surveyor of the ward;
- a **surveyor of the river and river men**, who was tasked with identifying which parts of the river were most in need of attention, and maintaining discipline amongst the labourers; and, finally,
- a **receiver/treasurer**, who was responsible for compiling accurate accounts, rendering them for audit, and for ensuring that the correct balance was safely secured at the end of the year.

The ordinance enabled the Norwich chamberlains to delegate certain powers to the new committee. Specifically, the surveyors substituted for the chamberlains by supervising cleaning work and handling other routine matters, although they did not take on responsibility for structural repairs to the cockeys, streets or bridges.[35]

The committee also had regular dealings with two other sets of city officers: the clavors and the water bailiff. The clavors – who were responsible for payments into and out of the civic treasury – received the surveyors' end-of-year balance. Their own accounts therefore formed part of the audit trail for expenditure on the river and streets.[36] Sometimes they also financed sanitary measures of their own. In 1551, for example, they funded the removal of 114 loads of muck from the castle ditches.[37] Only one water bailiff is mentioned in the pages of the surveyors' accounts – Thomas Hogges – and he was not referred to after 1572–73.[38] Hogges was occasionally employed to collect outstanding debts, and for summoning the surveyors to their election meetings.[39] In 1569–70, he was also commissioned to extract a small number of fines (or 'amercements') from people who were found to have polluted the environment or damaged the river.[40]

---

[35] For the chamberlains' ongoing responsibility for structural repairs to the cockeys, see, for example, NRO, NCR 18a/8, CA 1551–67, ff. 221v-23r (1561–62). The work included: identifying faults; building a dam to hold back water during the works; paving over sections of the cockeys and their banks in tile and stone; putting up posts to stop horses and carts from contaminating the water; and, finally, removing many loads of 'filth'.

[36] For example, see the clavors' accounts for the early 1560s in NRO, NCR 17b, City Revenues Book; and NRO, NCR 18d, Clavors' Book 2 1556–1640, ff. 5r, 7v.

[37] NRO, NCR 18d, Clavors' Accounts 1 1550–1601, f. 53v. On the use of the Castle ditches to dump rubbish, see E. Shepherd Popescu, *Norwich Castle: Excavations and Historical Survey, 1987–98, Part II: c.1345 to Modern*, East Anglian Archaeology Report 132 (Gressenhall, 2009), pp. 544–45.

[38] The post of water bailiff was created at a meeting of the civic assembly on 24 October 1543 (*RCN*, ii, pp. cxxx, 124–5). He was not concerned with the condition of the river, but was to report such matters as illegal exports, sale of goods on the water by false measure, and the use of unlawful nets.

[39] See the main text, f. 9r (1559–60) and f. 20v (1561–62).

[40] NRO, NCR 19b, Account Book ('River and Street') 1556–1641, no foliation (1569–70).

The accounts

Format and content

The river and street accounts were entered into a folio-sized volume which cost the committee 18*d.* in 1557.[41] It seems likely that the paper was bought as a single block, because the leaves are of a similar quality and type through-out. It was subsequently re-covered in 1571–72.[42] Much later, probably at some point in the nineteenth century, the volume underwent conservation work. There are no folio numbers in the volume; the numbers that appear in this edition have been added to assist the reader.

The committee's financial year began on 25 March, which the surveyors also reckoned as New Year's day. The accounts generally opened with an itemisation of the previous year's arrears, that is, with the balance from the last account. Next followed two sections comprising, firstly, a list of receipts and, secondly, a list of payments.[43] Each account ended with a note of the remaining balance. It was then checked and signed off by the mayor and/or at least two aldermen. In the 1570s, this duty was commonly discharged by the civic auditors whose tasks also included verifying the accounts of the Great Hospital.[44]

To begin with, the accounts were kept and produced by professionals. John Bacon (receiver, 1557–58) went on to become the city's chamberlain in 1559; Richard Toly (receiver, 1558–59) was a scrivener by trade.[45] Subsequently, the town clerk, Anthony Marker, was paid for engrossing the accounts, which is to say that he produced a fair copy in this book on the receiver's behalf (1559–60 and 1560–61).[46] Each of them submitted the finished product in a well-ordered format. But the next few accounts are rather idiosyncratic, reflecting the different approaches (and handwriting styles) of the individual record keepers. Thomas Layer, for example, started each page of his accounts with the word 'Jhus'.[47] Councillor Richard Sotherton (treasurer for 1562–63 and a grocer by trade), similarly included a pious invocation at the top of his account: 'as yt pleasyth God, so be ytt'.[48] The following year, John Revell miscalculated his figures and Marker was given the task of tidying them

[41] See the main text, f. 3r (1557–58).

[42] See the main text, f. 55r (1571–72).

[43] Payments were sometimes made in response to individual invoices or bills. See, for example, the bills presented by John Byrche and other men who worked on the surveyors' boats or supplied materials in 1575–6 (main text, ff. 68v–69v).

[44] T. Hawes, *An Index to Norwich City Officers 1453–1835* (Norfolk Record Society, lxx, 1989), p. xvi.

[45] Hawes, *Index*, 'Bacon, John'; for Toly, see the main text, f. 5v.

[46] Marker was town clerk between 1559 and 1578: Hawes, *Index*, 'Marker, Anthony'.

[47] See the main text, *e.g.*, f. 18v (1561–62).

[48] NRO, NCR 19b, Account Book ('River and Street') 1556–1641, no foliation (1562–63). Sotherton's account is not reproduced here. On the selection of accounts printed in this edition, see below, p.112.

up.[49] Alderman Robert Suckling subsequently inscribed a memorandum stating that the book had become 'disordered' and that he had 'sett [it] in perfect state' again.[50] This was not quite the case as a few pages from the 1560s remain in the wrong position.[51] Subsequent accounts were much more orderly. From 1569–70, Marker, assisted by competent receivers, established a precise pattern of setting out transactions.

Other matters too were sometimes recorded in the book. During the 1550s and 1560s, for example, a list of the individuals elected for the year was generally inscribed before each account, often in a different hand. A list of the surveyors' property was also included in the 1567–68 account, and a selection of the city's sanitary by-laws was transcribed after that for 1595–96.[52] Finally, the assessment for the Coslany rate for 1631, which recorded the names of people liable to pay the river and street tax and the amount that they owed, was inserted before the 1634–35 account. The book remained in use until 1642–43, although there is a gap in the series between 1618–19 and 1635–36.

Two separate periods are covered in this edition. The first comprises the accounts from 1557 to 1562; the second, the decade between 1570 and 1580. The records from the intervening years have not been reproduced for reasons of space, and because they largely repeat the content and pattern of the others. Notable occurrences during the period not published here are mentioned in the introduction. The sample roll gives a clear picture of the surveyors' responsibilities as they were first conceived and as they developed. They also provide a direct insight into the working lives of civic labourers and constitute a valuable index to wages and prices at a time of steady inflation.[53]

The nature of the accounts to 1580: income and expenditure

The opening accounts suggest that the receivers were coming to terms with the scale of their task in what proved to be difficult circumstances. A virulent outbreak of disease known as the 'sweat' hit the city in 1557, with further outbreaks recurring over the next two years. The impact on the population was devastating. Between June 1558 and the following February, almost half of the city's twenty-four aldermen lost their lives.[54] The surveyors' income duly

[49] As a result, there are two versions of the account for that year. Marker's was the one that was subsequently audited.

[50] NRO, NCR 19b, Account Book ('River and Street') 1556–1641, no foliation (1564–65).

[51] For example, see the main text ff. 9–10 (1559–60) and n. 29.

[52] The ordinances included: the 1552 order which inaugurated the committee of surveyors; and two others passed in April 1566 and February 1586 which made minor extensions to the surveyors' powers.

[53] For comparison the rate of price increase in London was *c*. 8% per decade for the 1560s and 1570s: S. Rappaport, *Worlds Within Worlds: Structures of Life in Sixteenth-Century London* (Cambridge, 1989), pp. 135–6.

[54] P. Slack, *The Impact of Plague in Tudor and Stuart England* (Oxford, 1985), p. 71, suggests that this was the greatest mortality crisis to hit England between 1485 and 1665, and estimates that the population fell by about 6% between 1556 and 1560. See also NRO, NCR 17b, Mayor's Book, p. 144 for a list of the names of the aldermen who died.

suffered from the late payment of rents, rates and annuities. External financial pressures also took a toll; the committee lost £5 3s. 8½d. owing to the debasement of the coinage following a royal proclamation on 27 September 1560.[55]

From the start, the surveyors paid generous wages to workmen to remove filth from drainage courses and to sweep up detritus in the market (run-off from which was liable to pollute the Great Cockey in particular). The amounts of waste involved were considerable. For example, in the year 1558–59, over 570 cartloads of 'filth' and 'cumpasse' were removed from across the city's four wards. Increasing expenditure was balanced by a rise in receipts during the 1560s, which indicates the surveyors' success in managing their income. By the provisions of the 1552 ordinance, the surveyors were granted an annuity of £14 from the chamberlain, £10 of which came out of his revenue from the rent of the city's water-powered corn mills (the 'New Mills', *figure* 2).[56] In addition, the surveyors claimed an annual payment directly from the miller to cover the costs of cutting weeds in the river.[57] A further annuity of £4 was paid by the foreign receiver, an officer who collected and accounted for all of the civic corporation's irregular sources of income.[58]

The 1552 ordinance also transferred to the surveyors the two gifts from aldermen Jannys and Wood that had been made to the corporation for the furtherance of earlier sanitary reforms.[59] Wood's gift was used to purchase stretches of land that were rented out by the river and street surveyors.[60] Another bequest, which was made directly to the surveyors, came from Katheryn Rogers (d. 1556), widow of William Rogers, a former alderman and mayor. She left the city corporation £20 towards works for the improvement of the river.[61] The sum was finally paid to the surveyors by her executor in 1576–77.

A final substantial annuity, starting in 1564, was granted to the surveyors by Thomas Howard, 4th duke of Norfolk, again to fund work on the river.[62] The gift was supposed to amount to 20s. *per annum*, but, not surprisingly, the payments fell into arrears after the duke's imprisonment in 1569. After his execution for treason three years later, the final instalments were paid by his treasurer and a former steward of Norwich, John Blenerhasset.[63]

[55] See the main text, f. 17v (1560–61).

[56] *RCN*, ii, p. 129.

[57] The miller was, however, entitled to contract with labourers directly to do the work, if he felt that he could strike a better deal that way. This is what George Manne and Nicholas Beston chose to do in 1577–78, when they were the mills' tenants. See the main text, f. 74v.

[58] Principally this income derived from admission fees paid by those who wanted to become freemen of Norwich but who did not automatically qualify for that privilege by birth.

[59] See above, pp. 107 and 108.

[60] The land is identified in NRO, NCR 16d/3, Assembly Proceedings 1553–83, f. 191r (pencil f. 200r). See the main text, f. 52v, for the land 'bowght of Mr Pede' (1571–72).

[61] There is some confusion in the accounts as to whether the bequest came from the wife or the husband, and William is cited in a reference to the as yet unpaid sum in 1574–75. However, the gift was in fact made in Katheryn's will. The National Archives, PROB 11/38/176.

[62] Further payments were received in 1566, 1572–73 (for three years in total), and 1574.

[63] See the main text, f. 52r (1570–71).

In addition to these gifts, the surveyors had the right to improve and let out portions of consolidated ground on the river margins. They duly received rents for pieces of ground 'won out of the river' from 1566 onwards.[64] Other properties which paid rent to the surveyors included a house at the former Blackfriars' site, and a piece of ground in the parish of St Martin at Oak.[65] The committee proved to be a rather generous landlord. In 1575–76, Robert Cocket, who consistently struggled to make payments, was granted a refund of 10s. on his rent after he paid a lump sum to reduce his debt substantially. Similarly, neither alderman Elias Bates nor (after his death), his widow, had their lease of a piece of ground terminated, even though they failed to pay any rent over a five-year period in the early 1570s.

To help fund their works, the surveyors were also authorised to raise taxes on the citizens and 'foreign inhabitants' living in Norwich and its suburbs.[66] A sliding scale of fees was levied at the beginning of the year; each of the city's two justices of the peace was required to pay 2s., its twenty-four aldermen, 18d., and the individual members of the 'company of the livery of St George'[67], 12d. An assessment on other eligible ratepayers was made across the four wards. A fair-copy of a single Tudor assessment (that for 1561) survives elsewhere in the corporation's archive. It records the names of about 550 householders who were required to pay rates of between 2d. and 2s. each.[68] Additional charges could be imposed on individuals who polluted the river; dyers, calenderers (who pressed cloth or paper), tanners, glovers, parchment makers and brewers were all named as likely culprits in the 1552 ordinance. With all these sources of funding, the surveyors possessed a considerable yearly income, and they quickly built up a substantial reserve. Perhaps in recognition of this fact, the civic assembly cancelled all rate collections by the surveyors in 1576–77. The reported reason was that 'greate errors' had been committed in the collection for previous years.[69]

In 1579, Norwich was yet again struck by plague. The epidemic killed c. 5,000 (or roughly 30%) of the city's inhabitants.[70] The mayor and aldermen – armed with orders from the Privy Council on how to prevent the further spread of disease – blamed Dutch and Walloon immigrants for exacerbating the

---

[64] See, for example, the main text, f. 50r (1570–71); and see *RCN*, ii, p. 130. Small islands in river, formed in this way, were known locally as 'bitmays'.

[65] See the main text, ff. 6r, 50r (1558–59 and 1570–71, respectively).

[66] Citizens – not to be confused with the inhabitants in general – were members of the freedom of the city of Norwich. Foreign inhabitants were non-citizens, and often incomers to the city. The latter were excluded from the civic franchise.

[67] The company comprised the former religious guild of St George which was reformulated after the Dissolution, and was closely associated with the mechanisms and personnel of the civic government. It had about 200 members in the early sixteenth century: N. Tanner, 'Religious Practice', in Rawcliffe and Wilson, eds, *Medieval Norwich*, p. 149.

[68] NRO, NCR 17b, City Revenues Book, ff. 23r-35r.

[69] See the main text, f. 71v.

[70] Slack, *Impact of Plague*, pp. 129–30.

outbreak.[71] This community, known as 'the Strangers', had been invited by the corporation to settle in Norwich in 1565, to help revive the city's flagging textile manufacturing sector.[72] Their numbers rapidly swelled, increasing the population by perhaps as much as 35%, and raising the total number of inhabitants to *c.* 15–16,000 by 1571.[73] This may have forced the new arrivals to crowd into whatever domestic accommodation was available, and sanitary provisions in some neighbourhoods became seriously overburdened.[74] It was alleged that some of them were seriously polluting the river and gutters with the by-products of their industry – the treatment of wool and woollen baize in particular requiring large quantities of free-flowing water and suitable sluices.[75] Strict controls sought to regulate both the places and the times at which these processes would be allowed in future. The impact that the new level of dense settlement had upon the infrastructure and condition of the urban environment may be reflected in the rising expenditure documented in the River and Street Accounts.

Developments in the later part of Elizabeth's reign and the next century merit separate investigation and are outside the scope of this edition.[76] It is worth noting here, however, that the steady increase in expenditure continued throughout the last part of the sixteenth century. This included a sudden peak in spending between 1589 and 1593, occasioned by essential work on the river, with costs totalling almost £120 in 1590.[77]

Stone mines and street paving

In the early period of their activities, the surveyors' work in maintaining thoroughfares was limited to ensuring a high standard of cleanliness in the marketplace. Property owners were obliged to take personal responsibility in this respect, and to pave and clean the highway in front of their doorsteps. Negligent residents were reminded of their obligations in no uncertain terms by a by-law passed on 21 September 1559. This required every owner of a house or grounds adjoining a paved public street to repair or resurface that street in stone within a period of three months, or risk a fine. As a direct response to the epidemic of the previous year, the by-law stressed the sanitary benefits of streets that were easy to clean; proper paving was, it claimed, 'a helthefull commodyte'.[78]

---

[71] The plague orders were based on advice supplied by the College of Physicians in London: Slack, *Impact of Plague*, p. 209.

[72] For the corporation's petition to central government to allow the textile workers to settle, see *RCN*, ii, pp. 332–3, and see R. Wilson, 'The Textile Industry', in *Norwich since 1550*, pp. 221–2.

[73] Pound, 'Government', pp. 35–6, 41–2.

[74] Slack, *Impact of Plague*, pp. 139–42.

[75] For an admonitory letter from the mayor of Norwich to the Strangers on this account, see *RCN*, ii, pp. 335–6.

[76] For the later period, see Pelling, 'Health and Sanitation to 1750'.

[77] NRO, NCR 19b, Account Book ('River and Street') 1556–1641, no foliation (1590–91).

[78] *RCN*, ii, pp. 133–4 (quote at p. 133). For national legislation on the same subject, see the following statutes for highways: 2 & 3 Philip and Mary c. 8 (1555); 5 Elizabeth I c. 13 (1562–63); 18 Elizabeth I c. 10 (1575–76).

In the 1570s, however, the surveyors began to diversify their activities in this area. Thus, in 1575–76, they commissioned several masons to survey the state of Norwich's highways and to report any problems.[79] On the basis of these findings, they paid the masons to re-pave the area around Charing Cross (near the junction of St Benedict's and Westwick Street in the parish of St Gregory). The committee also began to source and to sell stone, probably in order to provide paving material.[80] A seam of chalk and flint deposits can be found at the 50m contour of the Wensum valley, and this has been mined throughout most of the city's history for building materials. Today, flint can still be seen in the surviving portions of the Norwich city walls, and in medieval domestic structures and churches. Flint rubble was also used to metal some of the medieval streets.[81] Little is known about the extraction of flint in Norwich from other documentary sources, and so the river and street accounts provide important evidence for the industry.[82] City-wide, three main groups of quarries and subterranean tunnels have been located. The first is to be found along King Street and Ber Street; another extends either side of the walls along the line of Earlham Road and in the Westwick Street/Pottergate area; the final group lies to the east of the city and on Mousehold Heath (where sand and gravel were probably extracted). The Earlham Road system of galleries, which is almost 500m long, was in use in 1571.[83]

The first recorded involvement of the surveyors in the extraction of stone came in 1575–76, when they made a loan of £10 to one John Tewesdaye for 'charges at the stone myndes'.[84] The flints excavated by Tewesdaye and his team of labourers were divided into small, middle and large sizes, and were sold on to various individuals. There was also a particular flurry of activity in the period leading up to the arrival of Elizabeth I during her progress through Norfolk in August 1578; most of the stone extracted at this time was again sold on to private individuals, probably in order that they might fulfil their obligations with regard to paving.[85]

[79] See the main text, f. 69v.

[80] It is not clear from the accounts themselves to what specific use the stone was put, but paving seems the most likely explanation. Celia Fiennes, when she visited Norwich in 1698, remarked on Norwich's well-paved streets that were 'pitched', i.e., paved with stones set on end: B. Ayers, 'Building a Fine City: The Provision of Flint, Mortar and Freestone in Medieval Norwich', in D. Parsons, ed., *Stone: Quarrying and Buildings in England AD 43–1525* (Chichester, 1990), p. 223.

[81] B. Ayers, 'The Infrastructure of Norwich from the 12th to the 17th Centuries' in *Lübecker Kolloquium zur Stadtarchäologie im Hanseraum IV: Die Infrastrucktur*, Manfred Gläser, ed. (Lübeck, 2004), p. 37; P.A. Emery *Norwich Greyfriars: Pre-Conquest Town and Medieval Friary*, East Anglian Archaeology 120 (Gressenhall, 2007), pp. 26, 33, 38.

[82] M. Atkin, 'The Chalk Tunnels of Norwich', *Norfolk Archaeology* 38 (1983), p. 313.

[83] Atkin, 'Chalk Tunnels', pp. 314, 316.

[84] Main text, f. 70r. It is not clear from the accounts where this mine was located.

[85] For a comparison, see the repairs to the roads and bridges that were sanctioned by a civic assembly of 24 June 1578 on account of the impending royal progress: Galloway, *Norwich 1540–1642*, p. 244.

A note about scavengers

In 1570, the civic authorities temporarily appointed a number of 'scavengers'.[86] The initial impetus for these arrangements seems to have been the devastation wrought by a flood, although the measure was repeated in 1573 and again in 1580.[87] In addition to assisting in the clearing of streets and cockeys, the scavengers were responsible for ensuring not only that property holders swept up on a weekly basis – heaping the 'dust and compost' on their half of the street ready for collection – but also that they maintained the paving to a sufficient standard. A further tax on inhabitants and churchwardens, in addition to the river and street rate, was used to pay for the scavengers and for contractors to carry away the rubbish.

On one occasion, a cockey-cleaner appointed by the surveyors was referred to as a 'skavenger' (1579–80).[88] In general, however, the post of scavenger was a separate, parish-based one, and the surveyors do not seem to have had direct dealings with them.

The Norwich river and street surveyors in context

The extent to which the Norwich solution to the problem of city cleansing (namely, the establishment of a permanent committee to oversee routine matters and to identify the areas of greatest need) was also adopted in other English cities and towns, remains open to further inquiry. What follows is not a comprehensive survey, but some preliminary remarks may be useful.

We might expect London to be a special case owing to its size, but in fact provisions in the two cities were rather similar (albeit on different scales).[89] In both cities, sanitation was a matter of regulation for ward-level courts from an early date, and both used similar instruments in order to maintain standards, such as fines, rates and groups of semi-permanent overseers. However, London did appoint intermediate officers – scavengers and a serjeant of the canelles – at a far earlier date than Norwich.[90] Many other towns and cities employed scavengers and common carters by 1600 if not considerably before.[91] Nearby Ipswich engaged the latter from 1574, although here (in con-

---

[86] *RCN*, ii, pp. 141–2 (1570); NRO, NCR 16d/3, Assembly Proceedings 1553–1583, ff. 217v-18r (1573), f. 288r (1580).

[87] *RCN*, ii, p. 141.

[88] See main text, f. 86r.

[89] E. Sabine, 'City Cleaning in Mediaeval London', *Speculum* 12 (1937), pp. 19, 21–2; C. Barron, *London in the Later Middle Ages* (Oxford, 2004), pp. 261–2. On searching for obstructions and problems in the Thames, see B.R. Masters, ed., *Chamber Accounts of the Sixteenth Century* (London Record Society, xx, 1984), e.g. p. 85.

[90] On the duties of these officers, see Sabine, 'City Cleaning', p. 22, and Barron, *London*, p. 262.

[91] Surveys of when such measures were adopted in various places may be found in: Rawcliffe, *Urban Bodies*, chapter three; G.T. Salusbury-Jones, *Street Life in Medieval England*, 2nd edn (Oxford, 1948); and J.H. Thomas, *Town Government in the Sixteenth Century* (London, 1933).

trast to Norwich) the burden of routine cleaning remained a matter for the town's chamberlain.[92]

Committees with similar powers to the Norwich river and street surveyors may come to light. Liverpool – as yet a relatively small town – may have established a body for overseeing the cleaning of the streets by 1555–56.[93] A joint agreement between the mayor of Cambridge and the vice-chancellor of the University in September 1575 instituted a number of ward-based committees (made up of burgesses and university men) as part of a much bigger programme of sanitary and welfare reforms.[94] But a superficial survey seems to suggest that the wide-ranging mandate of the Norwich committee – which (in theory at least) dealt with watercourses as well as streets, sourced and supplied stone, collected taxes and fined irresponsible polluters – was very unusual.

Acknowledgements

My grateful thanks are due, firstly, to the trustees of the Scouloudi Historical Awards 2010, whose grant enabled me to conduct the research for this edition, and also to the Norfolk Record Office, for allowing me to reproduce the material presented here. I would also like to thank the following people: most especially, Elizabeth Rutledge, for encouraging me to produce this edition, for her careful guidance in the production of the text and many comments and suggestions for its improvements, and for her generous long-term interest and kindness; Sachiko Kusukawa, Nick Jardine and Liba Taub, from the University of Cambridge, also supported the volume's completion, and I am indebted to them.

I would also like to thank Ellie Phillips for sharing her thoughts (and this volume) with me; Carole Rawcliffe for introducing me to the subject of urban environmental reforms in the first place and for commenting on the introduction; and Mike Evans and Phillip Judge for their work on the maps. Finally, at the Norfolk Record Office, I would like to thank Nick Sellwood for his advice about the physical aspects of this volume, Tom Townsend for solving the occasional palaeographical problem, and the search room staff for their cheerful assistance. Any remaining errors are, of course, my responsibility alone.

[92] J. Webb, ed., *The Town Finances of Elizabethan Ipswich: Select Treasurers' and Chamberlains' Accounts* (Suffolk Records Society, xxxviii, 1996), pp. 112, 114, 127.

[93] J.A. Twemlow, ed., *Liverpool Town Books: Proceedings of Assemblies, Common Councils, Portmoot Courts etc. 1550–1862*, 2 vols (1918–35), i, pp. 60, 84, 147, 198.

[94] C.H. Cooper, *Annals of Cambridge*, 5 vols (Cambridge, 1842–53), ii, pp. 332–8, esp. p. 333.

Editorial conventions

SYMBOLS

[*italics*]	editorial remarks, words or letters omitted in the manuscript which have been supplied; accountant marks transposed into pounds, shillings and pence
[and streets]	words or letters which have been supplied because of damage to the manuscript, or because they are in the binding
[?The re]ste	as above, but there is doubt about the first word
[? ther workes]	as above, but there is doubt about both words
/*italics*/	marginal entry or annotation, brought into the text
< >	words which have been deleted
* *	words which have been inserted

PAGINATION

The text is not foliated. Folio numbers have been added to assist the reader in understanding the format and layout of the text.

NUMERALS AND DATES

In the original text, figures were generally written in Roman numerals, although Arabic numerals appear from time to time in dates and in accounting totals. All Roman numerals have been converted to Arabic. Four and eight were occasionally written thus: *iiij^{er}*, *viij^{te}*. Figures in the twenties were also sometimes presented with a superscript *ti(e)* as for example *xx^{tie}* ('twenty'); *xxv^{ti}* (i.e., 'five-and-twenty'). Numerals have been standardised and modernised.

Dates were sometimes written as follows: *ij^{de}* (2nd); *xxjth* ('one-and-twentieth'); *xxijth* ('two-and-twentieth'); *xxiijth* ('three-and-twentieth'), *etc*. Where present, these abbreviations have been modernised (2nd, 21st, 22nd, 23rd). The year of grace was always given in Arabic numerals in this text (e.g. '1557').

SPELLING

Standard contractions have been expanded without comment. 'U' has generally been inserted before a superscript 'r' except where it appears especially distracting for modern readers, e.g. *wo^{r}ke* is given as *worke* (rather than *wourke*), *ow^{r}* is given as *owr* (rather than *owur*). Similarly, either 'e' or 'o' have been inserted before a superscript 'r', where appropriate, for example *quart^{s}* is given as *quarters*, *collect^{r}* as *collector*. First names have also been expanded silently, (i.e. *Jo* to *John*, *Wm* to *William*, *Rich* or *Ric* to *Richard*, *Robt* to *Robert*), unless they are in doubt.

The following common abbreviations of words have also been expanded: *ald*, *alder* and *ald* as *alderman*; *a° as *anno*; *d* or *di* as *dimidia*; *dni* as *domini*; *it(m)* is given as *item*; *md* as *memorandum*; *p(d)* as *paid*;   *qr^r*, *q^art* or *qrt* as *quarter(s)*; *R*, *rec* or *res* as *received*; *tent* as *tenement*. *M* with a contraction sign has been given as *Mr* before proper nouns, but as 'master' if preceding a civic office (thus *m' mayer* and *mr mayer* have been given as *master mayer*). Variants of *sum* have been extended as *summa* in the totals but as English in the body of the account, except for ff. 18v-19r where *summa* may be indicated.

Additionally:

u   has been modernised to *v*

ff has been modernised to capital F at the start of a word, but is retained within a word

y   has been rendered *th*

Otherwise, original spelling has been retained. Capitalisation has been altered to modern usage. Punctuation has been lightly and silently modernised to assist with the sense.

MARGINALIA

Marginal entries in the text comprise headings, accounting subtotals and annotations.

Headings

Headings have been placed before the text (or block of text) to which they pertain, unless they simultaneously formed part of the sentence in which case they appear in the order dictated by the syntax.

Accounting subtotals

These might appear anywhere in the original text, but are generally to be found at the bottom of the page. They are not always present. They may be written as Roman and/or Arabic numerals, and/or as accounting marks (a series of dots and dashes). All subtotals have been standardised to £ s. d., and are shown in smaller type. Where enclosed in square brackets, they have been calculated from accounting marks using the rules given in C. Trice Martin, *The Record Interpreter*, 2nd edn (London, 1910), pp. xii-xiii, with the addition that dots appearing in a fourth column on the left were taken to represent multiples of £20.

The accountants' running totals might appear to either side of the main receipt/payment entry (which is to say, they might be placed to either side of the main text or the column of figures) or at the bottom of the page. The variable positioning has not been recreated here. Instead, to assist the reader, the accounting subtotals have been placed on a separate line after the entry they are closest to.

Annotations
Longer marginal annotations, such as those added at the end of a year's account during the auditing process, are entered onto a new line, but clearly marked using the convention given above (*i.e.*, */italics/*).

PLACES

Places mentioned in the notes have been identified using J. Kirkpatrick, *The Streets and Lanes of the City of Norwich*, ed. W. Hudson (Norwich, 1889) and J. Campbell, 'Norwich', in *The Atlas of Historic Towns: Volume 2*, ed. M.D. Lobel (London, 1975).

The Norwich river and street accounts, 1557–1562 and 1570–1580[1]

[1557–58]

[f. 1r] Herafter followythe the names off the surveyores of th[e river and streets][2]

Mr Fleccher alderman	Andrewe Deye	John Mapes
John Sotherton	Thomas Pettous	Edmond Thorston
Mr Graye alderman	John Lowe	Thomas Swanton
John Bacon	Ryccherd Tolye	Peter Applyard

Herafter followythe every man in hys offyce for thys yere followyng:[3]

John Bacon ys appoyntyd to be receyver & payer for thys yere

Andrewe Deye ys appoyntyd to surveye the strettes wythin hys ward[4]

John Lowe ys appoyntyd to collectyd the monye in that ward

John Mapes ys appoyntyd to surveye the strettes in that warde

Thomas Swanton ys appoyntyd to collecte the monye in that ward

John Sotherton ys appoyntyd to surveye the watermen in ther workes and to se that the watermen do not tracte no tyme and further to se wher that moste necessarye places be to be amendyd in the ryver and ony other thyng to be done by them

Ryccherd Tolye ys appoyntyd to survey the strettes in that ward

Thomas Pettous ys appoyntyd to collecte the monye in that warde

Edmond Thorston ys appoyntyd to surveye the strettes in that ward

Peter Applyard ys appoyntyd to collecte the monye in that warde

[f. 1v blank]

[f. 2r] Herafter followythe all sucche summs off monye as I John Bacon have receyvyd & shall receyve whyche dothe apperteyne to the mayntenaunce off the ryver & strettes wythin the cetye off Norwycche for thys yere followyng whycche ys *anno domini /1556/*[5]

---

[1] NRO, NCR 19b, Account book ('River and Street') 1556–1618.

[2] This page and the following half folios to 9v are damaged in the top right-hand (recto) /top left (verso) corners respectively. The missing words and letters have been assumed.

[3] For what immediately follows concerning the surveyors' roles, see the Introduction, pp. 109–10.

[4] The four great wards of Norwich were Conesford (with Berstreet), Mancroft, Wymer and Over/Beyond-the-Water (*figure* 3).

[5] The first account covers a period that slightly extends beyond the financial year, covering payments due on 25 March 1557 to May 1558. The date '1556' here appears to have been inserted in error.

In primis receyvyd off Thomas Pecke beffore master mayer and
owr companye off monye whycche remaynyd in hys handes of
the laste yeres accompte summe   £8 2*s.* 10*d.*

Receyvyd off George Walden chamberleyne for thys quarter
ended at Owr Ladye laste paste the summe of *wreton the
16 of Apprell 1557*   50*s.*

Receyvyd off Thomas Lowthes wyffe for the quarter ferme of
hyr howse dewe at Owr Ladye in Lente[6] laste paste   3*s.* 4*d.*

Receyvyd off the goodman mayer for hys quarter ferme of hys
howse ended at Owr Ladye in Lent laste paste   5*s.*

Receyvyd off Thomas Swanton in parte off payment off the
collectyon for the ward off Mancrofte   46*s.* 8*d.*

Receyvyd off Robart Hendrye the 2nd off Julye 1557 whycche
was dewe to be payd at Owr Ladye in Lent laste   20*s.*

Receyvyd off Thomas Lowthe for hys quarter ferme off hys
howse dewe at Mydsomer laste paste   3*s.* 4*d.*

Receyvyd off the goodman mayer for the quarter ferme of hys
howse endyd at Mydsomer laste paste   5*s.*

Receyvyd of the tayler at the corner howse for hys quarter ferme
endyd at Owr Ladye in Lente laste   8*s.* 4*d.*

Receyvyd off George Walden chamberleyne for thys quarter
endyd at <Owr L> Mydsomer laste paste wreton the 10 daye of
July 1557   50*s.*

Receyvyd off Peter Applyard the 14 daye off Julye 1557 in parte
off the colleccyon Over the Water   26*s.*

Receyvyd off Ryccherd Donkes the 17 daye of Julye 1557 for
the areragys off the laste yere the summe   31*s.*

Receyvyd off Thomas Elsye farren receyver the 12 daye off
Awguste for Mydsomer quarter   20*s.*

Receyvyd the 5 of September 1557 off Peter Applyard in parte
off the colleccyon Over the Water   25*s.*

/ *Summa* £22 16*s.* 6*d.*/[7]

[*f. 2v*] [Received] off Grene the mason for ones [*sic*] yeres ferme
of hys grownd   3*s.*

---

[6] That is, the feast of the annunciation of the Blessed Virgin Mary (25 March), which falls in
the period of Lent, as opposed to e.g., *inter alia*, the Purification (2 February) or the Assumption
(15 August).

[7] This total is given in both Roman and Arabic numerals.

[?The re]ste off hys ferme whycche ys for 3 yeres more order ys taken by master mayer & hys brotherne that ytt shalbe payd by the chamberleyne in consyderacion of servyce	9s.
Receyvyd off Thomaas [sic] Lowthe for hys quarter ferme dewe for hys howse at Mycchelmes paste	3s. 4d.
Receyvyd off the tayler at the corner howse in the markett for the rent off hys howse for halffe a yere dewe at Mycchelmes laste	16s. 8d.
Receyvyd off Thomaas [sic] Elsye farren receyver for Mycchelmes quarter the summe off	20s.
Receyvyd off Leonard Yonges the 24 daye of November 1557 for the quarter endyd at Mycchelmes laste	50s.
Receyvyd more off Leonard Yonges the same daye	£3

/£8 9s. 6d./

Receyvyd more the 23 daye off December 1557 off Thomas Beamond for the arerage off hys accompte made be fore Mr Steward & other[s]	£5 13s. 2d.
Receyvyd off John Lowe in parte off the colleccyon for Be[r]strete & Con[is]fforthe on Crystmes evyn 1557	20s.
Receyvyd off Thomas Pettous in parte off the colleccyon for the wardes of Wymer in parte off payment	£3
Receyvyd more the laste off December 1557 in parte off the colleccyon Over the Water off Peter Applyarde the summe off	11s. 4d.
Receyvyd off Thomas Lowthe for hys quarter ferme for hys howse ended at Crystmes	3s. 4d.
Receyvyd off Thomas Elsye farren receyver for Crysmes quarter	20s.
Receyvyd off the goodman mayer for the halffe yere rent of hys howsys that ys to seye at Mycchelmes & Crystmes ended the summe of	10s.

/<£43 15s. 4d.> £42 7s. 4d./

Received off John Lowe in parte off the colleccyon for Be[r]strete & Con[is]fforthe	15s.
Received off the goodman Swanton in parte off the colleccyon for Mancrofte	10s. 10d.
Receyvyd off Thoms Pettous in parte of the colleccyon for the ward off Wymer the 23 daye of Feveryere	26s. 6d.
Receyvyd off Peter Applyard in parte off the colleccyon Over the Water	9s. 1d.

/£44 19s. 8d./

Receyvyd of goodman Swanton in full payment off the colleccyon for the warde off Mancrofte	3s. 5d.
Receyvyd off John Lowe in full paymente for the ward off Be[r]strett & Cony[s]fford	8s. 4d.
Receyvyd off Thomas Pettous for the warde of Wymer	26s. 7d.
Receyvyd off Mr Blome for this quarter endyd at Crystmes	50s.
Receyvyd more of Mr Blome for the ryver	20s.
Receyvyd off the goodman mayer for the quarter ferme off hys howse ended at Owr Lady in Lent laste	5s.
Receyvyd off Thomas Lowthe for hys quarter ferme off hys howse ended at Owr Ladye	3s. 4d.

/ Summa £28 7s. 11d. /[8]

[Total of the year's receipts   £51 14s. 5d.]

[f. 3r] Deductyd & paid owrt off these receytes aforeseyd as herafter followythe partyculerlye

Paid fyrste for thys boke wherin everye accompte maye appere & so to be delyvered to the nexte receyver at the ende off the yere	18d.
Paid to John Cawston & Edmond Ryee the 30 daye off Marche 1557 for ther *halffe* quarters wagys dewe nowe at Owr Ladye daye	40s.
Paid for a rope off ten fadom for the bote	20d.
Paid to Andrewes for hys quarters wages the laste off Marche 1557	6s. 8d.
Paid to Cadbye for hys quarters wages for caryege for Over the Water endyd nowe at Owr Ladye in Lente	25s.
Paid for 6 lodes off fylthe caryed at severall cockeys[9] before Ester	2s.
Paid for the gatheryng to gether off 8 lodes off mocke at Seynt Awstens cockey at Ester	8d.
Paid for the caryge theroff	2s. 8d.
Paid to John Cawstond and Edmond Ryee the 2nd off Maye 1557 for ther halffe quarters wagys ended nowe at Crowchemes	40s.
Paid for 2 furryng sparres for ores	7d.
Paid for the caryng off 8 lodes off fylthe from dyversse cockes beffore the hyeryng off Marshame[10]	2s. 8d.

[8] This total is given in both Roman and Arabic numerals.

[9] For the location of the Norwich 'cockeys' (that is, its natural streams and man-made water channels), see the Appendix and *figure* 2.

[10] John Marsham was hired later in this year to collect and cart away material extracted from the cockeys by the cockey-cleaners. He was paid a wage for this task for the period of 15 May to 1 August (Lammas quarter) and again from 1 August to 1 November (Hallows): see below, f. 3v.

Paid to the manne that mendyd the bote for 5 dayes worke of hym selffe & hys manne for ther wagys & ther mete & drynke whyles thei ware mendyng off the bote	8s. 4d.
Paid for 2 stone pytche	3s. 4d.
Paid for a gallon off tarre	10d.
Paid for nayles, hardes, thromes, rede & wronges & the hyer off hys potte[11]	3s. 4d.
Paid for 88 fote off borde for the plancheryng theroff	5s.
Paid for C unche bord for twye bord	8d.
Paid for 3 peces of other tymber for the bote	6d.
Paid to the bote men the 16 daye of June 1557 for ther halffe quarter wagys endyd the 14 daye of thys monethe	40s.
Paid more to the laborer that dyd helpe them to cutt for 6 dayes worke uppon the ryver and mete & drynkes	4s.
Paid more to the laborer that dyd helpe them to cutte in the ryver for 5 dayes worke	3s. 1d.

/ Summa £9 12s. 6d. /[12]

[f. 3v] [Paid to And]rewe for hys quarters wages dewe at Mydsomer	6s. 8d.
[Paid to] the laborer that cuttythe in the ryver for 2 days worke	14d.
Paid for the hyer off a bote and a man for hys wagys at sucche tyme as Mr Graye, Edmond Thorston and I dyd goo downe to surveye the botemen whyles theye warre cuttyng in the ryver	12d.
Paid to the laborer that cuttythe in the ryver for 6 days worke	3s. 7d.
Paid to Catbye for hys quarter wages dewe to hym for caryge Over the Water ended nowe at <Owr Lad> Mydsomer laste paste	25s.
Paid to the laborer that cuttythe in the ryver for 2 days worke	14d.
Paid to the laborer that cuttythe in the ryver for 3 days worke	21d.
Paid more to hym for one days worke in the ryver	8d.
Paid more to hym for 3 days worke in the ryver	21d.
Paid more to hym for 7 dayes worke in the ryver	4s. 1d.
Paid more to the botemen for ther halffe quarter wages ended at Lammes laste	40s.
Paid more to John Marsham for hys wagys for Lammes quarter	£4

---

[11] For unfamiliar terms used here and below, please see the General glossary.
[12] This total is given in both Roman and Arabic numerals.

Paid more to Mr Bulward for 2 sythes & twys gryndyng off 2 payer
off sheres & mendyng off serten irenworke   7s.

Paid to Andrewe for hys quarter wagys dewe at Mycchelmes   6s. 8d.

Paid to the botemen for there halffe quarter wages endyd att
Mycchelmes laste   40s.

Paid more to a laborer that dyd helpe to cutte in the ryver for 5
dayes worke at 7d. a daye   2s. 11d.

Paid to the botemen for ther halffe quarter wagys endyd at Hallowes
laste   40s.

Paid to Thomas Pecke for the ferme off the howses *for the botemen*   20s.

Paid to Marsham for caryege from Lammes tyll Hallowes   £4

Paid to the botemen for ther *dimidia* quarter wagys ended at
Crystmes 1557   40s.

Paid for ropes for the botte   12d.

Paid to Andrewe for hys quarter wagys endyd at Crystmes   6s. 8d.

Paid for the caryage a waye off 7 lodes off mucke from the cockeys
and the markette & other placys ageynste Crystmes   2s. 4d.

Paid for the caryage a waye off 7 lodys off mucke from the cockeys
& other places a geynste Crystmes   2s. 4d.

/ *Summa £20 15s. 9d.*/

[*f. 4r*] Paid for the caryage a waye from the cockeys & the markett
stede off 6 lodes off mokke the 26 off Januarij 1557   2s.

Paid for the caryage a waye from the cockeyes at Seynt Martens,[13]
Seynt Symondes & Seynt Swethewnes, 4 lodes   16d.

Paid for a roppe off 5 faddom for ther bote   8d.

Paid to the botemen for ther halffe quarter wagys ended at Candelmes   40s.

Paid to Catbye for hys halffe yeres wagys dewe to hym for caryage
Over the Water ended at Crystmes laste the summe off   50s.

Paid to Ketryngham for the caryage a waye off 3 lodes off mucke   12d.

/ *£12 7s. 4d.*/

/ *<£35 <10s. 8d.> <*2s. 2d.*> £35 3s. 3d.*/

Paid to Andrewe for hys quarter wagys endyd at Owr Ladye in Lent   6s. 8d.

Paid to the boteman for ther halffe quarter wagys endyd at Owr
Ladye daye in Lente laste paste   40s.

---

[13] There were three parishes in Norwich dedicated to St. Martin: St Martin at Bale, St Martin
at Oak and St Martin at Palace (see *figure* 1). It is not known which one is referred to here.

Paid to Ketryngham for 10 lodes off fylthe from the cockeys	3s. 4d.
Paid to Catbye \<paid\> for hys quarter wagys endyd at Owr Ladye in Lente for caryage Over the Water	25s.
Paid for 6 lodes off mucke caryage from the stretes a bowgt the markette & the cockeys ther a bowgt	2s.
Paid more the 12 daye off Maye 1558 to the botemen for ther halffe quarter wagys ended at Crowchmes	40s.
Paid more for caryeng awaye off serten mocke in Seyntes Johns[14] & Seynte Lawrans & the markettestede & all the cockeys	7s.
Paid more to Thomas Cullye for baste rope delyvered be fore my tyme	16d.

/ Summa £11 4d./[15]

Summa *totallis* of the paymentes ys   £41 8s. 7d

So remayns in John Bacons handes at thys day wrettyn the 15 day of Maye *anno* 1558 s[um]   £14 5s. 10d.

[*signed*] by me Austen Styward, by me Robart Rugg
/ audytarres apoyntyd/

Reseived the 22 day of May *anno* 1558 the sayd s[um] of   £14 5s. 10d.
& put in to master meyeres locker[16] witness
[*signed*] by me Austen Styward, by me Robart Rugge

[*f. 4v*] Memorandum that ytt ys agreyd by the more parte off the companye and also grauntyd as well in owr tyme as in the yere beffore that the grownd that ys partable betwyxte the cetye & Crystes chirche lyinge on both sydes the ferrye by the meanes off a composycyon so made betwyxte the seyd partyes ys nowe grauntyd by us to Thomas Pecke grocer all & so mocche as ys longyng to the seyd cetye ther lying so farre and uppon condycyon that he the seyd Thomas maye attayne & gette the good wyll off the masters of Cryste chirche

[14] St John's: the parish of St John the Baptist, Timberhill. It is referred to as St John-at/on-the-Hill in these accounts from 1559/60.

[15] This total is given in both Roman and Arabic numerals.

[16] The treasury: see below, f. 5v (1558–59).

[1558–59]

[f. 5r] Heare folowith the namys of the surveyours

6 olde	6 newe
William Farrour alderman	Robert Mychels alderman
John Lowe	John Woodcokke
Thomas Swanton	George Walden
Richard Tolye	Thomas Wynter
Petir Appleyarde	Thomas Goche
John Soterton jun[ior]	George Redman

Memorandum *the hoale company* assembled the first daye of June *anno* 1558 and this daye is elected Richarde Tolye to be receyvour and payer for this yere

John Lowe is appoynted to survey the stretes within the warde of Berestrete & Cunnysforde

John Woodcoke is appoynted to collect the mony within the seid warde

Thomas Swanton is appoynted to survey the stretes in Mancroft warde

George Waldon is appoynted to collect the mony within the seid warde

Thomas Goche is appoynted to survey the stretes within the warde of Wymer

Thomas Wynter is appoynted to collect the mony within the said warde

Petir Appleyard is appoynted to survey the stretes within the warde Over the Water

George Redman is appoynted to be collectour of the mony of the said warde

John Soterton is appoynted to surveye the watermen in thir workes and to se that the watermen do no tract any tyme, and further to se wher that most necessary places be to be amendyd in the ryver

[f. 5v] Here after folowith all such somes of mony as I Richarde Toly skryvener have receyved toward the maytenaunce of the ryver and stretes <as h> within the citie of Norwich for this yere folowing /Anno 1558/

In primis receyved of Mr Henry Bacon then mayer of the seid citie *owt of the tresory*   £4

Item receyved of Thomas Hogges waterbaylyff parcell of the arrerages of the last yere   7s.

Item receyved of Thomas Lowth for the quarters ferme of his howse
endyd at Mydsomer *anno* 1558   3s. 4d.

<Item paid to Andrewe Robynson for his quarter wages endyd at
Mydsomer *anno* 1558   6s. 8d.>

Item received of Robert Mayer for the quarters ferme of his howse
endyd at Mydsomer *anno* 1558   5s.

Item receyved of William Farrour alderman the 6th daye of July
anno 1558 which he receyved of master mayer that ca[me] owt of
the tresorye   40s.

Item received of John Mundy myller the 12th of Julye *anno* 1558 for
the cutting *of* the ryver endyd at Mydsomer[17]   26s. 8d.

Item receyved of Thomas Elsy forren receyver to the use of the
ryver & stretes dewe at the feast of the natyvyte of Saynt John
Baptist *anno* 1558   20s.

Item receyved of Nycholas Man by thandes of Thomas Bemonde
in parte of payement of a certen arrerrages of £3 dewe for his
howse at the feast of the purificacion of Our Blissed Lady *anno* 1557   40s.

Item received of Mr Blome chamberlayn by the handes of Thomas
Parryshe the 13 day of August *anno* 1558 for his quarter endyd at
thanunciacion of Our Blissed Lady last past   £3 10s.

Item received of George Walden collectour for the warde of
Mancroft the 2nd daye of September *anno* 1558   23s. 4d.

Item received of John Woodcokke collectour for the warde of
Berstret [and] Cunnysford the 26 day of September   20s.

Item receyved of Mr Blome chamberleyn for his quarter endyd at
Mydsomer *anno* 1558   £3 10s.
/£[?][18] 5s. 4d./

[f. 6r] Receyved of Thomas Lowth for <his> *the* quarters ferme
of his howse endyd at Myhelmes *anno* 1558   3s. 4d.

Item of Mr Blome chamberleyn <for> by order taken by master
mayer & his brothern for Grene the mason for 3 yeres for a certayn
grownde that he fermyth of the cite   9s.

Item receyved of Thomas Wynter collectour for the stretes & ryver
for the warde of Wymer the first day of Octobre *anno* 1558   25s.

Item received of Robert Mayer for his quarters ferme of his howse
endyd at Myhelmes *anno* 1558   5s.

[17] For the millers at the civic water mills ('New Mills'), and their annual payments to the
surveyors, see the Introduction, p. 113.
[18] Page damaged.

Item received of Grene the mason for \<his\> the yeres ferme of his
grounde endid at Mihelmes *anno* 1558   3*s.*

Item receyved of Edwarde Reve for the half yeres ferme of his
howse endyd at Myhelmes *anno* 1558   16*s.* 8*d.*

Item received of Thomas Elsy forren receyve\<d\>*r* to the use of
the ryver & stretes dew at the feast of Saynt Michaell tharchaungell
anno 1558   20*s.*

Receyved of Nycholas Man for the half yeris ferme of his howse at
the *late* Black Fryers[19] dewe at the feast of Saynt Petyrs chaynes
called Lammes *anno* 1558   20*s.*

Receyved of Thomas Lowth for the quarters ferme of his howse
endyd at the feast of the burth of Our Lord God *anno* 1558   3*s.* 4*d.*

Receyved of Robert Mayer for his quarters ferme endyd at
Christmas *anno* 1558   5*s.*

Receyved of Thomas Wynter collector for the stretes & ryver of the
warde of Wymer the 20[20] daye of January *anno* 1558   46*s.*

Receyved of Thomas Elsy forreyn receyver to the use of the ryver
& stretes dewe at the feast of the birth of Our Lorde God *anno* 1558   20*s.*

Receyved of George Walden collectour for the warde of Mancroft
the first daye of Marche *anno* 1558   20*s.*

Receyved of Mr Blome for his quarter endyd at Myhelmes *anno* 1558   £3 10*s.*

/£13 6*s.* 4*d.*/

[*f. 6v*] Item receyved of George Redman collectour for the stretes
& ryver the 4th day of Marche *anno* 1558*   50*s.*

Item receyved of Thomas Wynter collectour the Munday after
myd-Lent Sonday[21]   6*s.* 6*d.*

Item of George Redman \<over\> the 6 daye of Marche *anno* 1558   5*s.*

Item receyved of George Walden the 6 daye of Marche *anno* 1558   7*s.* 8*d.*

/£3 9*s.* 2*d.*/

/£37 10*d.*/ *Memorandum* recevyd with Rychard Toly reseyvor of
thys mony for the rever fir 3 quarters rendyd at Cristmes last past
anno 1558 wyche mony that he have received ys   £37 10*d.*

---

[19] Blackfriars: the former Dominican friary in the parish of St Andrew, also referred to as the
'New Hall' in these accounts (e.g., in 1559–60). In 1540, the city government bought the site and
refurbished the church building as a hall for civic assemblies. Large parts of the garden and
smaller buildings were let out to tenants, like this house.

[20] Deletion of one illegible letter/numeral.

[21] Mid-Lent Sunday is the fourth Sunday of Lent, that is, Sunday 5 March 1559, which makes
the Monday in question, Monday 6 March 1559.

Recevyd the 8 day of Marche *anno predicto*
[*signed*] John Aldryche mayer, Austen Styward alderman

Deducted & paid owt of thes receytes aforsaid as hereafter folowith
particulerly

[*f. 7r*] Paid first to William Warner & John Marshall for thir paynes in rowyng the hoale company to Surlingham wood[22] to survey the cutting of the ryver and for the hier of the bote	12*d*.
Item paid for 4 fadom & *dimidia* [*4½ fathoms*] of bastyng rope	9*d*.
Item paid to <Joh> Nicholas Marshall, John White & Henry Usher for 2 dayes cuttyng the ryver & for the bote	4*s*.
Item paid to Nycholas Phillippes that ded helpe the botemen to cutt the ryver for the space of 15 dayes at 7*d*. the daye, som	8*s*. 9*d*.
Item paid for a newe oore for thir bote	8*d*.
Item paid for nayles for to mende the broken ore	1*d*.
Item paid to Wale for the grynding of the sheris	10*d*.
Item paid to Nicholas Phillippes for 6 dayes <w> cuttyng in the ryver with the bote men	2*s*. 6*d*.
Item paid to Nycholas Marshall, John White & Henry Usher for fyve dayes cuttyng the ryver	10*s*.
Item paid to Nycholas Marshall, John White & Henry Usher for 4 dayes cuttyng the ryver	8*s*.
Item paid to John Cawson & Edmunde Rye over Mydsomer day for thir half quarters wagis dewe at the said daye *anno* 1558	40*s*.
Item paid to Andrewe Robynson for his quarter wages endyd at Mydsomer *anno* 1558	6*s*. 8*d*.
Item paid to Nycholas Phillippes for fyve dayes helping the botemen to cut the ryver	2*s*. 11*d*.
Item paid to Nycholas Phillippes for 4 dayes helpyng the botemen to cutt the ryver	2*s*. 4*d*.

/ *£4 8s. 6d.* /

[*f. 7v*] Item paid to John Marsham for the caryage of 12 lodes of compasse the 8 daye of July *anno* 1558	4*s*.
Item paid to Nycholas Phillippes for fyve dayes worke in helping the botemen to cut the ryver	2*s*. 11*d*.

---

[22] Surlingham wood: situated in a village on the river about 6 miles south-east of Norwich. For an example of the provisions made for clearing reeds from the river between New Mills and Surlingham before the surveyors were inaugurated, see *RCN*, ii, 102 (1478).

Item paid to Nycholas Phillippes for 6 dayes worke in helping the botemen to cut the ryver   3s. 6d.

Item paid to Thomas Bemonde by the cummaundement of master mayer for a dett dew to hym upon the yelding of his accompt whan he was receyvor for the ryver & stretes   3s.

Item paid to John Cawston & Edmunde Rye over Lammes daye for thir half quarters wages endyd at the seid feast *anno* 1558   40s.

Item paid to Vincent Tesmonde for the ferme of his bote by the space of 7 wekys in cutting the ryver at 4d. the weke   2s. 4d.

Item paid to Catby the caryer for the caryage of 72 loodes of compace at 4d. the lood   24s.

Item paid more to the said Catby for <illegible deletion> 13 loodes that Bacon ded owe hym *for*   4s. 4d.

Item paid to Thomas Bettes for 5 dayes worke in cutting the ryver the second tyme   2s. 11d.

Item paid more to Thomas Styngate for 3 dayes worke in cutting the ryver   21d.

Item paid to the goodman Banges for the hier of his bot[e] above the mylle 6 daies   6d.

Item paid to Thomas Bettes for 2 dayes worke in helping the botemen to cutt the ryver   14d.

Item paid to Edward Grewe executour of Mr Bolward for gryndyng the sheris & othir toles & for a gryndston[e]   6s.

/£4 16s. 5d./

[f. 8r] Item paid to Ketryngham the caryer for the cariage of the fylth in Berstrete & Cunnysforde warde the 10th daye of Septembre *anno* 1558 for 39 lodes   13s.

Item paid more to the seid Ketryngham for the caryage of 43 lodes of cumpasse owt of Saynt Stevyns warde[23] the said 10th daye of Septembre *anno* 1558   14s. 4d.

Item paid more to the said Ketryngham for caryage of 33 lodes of cumpasse owt of the warde of Wymer   11s.

Item paid more to the seid Ketryngham for 50 lodys caryage owt of the warde of Saynt Petirs of Mancroft[24] the said 10th day   16s. 8d.

[23] St Stephen's 'ward': this was in fact a sub-ward, part of the great ward of Mancroft in the south of the city. Its boundaries were co-terminus with those of the parish of St Stephen. See *figures* 1 and 3.

[24] St Peter Mancroft 'ward': again, a sub-ward, and part of the great ward of Mancroft. Its boundaries were co-terminus with those of the parish of St Peter Mancroft. See *figures* 1 and 3.

Item paid to Passon for makyng clene the cockeys after that Andrewe Robynson was departed	12d.
Item paid to Andrewe Robynsons wyf for his quarters wages for makyng cleane the cockeis endyd at Myhelmes *anno* 1558[25]	6s. 8d.
Item paid for mending *of* the sherys	3d.
Item paid to Edmunde <d> Rye for his half quarter wages endyd at Myhelmes *anno* 1558	20s.
Item paid to John Casson for his half quarters wages endyd at Myhelmes *anno* 1558	20s.
Item paid to the seid John Casson & <John D> Edmunde Rye for the rest of thir wages that was dewe unto them whan they war put owt of thir worke[26]	21s. 8d.
Item paid to John Clarke for the fyeng of the cockeis for his quarters ferme endyd at Christmas *anno* 1558	6s. 8d.
Item paid to Ketryngham for the cariage of the fylth of <Mancroft> *Berstrete ward* over Chrismas even for 31 lodes	10s. 4d.

/£7 19d./

[f. 8v] Item paid to the said Ketryngham for caryage of 80 lodes of fylthe owt of Saynt Stevens parish and Saynt Peters of Mancroft over Christmas even	26s. 8d.
Item paid to Catby for caryage of 48 lodes of fylth owt of the warde Beyonde the Water the 22 day of January *anno* 1558	16s.
Item paid to John Crowe by thandes of Thomas Wynter for 77 lodes of fylth for the warde of Wymer	25s. 8d.
Item paid to Thomas Chapman botewright for the mending of the dydall bote & for wronges, nayles & othir necessaries as appere by a byll	10s. 1d.
Item paid to Mr Pecke for the ferme of his howse for the botemen	20s.
Item paid to Toly for engrosyng the boke	2s. 6d.
Item to Hogges the water baly	3s. 4d.
Item paid to Thomas Ketryngham caryer for the cariage of 31 lodes of fylth for Mancroft warde paid the 8th daye of March *anno* 1558	10s. 4d.
Item paid to the seid Ketryngham for caryage of the fylth in Saynt Stevyns parishe & from the cockeys 21 lodes the 8 *day* of March *anno* 1558	7s.

---

[25] This entry is preceded by a marginal drawing of a teardrop.
[26] This entry is preceded by a marginal drawing comprising a circle with cross inside it.

Item paid the said daye to the seyd Ketryngham for 19 lodes <for>
of fylth owt of Berstret & Cunnysford   6s. 4d.

Item paid to Crowe for caryeing of 20 lodes of fylth for the warde
of Wymer   6s. 8d.

            Summa of the paymentes as yt apere be fore wretyn   £23<9d.>13d.

Summa that dothe remayn ys   £14 save 3d.
Wych mony was reseived the 8 daye of Marche *anno* 1558 & put
i[n] to the bage in the coffyr afor master meyer
[*signed*] John Aldryche mayer, Austen Styward alderman

/<£[?]²⁷ *8s. 5d.*>/ /£6 <21d.> <14s. 6d.> <6d.> *14s. 7d.**/
/<£22 15s. 3d.> £23 <9d.> 13d./²⁸

[1559–60]

[*f. 9r*]²⁹ /*Anno 1559*/ Thaccompte of George Walden grosser as[well]
of all souche sumes of money as he have receyved also of all souche
summes of money as he have <receyv> payed and layde forthe
concernyng the making cleane of the ryver stretes and cockyes that
ys to saye from the feast of thanunciacion of Our Lady *anno* 1559
u[ntill] the feast of thanunciacion of Our Lady *anno* 155 10 [*1560*]³⁰
be[ing] a hole yeare as hereafter ensuithe

/*Receptes*/ Fyrst receyved of Thomas Lowthe for his quarters ferme
dewe at the feast of the anunciacion of Our Lady *anno* 1559   3s. 4d.

Item received of Robarte Mayhow for his quarters ferme dewe at
the seyde feaste   5s.

Item of Thomas Wynter collector for the warde of Wymer for
certeyne arrerages remaynyng in his handes and dewe for this yeare
of Our Lorde 1558   29s. 2d.

Item of Thomas Hogges for arrerages by hym receyved of diverse
persons whiche was dew at thanunciacion of Our Lady *anno* 1558   10s.

Item of Thomas Lowthe for his quarters ferme dewe at Mydsomer
anno 1559   3s. 4d.

---

²⁷ Page damaged.

²⁸ It is not clear what all these calculations relate to, although some are clearly attempts to determine or audit the annual total expenditure.

²⁹ Folios 9 and 10 seem to have been misplaced, perhaps when the volume was re-ordered by alderman Robert Suckling (see the Introduction, p.112). The proper order of the half folios was probably: 8v (end of the account for 1558–59); 10r (a list of transactions made around the turn of the new financial year); 10v (a list of office holders); 9r-9v (receipts); 11r (payments).

³⁰ As is the case throughout the text, the year of grace is given here in Arabic numerals. The numerals '155 10' signify 1550 years plus ten, which is to say, 1560.

Item of Thomas Mondy for money that he owght for cutting the rever in the yeare of Our Lorde 1558   26s. 8d.

Item received of John Revell for the halfe yeres dewty payde oute by the forren receyvour towardes the ryver stretes and cockes which was dewe at [blank]   40s.

Item of Richarde Toley skrevener for money that Nicholas [blank] owght dewe at Candelmas anno 1558   20s.

Item of Mr Blome late chamberlyne for money dewe from the chamber to the uses aforeseide, viz., for the feast of Our Lorde God 1558   70s.

[f. 9v] //[Re]ceptes/ Item more receyved for arrerages that remayned in myn owne handes at the feast of thanunciacion of Our Lady anno 1558   10s. 2d.

Item of Robert Mayhew for his quarters ferme dewe at Mydsomer anno 1559   5s.

Item receyved of Edwarde Reve for halfe a yeres ferme of the corner tenement nere to the Gwyldehall[31] and dewe at the anunciacion of Our Lady anno 1559   16s. 8d.

Item received of Christofer Barrett in parte of payment of his colleccion for the warde of Mancrofte   20s.

Item received more of the same Christofer Barrett the fyrst of October in parte of payment of his colleccion for the warde of Mancrofte   20s.

Item received of Robarte Mayhew for his quarters ferme dewe at Michelmas within the tyme of this accompte   5s.

Item received of Thomas Lowthe for his quarters ferme dewe at Michelmas within the tyme of this accompte   3s. 4d.

Item of John Revell foren receyvor for money that he payeth towardes the charges of the rever for Mychelmas quarter   20s.

Item of Mr Blome late chamberleyne for money from the chamber to the uses aforeseide dewe for the qwarter ended at Our Ladys daye anno 1559   70s.

Item of Edwarde Reve for the halfe yeres ferme of the tenement nere to the Gwylde Hall dewe at Michelmas 1559   16s. 8d.

Item of Nicholas Man for the halfe yeres ferme of his howse at the New Hall[32] ended at Lammas anno 1559[33]   20s.

---

[31] Guildhall: the administrative centre of the city's ruling government, situated on the northern edge of the market.
[32] New Hall: see above, n. 19.   [33] This entry is preceded by three dots in the margin.

Item of Nicholas Sotherton collector for the warde Beyonnde the
Water   20s.

[f. 10r][34] Wherof paide the Wedensdaye in passion weke to John
Warner <for> one of the botemen appoynted for the making cleane
the river and due to hym for *dimidia* <a> quarters [a half quarter's]
wages due to hym the 11th daye of Marche anno 1558   18s. 5d.

Memorandum paid to John Clarke for making cleane the cockes and
swepyng the markett the 25th of March anno 1559   6s. 8d.

Memorandum paid to Cawston for making clene the ryver for the
halfe quarter wages dewe at thannunciacion of Our Ladye *last paste*
/ Primo Aprilis anno 1559/[35]   20s.

Item paid to Alman the same daye for a fortenyght working in the
ryver which ended at Our <Lay> Lady daye aforesayde   6s. 2d.

Memorandum paid to Cadby the 8th of Apriell anno 1559 for dett due
to hym for carryeng the swepynges of the stretes which was due *to*
hym for the yere last past
/ Octavo Aprilis/[36]   3s. 4d.

Paid to Cawston and Wright laborers in the ryver for wages due to
them for halfe a quarter endyd at Whitsontyde last, viz., to eyther
of [them] 20s. / Primo Maii anno 1559/[37]   40s.

[f. 10v] Here foloweth the names of the survi<u>ours anno 155<8>9

6 olde	6 newe
Robert Michell alderman	Edmund Warden alderman
John Woodcok	Christofer Barrett
George Walden	William Butfylde
Thomas Wynter	John Suckelyng
Thomas Goche	<Richarde Bate> Edmunde Overt[o]n
George Redman	Nicholas Sotherton

Memorandum the 10 daye of Maye anno 1559 and this daye is elected
George Walden to be receyver & payer for this yere

John Woodcokke is appoynted to be surweyer of the stretes within
the warde of Berestrete & Connesforde

Edmunde Overt[o]n is appoynted to collect the money within the
seid warde

Christofer Barrett is appoynted to collect the money within the
warde of Mancroft

---

[34] See above, n. 29.
[35] 'The first of April in the year 1559'. This entry is bracketed with the next one.
[36] 'The eighth of April'.
[37] 'The first of May in the year 1559'.

William Butfylde is appoynted to survey the stretes within the seid warde

John Suckelyng is appoynted to collect the money within the warde of Wymer

Thomas Wynter is appoynted to survey the stretes within the seid warde

Nicholas Sotherton is appoynted to collect the money within the warde Beyonde the Water

George Redman is appoynted to survey the stretes within the seid warde

Thomas Goche with the assistence of Mr Warden is appoynt[ed] to surveye the watermen in ther workes to se that the watermen do not tract any tyme and further to se wher that most necessary places be to be amended in the ryver etc

[*f. 11r*] Item of John Suckelyng baker collector for the ryver and stretes for the warde of Wymer	20*s.*
Item of Edmonde Overton collector for the warde of Connesforde & Bestrete <and>	20*s.*
Item of Mr Blome late chamberleyne for money from the chamber to the uses aforeseide dewe for the quarter ended at Mydsomer *anno* 1559	70*s.*
Item of Robarte Mayhewe for his qwarter ferme dew at Cristmas *anno* 1559	5*s.*
Item of Thomas Lowthe for his quarters ferme dewe at Cristmas	3*s.* 4*d.*
Item of Grene the mason for rente of his grounde dewe at Michelmas	3*s.*
Item received more of John Revell foren receyvour for money that he payeth towardes the charges of the ryver and stretes for Christmas quarter	20*s.*
Item received of Christofer Barret collector for the ryver and stretes for the warde of Mancrofte	19*s.*
Item received of John Suckelyng baker collector for the ryver and stretes for the warde of Wymer	50*s.*

/[£10 4s. 8d.]/

/[£?³⁸ 4s. 8d.]/ /£30 4s. 8d./³⁹

---

³⁸ Accounting marks obscured in binding.

³⁹ In Arabic numerals. If this is intended to be the subtotal of the receipts for the year to this point in the text, the sum should in fact read '£29 14*s.* 8*d.*'.

Item of Nicholas Man for the halfe yeres ferme of his howse at the
New Hall ended at Candelmas *anno* 1559[40]   20s.

Item of Mr Blome late chamberleyne for money dewe from the
chamber to the uses aforeseyde dewe for the quarter ended at
Mychelmas *anno* 1559   70s.

/[£36 14s. 8d.]/

                                        Summa of the receiptes   £36 14s. 8d.

/*Wherof payde as followeth*/

[*f. 11v*] /*Paymentes*/ Payde to John Thurketyll for 9 dayes worke in
cutting the ryver at 7d. the daye   5s. 3d.

Item to Henry Holden for a barrow to karry the mucke owte of
the bote   2s.

Item to John Crow for 30 lodes carryng which was owing unto
hym of olde   10s.

Item payde to Thomas Wynter for 8 fadam of bast to draw the
cutting sherys with in the ryver   12d.

Item payde more to John Thyrketyll for 7 dayes worke in cutting
the ryver at 7d. the daye   4s. 1d.

Item payde to John Cadby the 4th of June for carryng 61 lodes
fylthe oute of the stretes and cokkes for the warde Beyonde the
Water at 4d. the lode   20s. 4d.

Item payde more to John Thyrketyll the 10th of June for 6 dayes
worke in rowyng of them that cut the rever at 7d. the daye   3s. 6d.

Item more to the same John the 17th of June for 6 dayes worke in
rowyng of them that cut the rever at 7d. the daye   3s. 6d.

Item payde more to the same John Thirketill the 24th daye of June
for 5 dayes worke in rowing them that cut the ryver at 7d. the daye   2s. 11d.

Item to John Clarke for his quarters wages for sweping the markett
and clensing the cockes dewe at Mydsomer   6s. 8d.

Item to John Cawston and William Wright for ther wages dewe for
halfe a quarter ending at Midsomer   40s.

[*f. 12r*] /*Paymentes*/ Item payd to John Marsham the 28th of June for
14 lodes of mucke carryng oute of the stretes in Weste Wymer[41]   4s. 8d.

Item payde to John Thyrketyll the fyrst of July for 5 dayes worke in
rowing of them that cut the ryver at 7d. the daye   2s. 11d.

---

[40] This entry is preceded by three dots in the margin.
[41] West Wymer: a sub-ward, see *figure 3*.

Item payde more to John Thurketyll the 15th of July for 7 dayes
worke in rowing them that cut the ryver at 7*d.* the daye 4*s.* 1*d.*

Item payde to Thomas Keteringham the 21st daye of July for 64
lodes of mucke carryng oute of St Peters at 4*d.* the lode 21*s.* 4*d.*

Item more the same daye to the seide Thomas Keteringham for
62 lodes of mucke caryed oute of St Stephans 20*s.* 4*d.*

Item more to the seide Keteringham the same daye for 33 lodes
mucke caryed oute of Bestrete and Consforde 11*s.*

Item payde to John Thurketyll the 20th of July for 5 dayes worke in
rowing them that cut the ryver at 7*d.* the daye 2*s.* 11*d.*

Item payed to John Marsham the 28th of July for carryng 7 lodes
mucke that is one lode from Mr Crokes backe gate 3 lodes oute of
St Stephans and 3 lodes oute of St John at the Hill 2*s.* 4*d.*

Item to John Thyrketyll the 29th daye of July for 5 dayes worke in
rowing of them that cut the ryver at 7*d.* the day 2*s.* 11*d.*

Item more to the same John for 6 dayes for the lyke beyng payde
the 6 of Aug[*ust*] 3*s.* 6*d.*

Item payde to John Cawston and William Wright the 6 daye of
August for the halfe quarters wages dewe to them at Lammas 40*s.*

[*f. 12v*] /*Paymentes*/ Item payde to John Thyrketyll the 12th of August
for 6 dayes worke in rowing of them that cut the rever at 7*d.* the daye 3*s.* 6*d.*

Item payde to John Cadby the 15th of August for 80 lodes mucke
carryed oute of the stretes within the warde Beyonnde the Water
at 4*d.* the lode 26*s.* 8*d.*

Item payde to John Thyrketyll the 19th of August for too dayes
worke in rowyng them that cut the ryver at 7*d.* the daye 14*d.*

Item paid more to the seide John Thyrketyll the 21st of August for
14 wekes of his botehyer [*boat hire*] at 5*d.* the weke 5*s.* 10*d.*

Item payde to John Thyrketyll the 26th of August in helping of them
that cut the ryver too dayes at 7*d.* the daye 14*d.*

Item payde to John Marsham the 12th daye of September of 4 lodes
of mucke carryng at 4*d.* the lode 16*d.*

Item paid more to the seide John Masham for thre lodes carryng
oute of St Lawrences 12*d.*

Item payde to John Perry the 14th of September for 3 dayes worke
in helping of the ryvermen at the New Mylles 2*s.*

Item payde to John Clarke for his quarters wages <for> sweping
of the markett and cockyes dewe at Michelmas 6*s.* 8*d.*

Item payde to John Cawston and William Wright kepers of the
ryver for ther halfe quarters wages dewe at Michell[*mas*]   40*s.*

[*f. 13r*] /*Paymentes*/ Item payde to Thomas Keteringham the 12[th]
of October for carryng 17 lodes mucke oute of Be[r]strete and
Connesforde   5*s.* 8*d.*

Item more to the seide Keteringham for 25 lodes carryng oute of
Weste Wymer   8*s.* 4*d.*

Item paid to John Clarke sweper of the markett in augmentacion
of his wages for the entente he shoulde carry awaye the fylthe hym
selffe begynnyg at Michell[*mas*]   20*d.*

Item paid to Thomas Wynter for thre fadom of baste for the cutters
of the ryver   5*d.*

Item payde to Edmonde Thurston for a fyrren sparre for a quante
for the ryvermen   6*d.*

Item payde to John Crowe the 30th daye of October for carryng
30 lodes mucke oute of Weste Wymer warde   10*s.*

Item paid to Thomas Keteringham the seconde of November for
58 lodes fylthe oute of St Peters [*Mancroft*] and St Stephans   19*s.* 4*d.*

Item payde to John Cadby for 80 lodes of mucke carryed oute of
the warde Beyonnde the Water[42]   26*s.* 8*d.*

Item payde to John Cawston and William Wright the 12 of
November for ther halfe quarters wages dew at Hallowmas   40*s.*

Item to Blewett the smyth for a spyndel for the barrow and a
quanthok   8*d.*

Item payde for 5 fadam of baste to teye bothe endes of the bote at
the Newe Mylles   9*d.*

[*f. 13v*] /*Paymentes*/ Item payde to John Marsham the 21st of
December for 14 lodes of mucke carryng, *viz.*, 6 lodes from St Johns
on the Hill, too lodes from St Michelles,[43] thre lodes from All
Hallowes,[44] and thre lodes from Seynt Margettes,[45] and St Lawrence   4*s.* 8*d.*

Item paid to John Clarke sweper of the markett and the cockeyes
for his quarters wages dewe at Cristmas   8*s.* 4*d.*

---

[42] This entry is preceded by a marginal drawing of a teardrop.

[43] St Michael's. There were three parishes dedicated to St Michael in Norwich: St Michael at
Thorn (Conesford), St Michael at Plea (Wymer) and St Michael Coslany (Over the Water). In
the 1530s, a cockey in the parish of St Michael Coslany is referred to in Norwich's chamberlains'
accounts, so this could be the parish intended here (NRO, NCR 18a/5, CA f. 30v). However, St
Michael at Thorn was adjacent to both All Saints and to St John's Timberhill, which are also
mentioned in this entry, and so it is perhaps more likely that this was the St Michael's in question.

[44] All Hallows': the parish of All Saints Timberhill.

[45] St Margaret's: the parish of St Margaret Westwick.

Item paid to John Cawston and William Wright kepers of the ryver
for ther halfe quarters wages dewe at Cristmas   40s.

Item payde to John Hewer bladesmyth for gryndyng the sherys
thryse and for-lockes makyng for them   3s. 4d.

Item payde to Warde of Cunesforde for persing[46] a qwante for the
bote   3d.

Item payde to Thomas Keteringham the 20[th] daye of January for
11 loodes of mucke carrying oute of Be[r]strete and Connesforde   3s. 8d.

Item payde to the seide Keteringham for 17 lodes carryng from the
parisshe of St Stephan and St Peter [*Mancroft*]   5s. 8d.

Item paid to the seide Keteringham for <12> 15 lodes carryng
oute of Myddell Wymer[47] at 4d. the lode   5s.

Item payde to John Cadby for 33 lodes mucke carryng oute of the
warde Beyonnde the Water and Wymer warde   11s.

[*f. 14r*] Item payde to John Cawston and William Wright for ther
halfe quarters wages dew at the purificacion of Our Lady last paste
40s.

/[£26 20s. 5d.] £27 5[d.]/

Item to Mr Pecke for too lodes of mucke carryng that he payd for to
Keteringham carryde from St Peters Hungate   8d.

Item to Anthony Marker for engrossing this accompte as hathe ben allowed in
former accomptes   2s. 6d.

Item paid to Mr Blome late chamberleyne for money dewe oute of Nicholas
Mans howse at the Blacke Fryers at Lammas *anno* 1559
20s.   20s.

                                    Summa of all the paymentes   £28 3s. 8d.
/[£28 3s. 8d.]/

And so remayneth in the handes of the seide George Walden   £8 11s.

Received thys £8 11s. and put yt in the hamper beffore master meyor the 27 day
of Marche 1560

[*signed*] *Richard Flecher mayor*, by me Austen Steward, by me Henry Bacon, be
me Rychard Davy

[*f. 14v blank*]

---

[46] 'Piercing' or perhaps 'piecing'. See 'pecyng' in the General glossary.
[47] Middle Wymer: a sub-ward, see *figure* 3.

[*1560–61*]

[*f. 15r*] Here folow the names of the surveyars in *anno* 1560

Edmond Wardan	Nycholas Norgatt
Crestofar Barrett	Robartt Tooke
Wyllyam Buttfeld	Henry Grenewood
John Soclenge	Thomas Layere
Rychard Ba<rr>tt	John Stengatt
Nycholas Sotherton	Matthew Plome

The 25 daye of Marche 1560 is elected & choson to recyve & paye for thes yere folowynge John Soclenge

John Stengatt is elected to be survear of the stretes of Consford and Be[r]strett <Edmonde Overton is>

Robart Tooke is choson recyvor of that ward

Crestofar Barrett is choson surveyar for the ward of Mancroft & Henry Grenewood collector for the same surcuitt

Thomas Layar is choson surveyar for the ward of Wymer

Rychard Batt is choson colector of thes same ward for the yere

Matthew Plome is choson <surveyar> colector for the ward Byyond the Wattar & Nycholas Sotherton surveyar

Wyllym Bottfeld is choson to survey the wattarmene in ther workes & to se thay do ther dewtes <in ther workes>

[*f. 15v*] /*Anno 1560*/ Thaccompte of John Suckeling baker aswell of all souche summes of mony as he have receyved as also of all suche sumes of mony as he have payed and disbursed aboute the making cleane the ryver stretes and cockeys that ys to saye from the feast of thanunciacion of Our Lady *anno* 1560 untyll the feast of thanunciacion of Our Lady *anno* 1561 beyng a hole yeare as hereafte ensueth

/*Receytes*/ Fyrst receyved of John Bacon chamberlyne of the cittie of Norwich for mony dewe from the chamber to the uses aforeseide, *viz.*, for Cristmas quarter 70*s.*, Our Lady 70*s.*, Mydsomer 70*s.*, and for Michelmas quarter 70*s.*, which amount in all to	£14
Item receyved of George Buttery for the hole yeres ferme of his house in the parisshe of Saynt Peter Mancrofte dewe at Cristmas last past	13*s.* 4*d.*
Item receyved of Reve the hosier for the ferme of his house dewe for the hole yeare ended at Michelmas *anno* 1560	33*s.* 4*d.*
Item receyved of Robart Mayhewe for the ferme of his house dewe for the hole yeare ended at Christmas *anno* 1560	20*s.*

Item receyved of John Revell forren receyvor for money dew to the uses aforeseide, *viz.*, for Our Ladys daye 20*s.*, Mydsomer 20*s.*, Michelmas 20*s.*, and for Cristmas 20*s.*, in all £4

Item of mony remaynyng in myne owne handes beyng one of the collectors the yeare now last past 7*s.*

Item receyved of John Welde myller of the Newe Mylles 15*s.*

[*f.16r*] /*Receytes*/ Item receyved of Robarte Toke collector for St <Stephans> *Connesforde & Be[r]strete* warde in full payment of souche mony as he have collected in the same warde dewe for the uses aforeseide 27*s.* 8*d.*

Item receyved of Henry Grenewoode collector for Mancrofte warde for mony that he have collected in the same warde to the use aforeseide 51*s.* 6*d.*

Item receyved of Richarde Bate collector for Wymer warde for money that he have collected in the same warde to the use aforeseide £5 4*s.* 1*d.*

Item receyved of Mathew Plom one of the collectors of the warde Beyonnde the Water for money by hym collected to the same uses 67*s.*

Item receyved of Nicholas Man in parte of payment of his house ferme at the New Hall 20*s.*

Item receyved of Nicholas Sotherton for money that he have gathered to the uses afore seide 29*s.* 7*d.*

Summa of the receyptes £37 8s. 6d.

/[£37 8s. 6d.]/

[*f. 16v*] Payed to John Cawson and William Wright for ther halfe quarters wages dewe unto them at Our Ladys daye *anno* 1560 40*s.*

Item payde to the same John Cawson and William Wright for ther halfe quarters wages dew at Crouchemas then next followyng 40*s.*

Item payed the 6th of Maye for one payer of owers for the mocke bote 2*s.*

Item payed to John Thyrketyll for 6 dayes rowyng of them that cut the ryver at 7*d.* the daye 3*s.* 6*d.*

Item payed to John Clarke for his quarters wages for swepyng the markett dewe at Or Ladys daye *anno* 1560 8*s.* 4*d.*

Item payed to John Thyrketyll the 7th of June for 13 dayes rowyng of them that cut the ryver at 7*d.* the daye 7*s.* 7*d.*

Item payed to Thomas Anott of Yarmothe the 20th of July for 12 fadom of pytched rope for a towe for the bote 20*d.*

Item payed to Mr Pecke the 6th of Maye for 6 fadam of baste at 2*d.* the fadam 12*d.*

Item payed to John Cawson and Nicholas Philips for ther halfe
quarters wages dewe unto them at Mydsomer *anno* 1560   40s.

Item payed the 13th of July to Richarde Bate for too sparres to make
with too quantes for the botemen   10d.

Item payed the same daye to Borde for shavyng and smothing of
them   8d.

Item payed to John Thurketyll for 6 dayes rowyng of them that cut
the ryver the 13th of July   3s. 6d.

[*f. 17r*] Item payed more to John Thyrketyll the 12th of August for 1
4 dayes rowyng them that cut the ryver at 7d. the daye   8s. 2d.

Item payed to John Thyrketyll the 13th of August for his boote hyre
for 3 wekes and too dayes   20d.

Item payed to John Cawson and Nicholas Philipps for ther halfe
quarters wages dewe unto them at Lammas *anno* 1560   40s.

Item payed to John Haywarde for gryndyng the sherys to the ryver
4 tymes and for for-lockes to them   4s.

Item payed to John Clarke the sweper of the markett for his quarters
wages dewe at Michelmas last paste   8s. 4d.

Item payed to John Cawson and Nicholas Philipps for ther halfe
quarters wages dewe unto them at Michelmas   40s.

Item payed to John Cadby the 22nd of October for carrying mucke
oute of the stretes and cockeyes[48]   40s.

Item payed to John Cawson and Nicholas Philipps for ther halfe
quarter wages dewe unto them at Hallowmas   40s.

Item payed to John Clarke sweper of the markett for his quarters
wages dewe at Cristmas *anno* 1560   8s. 4d.

Item payed to John Cadby for carryng mucke oute of the stretes
and cokys   23s. 4d.

Item payed to John Cawson and Nicholas Philipps for ther halfe
quarters wages dewe unto them at Cristmas *anno* 1560   40s.

[*f. 17v*] Item payed to Thomas Keteringham carryng mucke oute
of the stretes and cockyes   51s.

Item payed to John Cawson and Nicholas Philipps for ther halfe
quarters wages dewe at Candelmas *anno* 1560   40s.

Item payed to John Cawson and William Wright for ther house
ferme at Our Ladys daye in Lent *anno* 1560 by comaundement of
Mr Norgate and Mr Warden aldermen   20s.

---

48 This entry is preceded by a marginal drawing of a circle with a dot in it.

Item payed more the 23rd of Marche after that to John Cawston
for his house ferme for one quarter endyng at [*blank*]   10s.

Item payed to Nicholas Philipps the 23rd of Marche for his house
ferme for thre quarters of a yeare ending at [*blank*]   7s. 6d.

Item payed to John Clarke sweper of the markett for his quarters
wages dewe at Our Ladys daye in Lent *anno* 1561   8s. 4d.

Item payed to the smyth ageynt Seynt Andrewes[49] for a forked iren
for the quant   5d.

Item tobe allowed for the los of the mony that was in my hande at
the fyrst reclamacion made for the decrye of the mony which was
on Michelmas even[50]   103s. 8½d.

Item payed and allowed to Anthony Marker for making and writing
this accompte   2s. 6d.

Summa of all the paymentes   £32 6s. 4½d.

/[*£32 6s. 4½d.*]/

And so remayneth in thandes of the seide John Suckelyng   102s. 1½d.
*/Which £5 2s. 1½d. the seide John Suckelyng payed the 17th daye of Maye
anno 1561 and was put in the chest before master mayour in a paper by yt selffe/*

[*1561–62*]

[*f. 18r*] Hereafter followe the names of the surveyours in *anno domini* 1561

/6 olde/	/6 newe/
Nicholas Norgate alderman	Roberte Woode alderman
Robert Tooke	Peter Petreson
Henry Grenewood	John Lowe
Thomas Layer	Richard Sotherton
John Styngate	Raufe Pynne
Mathew Plombe	[*blank*][51] Marcon

The feaste of thanunciacion of Our Lady *anno domini* 1561 was chosen
and elected to be receyvour and paymaster Thomas Layer for this
yere next folowing

Robert Tooke is elected to be surveyour of the stretes of Consford
and Be[r]strete and John Lowe receyvour

---

[49] The parish church of St Andrew's.
[50] That is, the debasement of coins by a royal proclamation published on 27 September 1560.
On this, see R. Ruding, *Annals of the Coinage of Great Britain and its Dependencies*, 3 vols (London, 1840),
i, pp. 333–8.
[51] John Marcon: Hawes, *Index*, p. 102.

Henry Grenewoode is chosen surveyour for the warde of Mancrofte
and Petre Petreson receyvour

Richard Sotherton is chosen surveyour for the warde of Wymer and
Raufe Pynne receyvour

Mathew Plombe is chosen surveyour for the warde of Beyonde the
Water and [*John*] Marcon receyvour

John Styngate is chosen to survey the water men in their workes
that they do their duties about the river

[*f. 18v*] /*Jhus*/

/*Receytes*/ Thacount of Thomas Layer grocer of all suche *summa* of
monye recayved and allso payde a bowght the makyng clene [*of*] the
ryver, the strettes and cockyes from the feaste of theanunciacion of
Owr Ladi *anno* 1561

Fyrst recayved of Robart Mayhew for one qwarter ended at Owr Ladi daye	5*s.*
Item recayved of Gorge Buttreye for one qwarter ended at Owr Ladi daye	3*s.* 4*d.*
Item received of John Revell furrayn recayvor the 24 of Julye 1561 for 2 qw[*a*]rt[*ers*], Owr Ladi daye & Mydsomer, the *summa* of	40*s.*
Item received of Gorge Butterye for one qwarter ended at Mydsomer *anno* 1561	3*s.* 4*d.*
Item received of Edward Reve hosier for hallfe a yere ended at <Owr Ladye daye in Lent> *Myhellmes 1561*	16*s.* 8*d.*
Item recayved of Robart Mayhew for on qwarter ended at Mydsomer 1561	5*s.*
Item recayved of the chamberlyne *Pynchyne* the 1 daye of August 1561 in parte of payment	40*s.*
Item received of Raffe Pynne le 28 of August 1561 in parte of payment of a mor *summa*[52]	23*s.*
Received more of hyme le 2 of Decemb[*e*]r 1561	4*s.*
Received le 12 of December 1561	20*s.*
Received more of hyme 1562	6*s.*
Received more of hym	5*s.* 4*d.*

/£8 11s. 8d./

[*f. 19r*] /*Jhus 1561*/

---

[52] That is to say, in part payment of a greater sum. The collectors (here called the 'receivers')
are paying the taxes they have gathered in the wards to the treasurer in instalments. Cf. Peter
Peterson below, f. 19r.

/*Receytes*/ Received of Peter Peterson collecter for the ward of
Mancraft the fyrst of October 1561 in parte of payment   30s.

Received \<the\> of Robart Mayhewe for on[*e*] qwarter ended at
Myhellmes 1561   5s.

Received of Gorge Buttreye for one qwarter ended at Myhellmes
1561   3s. 4d.

Received of Pynchyn latte chamberlyne le 8 of Oct[*o*]ber 1561 in
parte of \<py\> payment \<£3\>   £3

Received of Grene the masone for rente of his grownd dew at
Myhellmes *summa*   3s.

Received more of the sayd Grene for the yere in *anno* 1560 that
was not payd   3s.

Received of goodman Pynchone *latt chamberlyng* le 20 of
Decembr 1561 the summ of £3 7s. wyche was payd unto Thomas
Ketteryngam   £3 7s.

Received of Peter Peterson for the warde of Mancraft the 23 daye
of Jenewary 1561   30s.

\<Received of John Bakone *the 26 of Jeneware 1561*chamberlyng
for one qwarter ended at the fest of Owr Lord God 1561   70s.\>
/ *This is cancelled becawse yt was payed to hym ageyne*/[53]

Received of John Revell the last of Jeneway 1561 for 2 qwarters
ended at Mychelles & Crystmes   40s.

/ £15 11s. \<8d.\> 4d./

[*f. 19v*] /*Jhus*/

Received of John Marcone the 15 of Marche 1561   £3

Received of the goodman Mayhewe the 27 of Marche 1562   5s.

Received of goodman Lowe the 27 of Marche 1562   34s.

Received of Gorge Buttarye the 27 of Marche 1562   3s. 4d.

Received of Raffe Pyne le 27 of Marche 1562   £3

Received of Edward Reve the 29 of Marche 1562 for his hallfe yer
ferme   16s. 8d.

/ £8 19s. 0d./

Received more of John Lowe   \<20d.\> 2s. 8d.

Received more of John Marcone   12s. 4d.

Received of Pynchon   £5 13s.
/ £15 7s. 0d./

[53] This entry is in a different hand.

Received of Peter Peterson   3s.

                                        Summa of all the receiptes   £36 3s.

/*£39 13s. 0d.* <Summa £39 13s. Paid of this, £23 17s. Rest, £15 16s.>/

[f. 20r] /Jhus/

/*Paymentes*/ Paid John Cawsone for one holle yere and hallfe a qwarter   £9

Paid father Cattbye the 20 of August   20s.

Paid goodwyff Hyndersone for a towe rope   20d.

Paid Harye Usher for 12 dayes worke wythe Cawsone at 8d.   8s.

Paid hyme more for 13 dayes & a hallfe   9s.

Paid that tyme to Jarram for 13 dayes worke in cuttyng the ryver   8s. 8d.

Paid John Clarke sweper of the markett his yeres wagis at 8s. 4d.
the *quarter*   <33s. 4d.> *25s.*

Paid for 2 whelbarowes the 5 of October 1561 and delyveryd to
Cawsone   4s.

Paid the smythe that tyme for 1 spyndell & 2 for-lokes for the whelbarowes   8d.

Paid father Cattbye le 9 of October   30s. 8d.

Paid John Cawson for his howse ferme ended at Myhellmes 1561   10s.

Paid John Thurketyll for his wagis   13s. 4d.

Paid Thomas Ketryngam the 21 of Decembr 1561   £3 7s.

Paid Jaram Rabe the 22 of Decembr for 12 dayes worke be for
Saynt Thomas daye[54]   8s.
and he intryd <s> in to wagis with John Cawsone & to be gyne his
yere on Saynt Thomas daye

Paid to John Cawsone for tarde ropes for his ankeres   8d.

Paid John Thyrketyll the 24 of Decembr for 49 dayes worke   19s. 4d.

For heyer of his bote 30 dayes   2s. 8d.

For mendyng of an ore   4d.

Paid Robart Blythe for careg of 54 lodes in the ward of Wymer the
7 of Jeneway [*January*]   18s.

Paid Kettryngam for 21 lodes   7s.

Paid Jaram Rabe for *dimidia* a quarter [*half a quarter*] ended at
Candellmes   20s.

Paid Jaram Rabe the 24 of Marche 1561   20s.

Paid Pynchone for that I received of Grene   3s.

/<£24 2s. 4d.> Rest, £23 <14> 17s. 0d./

---

[54] This entry is preceded by a marginal drawing of a teardrop.

[*f. 20v*] Also allowed to Thomas Hogges for warnyng[55] the 12
surveyours for the ryver and stretes for too yeares   3*s.* 4*d.*

                 Summa of all the paymentes   £24 4*d.*

And so remayneth in thandes of the sayde Mr Layer   £12 2*s.* 8*d.*

/Which money was payed and delyvered into the tresory the thred daye of Apriell anno 1562/
[*signed*] Robert Mychell alderman, Raphe Marshame, John Bacon

[1570–71]

[*f. 49r*] Surveyors chosen for the ryver and stretes for *anno* 1570 whose names
hereafter insuthe

Syxe ollde	Syxe newe
John Sucklyng allderman *tresurer*	Robert Sucklyng allderman
Raphe Marsham *surveyor of the ryver*	John Cottwyin *collector for Berestret*
Richard Swyffte	George Buttery *collector for
Richard Sottherton *Cunforth*	Mancrofft*
John Sadeler *collector Over the Water*	Richard Baker *surveyor of Wymar*
Robert Goslyng *surveyir Over [*the*] Water*	Thomas Dethick *collector for Wymar*
	Thomas Norgat

[*f. 49v*] */Anno 1570/* Thaccompt of John Sucklyng alderman treseror
and receyver of all the revenewes belonging to the ryver and stretes
aswell of all sutche sommes of mony as he have receyved as allso
of all paymentes made consernyng the same, *viz.*, from the feast of
thannunciacion of Our Ladye *anno* 1570 untill the feast of
thannunciacion of Our Ladye *anno* 1571 being one hole yeare as
hereafter insuith.

/Arrerages/ Inprimis the sayd accomptaunnt is charged with monye
by him receyved of Henrye Grenewoode alderman late treasoror
to the use aforesayd as monye remaynyng uppon thende and
determynacion of his accompt as in the foote of the same accompt
may appeare   £22 19*s.* 4½*d.*

                 Summa patet

/Receyptes/ Receyved of Thomas Gowche and Peter Petersonn
chamberlynns of the cytye in *anno* 1570 for monye dew owt of the
chamberlynnes offyce to the use of the ryver and stretes and here
charged for one hole yeare *ended* at the feast of the burthe of
Our Lord within the tyme of this accompt   £14

---

[55] That is, for summoning the surveyors to attend meetings and/or reminding them to perform
their duties.

Item receyved of the forren receyver for monye dew owt of the same
offyce to the use of the ryver and stretes for one hole yeare ended
at the feast of the birth of Our Lord in the tyme of this accompt   £4

Item receyved of Thomas Payman myllor for monye dew from him
to the use abovesaye for one hole yeare ended at the sayd feast   £2 13s. 4d.

Item receyved of Robert Cocket for the ferme of his tenement for
one hole yeare endyd at the sayd feast   20s.

Item receyved of George Butterye for the ferme of his tenement
for one hole yeare endyd at the sayd feast   13s. 4d.

[f. 50r] /Receyptes/ Item receyved of Edwarde Reve for one hole
yeares rent ended at the feast aforesayd   33s. 4d.

Item received of Mr Some alderman for the ferme of a parcell of
grownde in the parisshe of St Martyn at the Oke dew for one hole
yeare ended at the feast of St Mychahell tharchangell within the
tyme of this accompt   3s.

Item received of Mr Thomas Farror for the ferme of twoo peces of
grownde withowt Bisshoppes gate dew for one hole yeare ended at
the feast of thannunciacion of Our Lady 1570   7s. 4d.

Item received of Mr Elyas Bate alderman for the hole yeares ferme
of a pece of grownde wonne owt of the ryver[56] and dew at the
same feast   20d.

Item received of Mr John Sutterton for the hole yeares ferme of a
pece of grownde that is also wonne owt of the ryver & dew at the
same feast   2s.

Item received of Mr Thomas Winter alderman for monye collected
towardes the reperacions of Trowse bridge[57]   40s.

Receyved of John Bexswell for amersement for anoyeng the ryver
[the] somme [of]   2s.

Receyved of John Sadeler collector for the ward Beyonde the Water   £6 4s. 4d.

Receyved of George Buttery collector of Mancroft ward for monye
dew for the same ward   £4 9s.

Receyved of Thomas Dethick collector of Wymer ward for monye
dew from the same ward   £8 2d.

Receyved of John Cotwynne collector for the ward of Conysforth,
Be[r]strete and Trowse for monye dew for the same ward   £3

---

[56] On the surveyors' right to improve and rent out land reclaimed from the river, see the
Introduction, p. 114, and *RCN*, ii, p. 130.

[57] Trowse bridge: a bridge that spans the river Yare at Trowse, about 1½ miles south east of
Norwich. This was a special collection to fund repair works.

/ *Summa* £48 9s. 6d./

    Summa totalis aswell of the arrerages the last yeare as also of the
receyvetes this yeare £71 8s. 10½d.

[*f. 50v*] /*Paymentes*/ Payed to Peter Wygot a laborer hired for the
ryver for his wages dew to him for one hole yeare ended at the
annunciacion of Our Ladye 1571   £8

Item to John Cannell hired for the same offyce & paid to him for
3 quarters of a yeare and a half & 10 dayes and then he fell syck
so paid to him for his tyme   £7 5s.

Item payd to William Granger which wrowght in his place after he
was departed 21 dayes at 8d. the day   14s.

Item paid to Odder Johnsonne for sweping the cockies and market
place and carieng away the meanor for one yeares wages ended at
the feast ab[o]vesayd   £8

Item paid to William Littellwoode for his paynes for overseing the fyers
and cutters of the ryver for one hole yeare ended at the sayd feast   26s. 8d.

Item to Palmer & Wapoll for making the walle at Trowse bridge   £4 10s.

Item payd to Blewet carpender for 2 loopes for the grates there and
lintalles to them   13s. 4d.

Item paid to Fresson smythe for the iern work to the sayd grates
q[*uibus*] 1 *C* a quarter at 2¼d. the *li.*[58]   26s. 3d.

Item paid for 11 faddam of rede at 3d.   2s. 9d.

Item paid for 2 lode of clay   20d.

Item paid for straw   4d.

Item paid for 2 dayes work & *dimidia* [*two and a half days' work*] of 2
men at Trowse bridge thone at 8d. the day and thother at 10d. the day   3s. 9d.

Item to William Granger the 14th of May for 6 dayes cutting in
the river   4s.

Item to John Smythe the same day for 6 dayes work   4s.

Item the 21 of May to William Granger for 4 dayes cutting the ryver   2s. 8d.

Item to John Smythe for 4 dayes work   2s. 8d.

Item to William Granger the 28 of May for 6 dayes cutting the ryver   4s.

Item to John Smythe for 6 dayes work   4s.

/£33 5s. 1d./

---

[58] The purchase of two grates is recorded here: 'for which ('*quibus*') 1 hundredweight and a
quarter (*i.e.,* 140 *lb*) of iron was purchased at 2¼d. per *lb*.'

[*f. 51r*] /*Paymentes*/ Item the 28 of May to John Bexswell for 16 dayes work in the bote	10s. 8d.
Item the 4th of June to William Granger for 6 dayes work in the ryver	4s.
Item to John Smythe the same day for 6 dayes work	4s.
Item the sayd day to Bexswell for 6 dayes work in the bote	4s.
Item to William Granger the 11 of June for 6 dayes work in the river	4s.
Item to John Smythe for 6 dayes work	4s.
Item to John Pye for working in the bote one day	8d.
Item the 18 of June to John Bexswell for 15 dayes work	10s.
Item to Granger for 5 dayes work *& *dimidia**	3s. 8d.
Item to John Smythe for 5 dayes & *dimidia*	3s. 8d.
Item to William Granger the 24 of June for 4 dayes work	2s. 8d.
Item to John Smythe for 4 dayes work	2s. 8d.
Item the 2 of Julye to William Granger for 5 dayes work	3s. 4d.
Item to John Smythe for 5 dayes work	3s. 4d.
Item to Myhell Coke for 5 dayes work in the bote	3s. 4s.
Item the 9 of Julye to William Granger for 6 dayes work	4s.
Item to John Smythe for 6 dayes work	4s.
Item to Myhell Coke for 6 daye work in the bote	4s.
Item to William Granger the 16 of Julye for 6 dayes work in the ryver	4s.
Item to John Smythe for 6 dayes work	4s.
Item to Myhell Coke sayd day for 6 dayes work in the bote	4s.
Item to William Granger the 23 of Julye for 6 dayes work in the ryver	4s.
Item to John Smythe for 6 dayes work	4s.
Item to Myhell Coke the same day for 6 dayes work in the bote	4s.
Item the 30 of Julye to William Granger for 5 dayes work in the ryver	3s. 4d.
Item to John Smythe for 5 dayes work	3s. 4d.

/£5 6s. 8d./

[*f. 51v*] /*Paymentes*/ Item to Myhell Coke the 30 of Julye for 5 dayes work in the bote	3s. 4d.
Item the 7th of August to William Granger for a wekes work	4s.
Item to John Smythe same day for the leke	4s.
Item to Myhell Coke for 6 dayes in the bote	4s.
Item to William Granger the 14 of August for 5 dayes work & *dimidia* at	3s. 8d.
Item to John Smythe sayd day for the leke	3s. 8d.

Item the sayd day to Myhell Cooke for working in the bote	3s. 6d.
Item to William Granger the 19 of August for a wekes work in the ryver	4s.
Item to John Smythe the sayd day for the leke	4s.
Item the sayd day to Myhell Cooke for 6 dayes work in the bote	4s.
Item to William Granger the 24 of August for 3 dayes work in the ryver	2s.
Item the sayd day to John Smythe for the leke	2s.
Item the 26 of August to Myhell Coke for 5 dayes work in the bote	3s. 4d.
Item to the myller the seconde day of September for 3 mennes wages that wrowght 7 dayes a pece in all 21 dayes at 10d. the day	17s. 6d.
Item for a quare of paper to wright in the paymentes	4d.
Item for 2 furryng sparres for the bote	12d.
Item for a wheatstone	9d.
Item for a barre iern to make a crowe for the use of the ryver	3s. 6d.
Item for mending of the cutting bot	12d.
Item for a payer of new owers	2s. 8d.
Item for 6 faddam bast	9d.
Item the 6th of <bast> May a pece bast	20d.
Item for packthread	4d.
Item for 7 faddom of bast	9d.
Item for 6 faddom bast 5th September	9d.
Item to John Heward for 6 payer sheres grinding	6s.
Item for forelockes for the sheres & for a lock & a staple	13d.

/£4 3s. 7d./

[f. 52r] Item payd for a yeares rent of a storehowse for the watermens tooles	6s. 8d.
Item payd to Nawght botewright for mending of the cutting bote the 24 of Marche, somme	10s.
Item to Nawght for making of a new bote for the myll damme	£5 13s. 4d.
Item for 7 C dimidia [7½ hundreds] of plank to the same bote at 7s. [per] C	£2 12s. 6d.
Item for 2 cuppell sparres to the same bote	16d.
Item for a chene to the bote	2s.
Item for setting the same bote aflote & carieng yt over the myll damme	2s.
Item to John Wright for 2 payer bootes	13s. 4d.
Item paid for ingrossing of this accompt as hathe bene used to be payd	2s. 6d.

/£10 3s. 8d./

Summa of all the paymentes and allowances aforesayd   £52 19*s.*

And so remayneth in the handes of this accowntant uppon the determynacion of this accompt   £18 9*s.* 10½*d.*

/ *The which sume of £18 9s. 10½d. was payed & delyvered to Christofer Layour alderman the 12th of June anno 1571/*

/ *R[ecipitur] per me [Christofer]*[59] *Laier/*

/ *Remaynyng/* In the handes of Mr John Hasset esquier for a yearelye revenew geven to the ryver by the Duke of Norff[olk][60] his grace the some of 40*s.*, wherof 20*s.* was dew to the last yeares accompt as appearethe & the other 20*s.* dew for this yeare 1570 & to this accompt, I say   40*s.*

/ *This 40s. ys yet remaynyng in Mr Hassetes handes on payed [unpaid]/*

/ *Examinatur per nos/*

[*signed*] Thomas Whall, Robert Sucklyng, Nycholas Sotherton, Thomas Stokys

[1571–72]

[*f. 52v*] / *Anno 1571/* Thaccompte of Christofer Layour alderman treasorour and receyvour of all the revenewes belonging to the ryver and stretes aswell of all souche somes of money as he have receyved as also of all paymentes made concernyng the same, *viz.*, from the feaste of the anunciacion of Our Lady *anno* 1571 untill the feaste of the anunciacion of Our Lady *anno* 1572 beyng one hole yeare as hereafter ensueth

/ *Arrerages/* Inprim[i]s the sayde accomptaunt is charged with mony by hym receyved of John Suckeling alderman late treasorour to the use aforesayde as mony remaynyng upon thende & determinacion of this accompte as in the fote of the same accompt maye appeare   £18 9*s.* 10*d.*

                             Summa patet

Receyved of Peter Peterson chamblyne of the cittie in *anno* 1571 for money dewe owte of the chamberlyns office to the use of the ryver and stretes and heare charged for one hole yeare ended at the feaste of [*blank*][61]   £14

Item receyved of Randolf Smyth forren receyvour for money dewe owte of the same office to the use of the ryver and stretes for one hole yeare ended at the feaste of [*blank*]   £4

[59] Here and occasionally below, Layer signs his first name with a monogram.

[60] Thomas Howard, 4th duke of Norfolk (1536–72). On the Duke's annuity, see the Introduction, p. 113.

[61] In the previous year the sum was paid at Christmas. Later in the decade, however, it was settled at the feast of the Annunciation (25 March): see f. 70v below.

Item receyved of Thomas Payman myller for money dewe from
hym to the use above sayde for one hole yeare ended at the feaste
above sayde   53*s.* 4*d.*

Item receyved of John Gygges for the hole yeres ferme of a close
bowght of Mr Pede at St Stephans gates   66*s.* 8*d.*

Item of Edemonde Style & William Irenson for the ferme of too
orteyardes that were bowght of Mr Pede in St Stephans   42*s.*

[*f. 53r*] /*Receiptes*/ Item received of Robarte Cockett for the ferme
of his tenement for one hole yeare endyd at the sayde feaste   20*s.*

Item receyved of George Buttery for the ferme of his tenement for
one hole yeare ended at the sayde feaste   13*s.* 4*d.*

Item received of Edwarde Reve for one hole yeares ferme for his
tenement which ended at the same feaste   33*s.* 4*d.*

Item received of Mr Some alderman for the ferme of a parcell of
grownde in the parisshe of St Marten at the Oke dewe for one hole
yeare ended at the feaste of Saynt Michell tharchaungell within the
tyme of this accompte   3*s.*

Item received of Mr Thomas Farrour for the ferme of too peces of
grownde withoute Bisshippes gate dewe for one hole yeare endyd
at the feaste of thanunciacion of Our Lady 1572   7*s.* 4*d.*

Item received of Ellys Bate alderman for the hole yeares ferme of a
pece of grownde won owte of the ryver and dewe at the same feaste   <20*d.*>[62]

Item received of Mr John Sotherton for the hole yeares ferme of a
pece of grounde that ys also won owte of the ryver & dewe at the
same feaste   2*s.*

Item receyved of John Sadler collectour for the warde Beyonde the
Water   £5 10*s.*

Item received of John Brantingham collectour for the warde of
Wymer   £6 12*d.*

Item received of John Cotwyn collectour for the warde of
Connesford, Berestrete & Trowes   £3

Item received of George Buttery collectour for the warde of
Mancrofte   74*s.*

     Summa totalis aswell of the arrerages as of the receptes this yere   £66 15*s.* 10*d.*

[*f. 53v*] /*Paymentes*/ Payed to Peter Wigot a laborer hyryd for the
ryver for his wages dewe to hym for one hole yeare ended at the
feaste of thanunciacion of Our Lady 1572   £8

[62] The sum is deleted, but no other figure is supplied.

Item to William Granger his fellowe for the lyke tyme & hyryd for the same purpose	£8
Item payed to Odder Johnson for sweping the cockys and marketplace and carring awaye the mennour for one yeares wages ended at the feaste aforesayde	£8
Item to William Lyttelwoode for his paynes for overseyng the fyers and cutters of the ryver for one hole yeare ended at the sayde feaste	26s. 8d.
Item to Mr Beamonde the 21st of June *anno* 1571 for making certeyne plowes to gather the gravell owte of the ryver and for diverse other charges as by his bill maye appeare	£4 2s. 4d.
Item payed to Richarde Sadler for thre dozen sholves bought at London in June *anno* 1571	21s. 2d.
Item to Preston the smythe for too new mattockes	3s. 6d.
Item for helving of the same mattockes	4d.
Item to George Wattes the 20th of Maye *anno* 1571 for 6 dayes worke in the cutting bote	4s.
Item to John Smythe & John Sharpp eyther of them being in the same bote the sayde 6 dayes at 8d. a daye a pece	8s.
Item to George Wattes the 26 of Maye for 6 dayes in the cuttingbote at 8d. the daye	4s.
Item to Sharpp and Smyther eyther of them beyng in the same bote 5 dayes at 8d. the daye a pece	6s. 8d.

/[£31 16s. 8d.]/

[*f. 54r*] /*Paymentes*/ Item to Wattes, Sharpp and Smyth the <6th> *2nd* of June 1571 eyther of them 6 dayes in the cutting bote at 8d. a daye a pece	12s.
Item to John Smythe, John Kadell and John Sherpp the 9th of June eyther of them 4[63] dayes at 8d. a daye	8s.
Item to John Smythe, John Sharpp and Mihell Cooke the 16 of June 1571 eyther of them 6 dayes in the cuttingbote at 8d. a daye a pece	12s.
Item to John Sharpp, John Smyth and Myhell Cooke the 23rd of June 1571 for 6 dayes in the bote at 8d. a d[a]ye a pece	12s.
Item more to the same thre men the 30th of June 1571 eyther of them 5 dayes in the cutting bote at 8d. a daye a pece	10s.
Item more to the same thre men the 7th of July *anno* 1571 for 6 dayes at 8d. a daye a pece	12s.

---

[63] The phrase 'of them 4' is repeated here, in error, following a line break.

Item to Sharp, Smythe and Cooke the 14th of July 1571 eyther of
them 6 dayes in the cutting bote at 8*d.* a daye a pece   12*s.*

Item more to them the 21st of July 1571 for eyther of them 6 dayes
in the cutting bote at 8*d.* the daye a pece   12*s.*

Item more to them the 28 of July 1571 for 5 dayes worke eyther of
them in the cuttingbote at 8*d.* a daye a pece   10*s.*

Item more to the same Sharpp, Smythe & Cooke the 4th of August
1571 eyther of them 6 dayes in the cutting bote at 8*d.* a daye a pece   12*s.*

Item more to the same thre men the 11th daye of Auguste *anno*
1572 for 6 dayes <at> eyther of them at 8*d.* a daye   12*s.*

Item to them the 18th of August 1571 eyther of them 6 dayes at 8*d.*
a daye a pece savyng one daye abatyd for Smythe   11*s.* 4*d.*

Item more to Smythe, Sharpe and Cooke the 25th of August eyther
of them 5 dayes in the bote at 8*d.* a daye a pece   10*s.*

/[£7 5*s.* 4*d.*]/

[*f. 54v*] /*Paymentes*/ Item payed to Hewer the smythe for new <men>
mending and gryndyng the ryver sheres as by his bill maye appeare   26*s.* 6*d.*

Item payed the 16 & 17 of Maye 1571 to diverse laborers that
wrought in the ryver with the plowes   14*s.* 8*d.*

Item payed the <10>13th of August 1571 to 23 laborers that
wrought in the ryver with the plowes   15*s.* 4*d.*

Item payed the 16th of Auguste 1571 to 8 laborers that wrought in
the ryver with ther plowes   5*s.* 4*d.*

Item payed the 17th of August to 9 laborers that wrought in the
ryver with the plowes   6*s.*

Item payed the 18th of August to 10 laborers that wrought in the
ryver with the plowes   6*s.* 8*d.*

Item payed to Bane for too dayes worke & 4 dayes standing in the
water   2*s.*

Item payed for the wages of 7 men one daye that wrought in the
water   4*s.* 8*d.*

Item to Frauncys Allen for 10 small skepps   2*s.* 2*d.*

Item to Preston the smythe for an iron for a qwante   6*d.*

Item payed to Hagon the botewright from the 22 of June untill
the 21 of July for trymmyng the greate bote   55*s.* 2*d.*

Item payed to William Nowght botewight the 23 of July *anno* 1571
for workyng upon the greate bote with Hagon as by his bill maye
appeare   47*s.* 6*d.*

Item payed to Andrew, smyth,[64] the 7th of July for clynke nayles & roffes for the greate bote as by his bill maye appeare   28s.

Item payed to John Byrche for tymber & borde for the mending of this greate bote as by his byll maye appeare   35s. 4d.

Item to Payman the myller for cutting of the ryver   53s. 4d.

/[£14 13s. 2d.]/

[f. 55r] /Paymentes/ Item payed to William Nowght the 3rd of Marche 1571 for [?]deanyng the greate bote as by his bill maye appeare   28s. 4d.

Item to Naylour the smyth for nayles for the same bote   3s. 9d.

Item to John Byrche for 40 fote of thycke planke to laye on the syde of the greate bote   6s.

Item to hym for working and laying it into the bote   4d.

Item payed for 3 furren sparres for quantes and *dimidia* stone of towyng rope pitched   3s. 6d.

Item to Preston the smyth for a quant iron   7d.

Item to Wright the shomaker for too payer of botes for the ryver men   14s.

Item to William Browne for one doz[en] and halfe of shod sholves *at 8d. a pece*   12s.

Item for a new covering for this boke of accompte   4d.

Item payed to Mr Roberte Suckeling alderman the 22 of June for a payer of owers   4s.

Item for a dry hoghed   14d.

Item for a barrell of pitche   10s. 8d.

Item for money payed by Mr Suckeling to Andrew Nayler for nayles   6s. 8d.

Item to Richarde Rose the 13th of August for one dayes worke in the ryver   8d.

Item for 3 rowles for the plowgh   8d.

Item for howse hyer to laye in the plowes ropes and other thinges   10s.

Item 4 *C* lesse 20 fote planke for the bote   34s. 8d.

Item for carryng them to the brigg   8d.

Item to Anthony Marker for writing of this accompte   2s. 6d.

/[£6 18s.]/

---

[64] Here, 'Smyth' might be a surname or an occupation. An alternative reading would be: 'payed to Andrew Smyth the 7th of July ...'. I have opted for the occupation because of the following references f. 55r: 'Item, to Naylour the smyth for nayles ...', '... to Andrew Nayler for nayles'.

[*f. 55v*]   *Summa totalis* of all the paymentes aforesayde   £61 <10> 5*s*. 8*d*.

And so restith in the handes of this accomptaunt upon
thende and determinac[*ion*] of this accomptes   <£6 2*d*.> 110*s*. 2*d*.
Examinatur per nos
[*signed*] Robert Sucklyng, Thomas Whall, Nicholas Sotherton,
Thomas Stakys

[*1572–73*]

[*f. 56r*] /*Anno 1572*/ Thaccompte of Christofer Layer alderman
treasorour and re[*ce*]ivor of all the revenewes belonging to the river
and streates aswell of all souche sommes of money as he have
receyved as also of all paymentes made concernyng the same, *viz*.,
from the feaste of the anunciacion of Our Lady *anno* 1572 untill the
feast of the anunciacion of Our Lady *anno* 1573 being one hole yeare
as hereafter ensueth

/*Arrerages*/ Inprimis the sayd accomptaunt is charged with money
which remayned upon thend and determinacion of <of> his last
accompte as in the fote of the same accompt maye appeare   110*s*. 2*d*.

                                                              Summa patet

/*Receytes*/ Receyved of Peter Peterson chamberlyne of the cittie in
anno 1572 for money dewe owte of the chamberlyns office to the use
of the ryver and streates and here charged for one hole yeare ended
at the feast of [*blank*]   £14

Item receyved of Randolf Smith and Richard Sotherton forren
receyvours for money dewe out of the same office to the use
abovesayd for one hole yeare ended at the feast aforeseyd   £4

Item receyved of Thomas Paman myller for money dewe from
hym to the use above sayd for one hole yeare ended at the feast
abovesayd   53*s*. 4*d*.

Item receyved of John Gigges for the hole yeares fearme of a close
bowght of Mr Ped at St Stephans gates   66*s*. 8*d*.

[*f. 56v*] /*Receiptes*/ Item receyved of Edmond Style for the hole
yeares fearme of an orte yarde bought of Mr Pedde in St Stephans   20*s*.

Item receyved of William Irenson for the hole yeares fearme of an
orte yarde bought of Mr Peed in St Stephans   22*s*.

Item receyved of Roberte Cocket for the ferme of his tenement for
one hole yeare ended at the said feast   20*s*.

Item receyved of George Buttry for the fearme of his tenement for
one hole yeare ended at the said feast   13*s*. 4*d*.

Item received of Edwarde Reve for the fearme of his tenement for one hole yeare<s> ended at the feast   33s. 4d.

Item received of Mr Blenerhasset for the late duke of Norff[olk] his grace for an annuite geven yearly to the same use for 3 yeares <at> ended at the feast of the birth of Our Lord God *anno* 1572   60s.

Item receyved of Mr Some alderman for the fearme of a parcell of grownde in the parishe of St Martyne at the Oke dew for one hole yeare ended at the feast of St Michaell tharchangell within the tyme of this accompte   3s.

Item receyved of Mr Thomas Farrour for the fearme of too peces of grownd without Bisshopps gate dew for one hole yeare ended at the feast of thanunnciacion of Our Lady 1573   7s. 4d.

Item receyved of Mr Ellis Batt alderman for the hole yeares fearme of a pece of grownd that is won out of the ryver and dew at the same feaste   ni[hil]

[*f. 57r*] /*Receiptes*/ Item receyved of Mr John Sotherton for the hole yeares fearme of a pece of grownde that is also won out of the ryver and dew at the same feaste   2s.

Item receyved of John Cotwyn collector of the ward of Connesford, Berestret & Trowes   52s.

Item received of Robart Coller collectour of the warde of Mancrofte   £4 5s. 10d.

Item received of Oliver Aynsworth collectour of the warde of Wymer   £7 1s.

Item received of John Sadler collectour of the warde Beyonde the Water   £4 10s.

Item receyved of John Brantingham for *the rest of* his colleccion which was dew upon thend and determinacion of the last accompte   38s.

Item receyved of Litlewood for the rest of his colleccion which was dew upon thend and determinacion of the last accompte   9s. 8d.

     Summa totalis aswell of the arrerages as of the receiptes this yeare   £59 7s. 8d.

[*f. 57r*] /*Paymentes*/ Payd to Peter Wigott a laborer hirid for the ryver for his wages dewe to hym for one hole yeare ended at the feast of thanunnciacion of Our Lady 1573   £8

Item to William Granger his fellowe for the like tyme & hired for the same purpose   £8

Item payd to Odder[65] Johnson for sweping the cockes and market place and caring awey the mennour for one yeares wages ended at the feast aforesaid   £8

---

[65] The scribe originally entered 'Otter' here. He corrected the mistake by overwriting '*tt*' with '*dd*'.

Item payed to William Litlewood for his paynes for overseing the
fiers and cutters of the river for one hole yeare ended at the sayd feast   26s. 8d.

Item payd to Heward the smyth for grinding the great sheres   5s.

Item paid to Sharpe, *Caudell* and Jankenson the 24th daye of
Maye *anno* 1572 to eyther of them being in the river bott and
cutting botte 6 dayes at 8d. the daye apece   12s.

Item payd to Sharpe, Caudell and Jankynson the 31 daye of Maye
anno 1572 to eyther of them being in the same bottes 4 dayes at 8d.
the daye   8s.

Item paid by Hogges to diverse workemen at the milles in the
water worke the 2nd of June *anno* 1572   16s. 5d.

Item paid to Sharpe, Janckinson and Cawdell the 7 of June *anno*
1572 to eyther of them for 6 dayes worke at 8d. the daye apece   12s.

Item more to Sharpe, Janckinson and Cawdell the 14th of June *anno*
1572 for 6 dayes worke at 8d. the daye apece   12s.

[*f. 58r*] /*Paymentes*/ Item payd to Sherpe, Janckingson and Cawdell
the 21 daye of June *anno* 1572 for 6 dayes worke at 8d. [*the*] daye a
pece   12s.

Item paid to Sharpe, Janckinson and Cawdell the 28 daye of June
anno 1572 for 5 dayes worke<s> at 8d. the daye apece   10s.

Item payd to Sha*r*pe, Janckinson and Cawdell the 5 daye of
July *anno* 1572 for 6 dayes worke at 8d. the daye apece   12s.

Item payd to Sharpe, Janckenson and Cawdell the twelve daye of
July *anno* 1572 for 6 daies worke at 8d. the daye apece   12s.

Item payd to Sharpe, Janckenson and Caudell the 19 daye of July
anno 1572 for 6 dayes worke at 8d. the daye a pece   12s.

Item payd to Sharpe and Cawdell the 26th daye of July *anno* 1572
for 4 dayes worke at 8d. the daye a pece   5s. 4d.

Item payd Janckinson the 26 daye of July *anno* 1572 for 4 dayes
at 8d. the daye   3s. 4d.

Item paid to Sharpe, Janckinson and Cawdell the [*blank*] of July
anno 1572 for 6 dayes worke at 8d. the daye a pece   12s.

Item payd to[66] Hagon the botman for the rest of the great bott
mending which should have ben put in the last accompt   14s. 8d.

Item payd to Preston the smith for an iron <of a> *for the* qwant   4d.

Item payd to Richard Browne for one deyes worke in cutting of
the ryver the 11 of October   8d.

---

[66] The word 'to' is repeated here in error.

Item geven to Mr Hassettse sonne at the receite of <of> my lordes
grace ryver money   4d.

Item payd Wright the shomaker for 2 payer of bottes [*boots*] for
Wiet and Granger   16s.

Item payd to Preston for mending the great bottes [*boat's*] jemers   3d.

Item paid to Granger for an anker stoke   6d.

[*f. 58v*] Item to Heward the smyth for grynding the great cutting
sheres for somer worke 1572   5s.

Item paid for too new quantes   2s.

Item paid Paman the myller for cutting the river   53s. 4d.

Item payd by Mr Robert Suckelyng maior for howse hier to layng
the plowes ropes & other thinges   20s.

Item payd to Anthony Marker for writing of this accompte   2s. 6d.

Item payd to Litlewood the 8 daye of Marche 1570 for a pece of
large baste   22d.

Item paid more to hym the 12 daye of Maye 1571 for 2 peces of
large past [*bast*]   3s. 8d.

Item more to hym the 29 daye of July 1571 for 3 fadome and
an halfe   6d.

Item to hym more the 17 daye of Maye *anno* 1572 for a pece of
large baste   22d.

Item more to hym the 8 daye of February *anno* 1573 for one pece
of large baste   22d.

Item for pakethred   2d.

Summa totalis of all the paymentes aforesayde <£59 7s. 8d.>
                                                                                                £38 16s. 2d.

And so restith in the handes of this accomptaunt upon thende and
determinacion of this accompte   £20 11s. 6d.

Examinatur per nos
[*signed*] John Aldryche alderman, [*Christofer*] Layer, Thomas Stokys

[*1573–74*]

[*f. 59r*] Surveyours chosen for the river and stretes at an assemble holden on St
Mathies daye *anno* 1572 which surveyours ar to contynue for one hole yeare then
next following whose name hereafter do ensew

/*Surveiour*/ 6 olde

Roberte Suckeling alderman

John Cotwyn *collector for Berestr[*ete*]*

Roberte Collour *Collector for
<?Yarmath> Mancrofft*

Oliver Eynsworth *collectour* for
Wymer

Henry Shipdam surveyor to the stretes

/*ab*/ John Sadler surveyor

6 newe

Christofer Layer alderman tresurour

/*ab*/[67] Raff Marsham surveyor

/*ab*/ George Bowgen surveyor

Fraunces Morley surveyor to the ryver

James Richeman surveyor to the
stretes

/*ab*/ Peter Gold *coll[*ector*]* Over the
Water

[*f. 59v*] /*Anno 1573*/ Thaccompte of Christofer Layer alderman
treasorour and receyvour of all the revenews belonging to the river
and streates aswell of all <?>[68] souche sommes of money as he have
receyved as also of all the paymentes made concernyng the same,
vidz., from the feast of thanunciacion of Our Lady *anno* 1573 untill
the feast of thanunciacion of Our Lady *anno* 1574 being one hole
year as hereafter ensewith

/*Arrerages*/ *Inprimis* the sayd accomptaunt is chardged with money
which remayned upon thend & determinacion of his last accompt
as in the fote of the same accompt maye appeare

£20 11*s.* 6*d.*

Summa patet

Receyved of Peter Peterson chamberleyn of the cittie of Norwich
in *anno* 1573 for money dewe out of the chamberleyns office to the
use of the river and streates and here chardged for one hole yeare
ended at the feast of [*blank*]

£14

Item receyved of Richard Sotherton [*blank*] forreyn receyvours for
money dew out of the same office to thuse abovesaid for one hole
yeare ended at the feast aforesaid

£4

Item receyved of Thomas Paman miller for money dew from hym
to the use abovesaid for one hole yeare ended at the feast abovesaid

53*s.* 4*d.*

Item receyved of John Gigges for the hole yeares fearme of a close
bought of Mr Pede at St Stephans gates

£3 6*s.* 8*d.*

[*f. 60r*] /*Receites*/ Item receyved of Edmond Style for the hole yeare
fearme of an orteyarde bought of Mr Peade in St Stephans

20*s.*

Item receyved of William Irenson for the hole yeares ferme of an
orteyarde bought of Mr Pead in Sainct Stevens

22*s.*

Item receyved of Robart Cocket for the fearme of his tenement for
one hole yeare ended at the sayd feast

20*s.*

[67] It is not clear what is intended here, although 'ab.' may signify that the individual was absent
from the meeting when the officers for the next year were elected.

[68] One illegible letter is deleted here.

Item receyved of George Buttery for the fearme of his tenement for one hole yeare ended at the feast aforesaid   13s. 4d.

Item receyved of Edwarde Reve for the fearme of his tenement for one hole yeare ended at the sayd feast   33s. 4d.

Item receyved of Mr Christofer Some alderman for the fearme of a parcell of grownd in the parishe of St Marten at the Oke dewe for one hole yeare ended at the feast of St Michaell tharchangell within the tyme of this accompte   3s.

Item receyved of Mr Ellis Bate alderman for the hole yeares fearme of a pece of grownde that is won out of the ryver and dew at the feast of the annunciacion of Our Lady *anno* 1574   n[ihil]

Item receyved of Mr Thomas Farrour for the fearme of too peces of grownde with out Bisshopps gates for one hole yeare ended at the feast aforesaid   7s. 4d.

Item receyved of Mr John Sotherton for the hole yeares fearme of a pece of grownde that is also wone of the ryver ended at the[69] same feaste   2s.

[*f. 60v*] Item receyved of John Cotwyn collectour of the warde of Connesford, Berestred, & Trows   40s.

Item receyved of Roberte Coller collectour of the warde of Mancroft   £4

Item receyved of Oliver Eynsworth collectour of the ward of Wymer   £6 13s. 4d.

Item receyved of Peter Golde collectour of the ward Beyonde the Water   £4

Item receyved of Robert Coller for the rest of his colleccion which was dew upon thend and determinacion of the last accompte   12d.

Item receyved of John Sadler for the rest of his colleccon which was dew upon thend & determinacion of the last accompte   6s. 8d.

Item receyved of Oliver Eynsworth for the rest of his colleccion which was dew upon thend and determynacion of the last accompte   37s. 8d.

Summa totalis aswell of the arrerages as of the receiptes this yeare   £69 11s. 2d.

[*f. 61r*] /*Paymentes*/ Payed to William Granger a laborer hired for the ryver for his wages dew to hym for one hole yeare ended at the feast of thannunciacion of Our Lady *anno* 1574   £8

Item payd to Peter Wyet his fellow for the like tyme & hired for the same purpose   £8

Item payed to Richard Furneys for sweping the cockes and market

---

[69] The word 'the' is repeated here in error.

place and carying awey the mennour for one hole yeares wages
ended at the feast aforesaid   £8

Item payd to William Litlewoode for his paynes for overseing the
fyers and cutters of the ryver for one hole yeare ended at the said
feast   26s. 8d.

Item payd to Foster for making cleane of cockeys the 30 daye of
Maye *anno* 1573   6d.

Item payd to Coper the botewrite for mending of the litle bote the
first daye of June *anno* 1573   15s.

Item payd more to hym for a payer of owers the 13 of June *anno*
1573   2s.

Item payd the same daye for one <of> baste rope and one penner
of packethred   21d.

Item payd to Sharpe, Jankensen and Austen the 20 daye of June
anno 1573 to eyther of them being in the river bott & cutting bottes
6 dayes at 8d. the daye a pece   12s.

Item payd to Sharpe, Jankinson and Austen the 27 daye of June
anno 1573 to either of them being in the same bottes 5 dayes at 8d.
the daye a pece   10s.

[*f. 61v*] /*Paymentes*/ Item payd Sharpe, Jankinson and Austen the
4 daye of July *anno* 1573 to either of them being in the same bott
5 dayes at 8d. a daye apece   10s.

Item payd more to Sharpe, Jankinson & Austen the 11 daye of July
anno 1573 to either of them being in the same bottes 6 dayes at 8d.
a daye   12s.

Item payd to Baxter the 11 daye of July for serchin the Great
Cockey[70] for carreyn   4d.

Item paid to Sharpe, Jankinson and Austen the 18 daye of July *anno*
1573 to either of them being in same bottes 6 dayes at 8d. day a pece   12s.

Item payd more to them the 25 daye of July *anno* 1573 to eyther of
them being in the same bottes 5 dayes at 8d. daye a pece   10s.

Item paid to Sharpe and Austen the first daye of August *anno* 1573 to
either of them being in[71] the same bottes 5 dayes at 8d. daye a pece   6s. 8d.

Item paid to Jankinson the same daye for 2 dayes at 8d. the daye   16d.

Item paid to Sharpe and[72] Austen the 8 daye of August *anno* 1573 to either of
them being in the same bote 6 dayes at 8d. a daye a pece   8s.

---

[70] This is the first time that the Great Cockey is mentioned by name in this edition. For its
location, see *figure* 2.

[71] The word 'in' is repeated in error.

[72] An illegible word is deleted here.

Item payd to Jankinson that daye for *2* dayes at 8*d*. a daye   16*d*.

Item payd to Sharpe, Austen & Jankinson the 15 daye of August
anno 1573 to either of them being in the same bottes 6 dayes at 8*d*.
a daye a pece   12*s*.

Item payd more to them the 22 daye of August *anno* 1573 to either
of them being in the same bottes 6 dayes at 8*d*. a daye apece   12*s*.

Item payd to John Wright the shomake for 2 payer of bottes for
the river men   16*s*.

[*f. 62r*] Item to Paman the myller for cutting of the ryver   53*s*. 4*d*.

Item to Litlewood for a bast rope for the greate bote   9*d*.

Item to Preston the smyth for mending of the ancker   8*d*.

Item to Robert Suckeling alderman for *a* howse hier to laing the
toles [*lay in the tools*]   20*s*.

Item to Anthony Marker for writing of this accompte   2*s*. 6*d*.

Item payd for a bast rope   18*d*.

Item payd for a whetston   9*d*.

Item payd for a tylte   4*s*. 8*d*.

Item payed for a payer of owers   2*s*. 6*d*.

                          Summa totalis of all the payementes aforsaid   £36 16*s*. 3*d*.

And so restith in the handes of this accomptaunt upon thende and
determinacion of this accompte   £32 14*s*. 11*d*.

Examinatur per nos
[*signed*] John Aldryche alderman, [*Christofer*] Layer, Raphe Marsham

[*1574–75*]

[*f. 62v*] /*Anno 1574*/ Thaccompte of Christofer Layor alderman
treasurour and receivour of all the revenews belonging to the river
and streates aswell of all souch somes of money as he have received
as also of all the paymentes made concernyng the same, *viz*., from
the feast of the anunciacion of Our Lady *anno* 1574 untill the feast
of the annunciacion of Our Lady *anno* 1575 being one hole yeare
as hereafter ensewith

/*Arrerages*/ *Inprimis* the said accomptaunt is chardged with money
which remayned upon thend and determinacion of his last
accompt as in the fote of the same accompte maye appeare   £32 14*s*. 11*d*.

                                                  Summa patet

Receyved of Peter Peterson chamberleyne of the cittie of Norwich
in *anno* 1574 for money dewe out of the chamberleynes office to the
use of the river and streates and her chardged for one hole yeare
ended at the feast of [*blank*]   £14

Receyved of Randolfe Smyth [*blank*] forreyn receivours for money
dew out of the same office to thuse abovesaid for one hole yeare
ended at the feast aforesaid   £4

[*f. 63r*] /*Receiptes*/ Item receyved of <Thomas> John Paman myller
for money dew from hym to the use abovesaid for one hole yeare
ended at the said feast   53*s.* 4*d.*

Item receyved of John Gigges for the hole yeares fearme of a close
bought of Mr Peade at St Stevens gates   £3 6*s.* 8*d.*

Item receyved of Edmond Style for the hole yeares fearme of one
orteyarde bought of Mr Peade in St Stevens   20*s.*

Item received of John [*blank*] for the hole yeares fearme of one
orteyarde bought of Mr Peade in St Stevens   22*s.*

Item received of Robert Cocket for the fearme of his tenement for
one hole yeare ended at the said feast   20*s.*

Item receyved of George Buttry for the fearme of his tenement for
one hole yeare ended at the feast aforesaid   13*s.* 4*d.*

Item receyved of Edward Reve for the fearme of his tenement for
one hole yeare ended at the feast aforesaid   33*s.* 4*d.*

Item receyved of my Lord of Surrey[73] his grace for annuity given
yearely to the same use for 2 yeares ended at the feast of the byrth
of Our Lorde God *anno* 1574   40*s.*

[*f. 63v*] /*Receiptes*/ Item receyved of Mr Ellis Bate alderman for the
hole yeares fearme of a pece of grownde that is won out of the river
and dew at the feast of thanun[*ncia*]cion of Our Lady *anno* 1575   [*no sum given*]

Item received of Mr Christofer Some <maior> alderman for the
fearme of a parcell of grownd in the parishe of St Marten at the
Oke dewe for one hole yeare ended at the feast of St Michaell
tharchangell with in the tyme of this accompte   3*s.*

Item receyved of Mr Thomas Farrour for the fearme of too peces
of grownde<s> with out Bisshopps gates for one hole yeare ended
at the feast of <a> the annunciacion of Our Lady *anno* 1575   7*s.* 4*d.*

Item receyved of Mr John Sotherton for the fearme of a pece of
grownde that is also won out of the river ended at the same feast   2*s.*

[73] Earl of Surrey: Philip Howard, (1557-1595), the eldest son of Thomas, 4th Duke of Norfolk.
For the annuity given by his father, see the Introduction, p. 113.

Item receyved of John Cotwyn for the rest of his colleccion which was dew upon thend and determinacion of the last accompt   9s. 6d.

Item receyved of Oliver Eynsworth for the rest of his colleccion which was dew upon thend & determinacion of the last accompt   54s.

Item receyved of John Cotwyn collector of the warde of Connesford, Berestrete & Trowes   48s.

[f. 64r] Item received of Robert Coller collector of the warde of Mancroft   £4

Item received of Fraunces Morley collector of the warde of Wymer   £9 15s. 1d.

Item received of Peter Golde collector for the warde Beyond the Water   £4 10s.

Item received of Smyth and Sharpe for that our men did worke 2 dayes in ther worke   3s.

Item received of Peter Golde for arrerages that was lefte on gathered [ungathered] in the yeare last past   10s.

    Summa totalis aswell of the arrerages as of the receiptes this yeare   £89 5s. 6d.

/ Wherof/

Item payd to William Granger a laborer hired for the ryver for his wages dew to hym for one hole yeare ended at the feast of thannunciacion of Our Lady *anno* 1575   £8

Item paid to Peter Wyet for one quarter ended at the feast of St John Baptist last for the same purpose   40s.

[f. 64v] /Paymentes/ Item to Richard Furneis for sweping of the cockes and market place and carrieng awey the mennor for one yeares wages ended at the feast aforesaide   £8

Item to William Litlewood for his paynes for overseing the fiers and cutters of the river for one hole yeare ended at the said feast   26s. 8d.

Item to Sharpe and Smyth and ther fellowes for cutting the river this yeare from the hospitall tower to Hadly Crosse[74]   £6

Item to Litlewood for one bast rope   9d.

Item to Preston the smyth for mending of too mattockes which were broken in having out of Chamberleyns wall out of the ryver at Coslany bridge   12d.

---

[74] The hospital tower ('Cow Tower') was a defensive structure built by the city's governors in the late fourteenth century. It is located by a bend in the river Wensum on what was then pasture land belonging to the Hospital of St Giles (the Great Hospital). Hardley Cross, about fifteen miles down stream, marked the extent of the corporation's jurisdiction over the river Yare, with which the river Wensum converges near Trowse: *RCN*, i, 143.

Item to Cowper for mending of the litle bott the 8 daye of Maye *anno* 1574	17*s*.
Item to Foster for making cleane of \<too\> cockes the 20 daye of June *anno* 1574	4*d*.
Item to B[*blank*] for 3 dayes worke in the cutting bote at 8*d*. the daye	2*s*.
Item payd at that tyme for a bote hier	4*d*.
Item for thre litle iron \<stabl\> staples and packethred	4*d*.
Item for an iron didole with the net & pole	3*s*.
Item to William Davy the 8 daye of July *anno* 1574 for 4 dayes worke in the cutting bote	2*s*. 8*d*.

[*f. 65r*] /*Paymentes*/ Item to George Marshall the 10th daye of \<July\> July *anno* 1574 for 7 dayes worke in the river bote	4*s*. 8*d*.
Item to William Davy 17 daye of July *anno* 1574 for 5 dayes worke in the cutting bote	3*s*. 4*d*.
Item to George Marshall at that tyme for 5 dayes worke in the same bote	3*s*. 4*d*.
Item to [*blank*] Mannyng at that tyme for a bote hier	8*d*.
Item to [*blank*] Heyward the smyth for grinding the river sheres 6 tymes in *anno* 1573 and the forlockes	6*s*. 6*d*.
Item more to hym for grinding the sheres this yeare *anno* 1574	6*s*.
Item more to hym for 2 sithes for the river	5*s*. 8*d*.
Item to [*blank*] Preston the smyth for an iron for the quante	6*d*.
Item to George Marshall the 23 daye of July *anno* 1574 for 6 dayes worke \<in\> in the river bote at 8*d*. the daye	4*s*.
Item to him the 8 daye of August 1574 for 14 dayes in the river worke at 8*d*. the daye	9*s*. 4*d*.
Item more to hym the 14 daye of August *anno* 1574 for 6 dayes in the river worke at 8*d*. the daye	4*s*.
Item to Cawdell at that tyme for 6 dayes worke in the cutting bote at 8*d*. the daye	4*s*.

[*f. 65v*] /*Paymentes*/ Item to George Marshall the 21 daye of August 1574 for 6 dayes in the river worke at 8*d*. the daye	4*s*.
Item for a bott hier at that tyme	6*d*.
Item to Lister of Yarmouth for a parte of a pitchide cabell for ancker rops	6*s*.
Item to George Crane the 21 daye of September *anno* 1574 for 6 dayes worke in the cutting bott	4*s*.

Item to Peter Wyet the 1 daye of September *anno* 1574 for too
dayes worke in the cutting bote   16*d.*

Item to George Crane the 4 of September *anno* 1574 for 8<*d.*>
dayes and *dimidia* in the river worke at 8*d.* the daye   5*s.* 8*d.*

Item more to hym for 5 dayes worke the 11 daye of September
anno 1574 at 8*d.* the daye   3*s.* 4*d.*

Item more to him the 18 daye of September for 3 dayes worke &
dimidia at 8*d.* the daye   2*s.* 4*d.*

Item more to hym the 8 daye of October *anno* 1574 for 10 dayes
in the river worke at 8*d.* the daye   6*s.* 8*d.*

Item to Janckinson the 3 daye of November *anno* 1574 for 6 dayes
worke at 8*d.* the day   4*s.*

Item to Janckinson at sundry tymes for 106 dayes worke in the
river bote betwe[en] the 3ʳᵈ daye of November *1574* & the 25 daye
of Marche *anno* 1575 at 6*d.* the daye   53*s.*

[*f. 66r*] Item to Preston the smyth for too new Spanishe iron anckers,
the one weieng 32 *li.* & thother 34 *li.* & *dimidia* *& a new ancker
hooke at 3½*d.* the *li.**   19*s.* 4*d.*

Item to <Ch> Clifford for 4 paper bokes for the collectours   6*d.*

Item to John Byrche for stockeng of the 2 anckers   16*d.*

Item to Maior the shomaker for one payer of bottes for Granger   9*s.*

Item to Mr Richard Bate for 3 spares for quantes   2*s.*

Item to Granger for howse room <of> for the implementes
belonging to the cittie   10*s.*

Item to Anthony Marker for writing of this accompt   2*s.* 6*d.*

Item to Jankynson in rewarde in consideracion of his dilygens and
paynes that he have taken by the appoyntment of master surveyors   3*s.* 4*d.*

          Summa totalis of all the paymentes aforesaid   £36 4*s.* 11*d.*

And[75] so restith in the handes of this accomptaunt upon thende &
determinacion of this accompte   £53 7*d.*

Also ther restith in this accomptauntes handes one <of> obligacion
of Thomas Smythe of Yarmoth of £20 which shalbe dewe at
Christmas *anno* 1576 and is for the legacy geven by Mr William
Rogers to the ryver & stretes[76]   £20

Examinatur per nos
[*signed*] John Aldryche, [*Christofer*] Laier, Nycholas Sotherton

---

[75] This word obscures some accounting marks.
[76] The gift was actually made by Rogers' wife, Katheryn: see the Introduction, p. 113.

[*f. 66v blank*]

[*1575–76*]

[*f. 67r*] Thaccompte of Christofer Layer alderman treasorour and receivour of all the revenues belonging to the river and streates aswell of all souche somes of money as he have received as also of all the paymentes made concerning the same, *vidz.*, from the feast of thannunci*aci*on of Our Lady *anno* 1575 untill the feast of thannunciacion of Our Lady *anno* 1576 being one hole yeare as hereafter insuith

/*Arerages*/ Inprimis the sayd accomptaunt is chardged with money that remayned upon thend and determinacion of his last accompt as in the fote of the same accompte maye appeare £53 7d.

Summa patet

Receyved of Peter Peterson chamberleyne of the cittie of Norwich \<in\> *anno* 1575 for money dew out of the chamberleyns office to the use of the river and streates and here chardged for one hole yeare ended at the feast of [*blank*] £14

Receyved of Mathew Plome forreyn receivor for money dew out of the same office to thuse abovesaid for one hole yeare ended at the feast of [*blank*] £4

[*f. 67v*] /*Receiptes*/ Item received of George Manne and Nicholas Beston millers for money dew from him [*to*] the use aforesaid for one hole yeare ended at the feast aforesaid 53s. 4d.

Item of John Gigges for the hole yeares fearme of a close bought of Mr Peade at St Stevens gates 66s. 8d.

Item of Edmond Style for the hole yeares ferme of an \<ote\> orteyarde bought of Mr Pead in St Stevens 20s.

Item of John [*blank*] for the hole yeares ferme of an ortcharde bought of Mr Peade in St Stevens 22s.

Item of Robert Cocket for the fea[*r*]me of his tenement for one hole yeare ended at the said feast 30s.

Item of Georg Buttry for the hole yeares ferme of his tenement ended at the said feast 13s. 4d.

Item to [*sic*] Edward Reve for the hole yeares ferme of his tenement ended at the said feast 33s. 4d.

Item of Mrs Bate wedow for the hole yeares ferme of a pece of grownd that is won out of the river and dew at the feast of Our Ladye 1576 [*no sum given*]

Item of Mr Some alderman for the fearme of a parcell of grownd
in the parishe of St Marten at the Oke dew for one hole yeare
ended[77] at the feast of St Michaell tharchangell within the tyme of
this accompte　　　　　　　　　　　　　　　　　　　　　　　　　　　3s.

[f. 68r] Item of Mr Thomas Ferrour for the hole yeares fearme of
too peces of grounde with out Bisshoppes gates ended at the feast
of the annunciacion of Our Lady *anno* 1576　　　　　　　　　7s. 4d.

Item of Mr John Sotherton for the hole yeares ferme of a pece of
grownde that is also won out of the river ended at the same feast　　2s.

Item of Robert Cocket for the arrerages of his howse which was
behind and unpaid and was due for 8 yeares and three quarters of
a yeare at 10s. a yeare　　　　　　　　　　　　　　　　　£4 7s. 6d.

Item of Richard Sotherton collectour of Connesford, Berestreat &
Trowse　　　　　　　　　　　　　　　　　　　　　　　　46s. 8d.

Item of Robert Davy collectour of the warde of Mancrofte　　73s. 4d.

Item of Robert Ezod collectour of the warde of Wymer　　　　£8

Item of John Wilkinson collectour of the ward Beyond the Water　106s. 2d.

<Item for pitche>　　　　　　　　　　　　　　　　　　　<4d.>

Rest to accompt for that Janckinson one of the rivermen died this
yeare and Smyth came not in 8 or 10 dayes after　　　　　　3s. 4d.

Item receyved of Peter Golde for arrerages that remayned the
last yeare　　　　　　　　　　　　　　　　　　　　　　12s. 9d.

　　Summa totalis aswell of the arrerages as of the receiptes this yeare　£108 1s. 5d.

[f. 68v] /*Paymentes*/ Payd to William Granger laborer being hired
for the ryver for his wages dew to him for one hole yeare ended at
the feast of the annunciacion of Our Lady *anno* 1576　　　　£8

Item to Jankinson and John Smyth either of them for halfe a yeare
for the same purpose　　　　　　　　　　　　　　　　　　£8

Item to Ebbottes for sweping of the cockis and market place and
for carrying awey of the mennor for one yeares wages ended at the
feast aforesaid　　　　　　　　　　　　　　　　　　　　　£8

Item to John Keddell for his paynes taking in overseing the fiers
and cutters of the [river] for one hole yeare *laking 3 wekes* ended　<30s.>
at the said feast　　　　　　　　　　　　　　　　　　　*50s.* 4d.

Item to Richard Lussher for the making of too bondes　　　　10d.

Item to Smyth and Sharpe for cutting of the <m> river from the
milles downe warde this yeare　　　　　　　　　　　　　£6 6s. 8d.

---

[77] The word 'ended' is repeated here in error.

Item the 2nd daye of Aprill 1575 to Hagon the botwrite for himselfe
his man and his lade for 7 dayes worke in mending of 3 bootes at
2s. 6d.[78] the daye and 2d. over   17s. 8d.

Item to Kedell for his chardges about the bootes at that tyme as by
his bill appearith   8s.

Item for nayles at that tyme   3s. 6d.

[f. 69r] /Paymentes/ Item to John Byrche for bord and other thinges
at that tyme as by his bill appearith   21s.

Item to Thomas Secker in Aprill 1575 for a bast rope and
packthred   <19d.> *21d.*

Item to Preston the smyth for an iron for a quante   6d.

Item for making cleane the olde drayn at St Giles churche yarde   3d.

Item to Yonges for 2 payer of botes for the river men   16s.

Item to Mr Bate for 2 spares for quantes   16d.

Item to Henry Davy for one bast rope   22d.

Item for packthred   1d.

Item to Cawdell the 2nd July for 5 dayes worke in cutting the river
above the mylles   3s. 4d.

Item the 7 of July to Cawdell for 3 dayes worke in cutting of the ryver   2s.

Item for a payer of oers   16d.

Item to Kedell and the miller the 4th of September 1575 for 6 dayes
worke in cutting of the ryver above the milles at 8d. the daye   8s.

Item to them the 10th of September for 5 dayes worke in cutting
the river   6s. 8d.

Item to Mrs Wynter for one bz [bushel] of pitch   9s.

[f. 69v] /Paymentes/ Item to Robert Cane botwright in October 1575
for mending of the great and lesser bote as by his bill appearith   17s. 4d.

Item to John Byrche for borde to mend the botes at that tyme as
by his bill appearith   5s. 7d.

Item for nayles for the botes as appearith by Kedelles bill   7s. 8d.

Item to Kedell for diverse chardges for the botes as by his bill
appearith   6s. 3d.

Item to William Litlewood for a lock and key for the cockey dore
at the Blacke Fryers   13d.

Item to Fayerchilde for bringing in [a] bill of the defaltes in the
st*r*eates in the warde Beyond the Water   8d.

---

[78] One illegible word is deleted here.

Item to Hew Burton and diverse other masons for too dayes paynes in vewing certeine defaltes in the stretes and bringen in a bill in writing	5s.
Item to them for the chardge of ther bill making	16d.
Item to Hawerd for mending and grinding the cutting sheres this yeare as by his [bill] appearith	10s.
Item to Clifford for 4 litle paper bookes for the collectors	4d.
Item to Granger for howse rome for the implementes belonging to the cittie	6s. 8d.

[f. 70r] Item to Robert Coller for that he could not get nor gather upp of the colleccion *in* <of> his accompt ended at the feast of thannu[ncia]cion of Our Lady 1575	4s.
Item allowed to Robert Cocket with the consent of the auditours for bycause *he is* a poore *man* and for that he paied £4 7s. 6d. which was the arrerages that was behinde unpaid for his howse	10s.
Item payd to Fraunces Morley for pathing of the streat about the Shering Crosse[79] as by his bill appearith	6s. 2d.
Item to Anthony Marker for writing of this accompte	2s. 6d.
Item for pitche	4d.
Summa totalis of all the paymentes aforesayde	£42 5s.

/[£42 4s. 12d.]/

And so restith dewe upon this accompte	£65 16s. 5d.
/ Wherof there was lent to John Tewesdaye by the commaundement of master mayour and other of the justices towardes the charges at the stone myndes[80] which he have promysed to repaye ageyne	£10
And lent also to [blank] Ebottes towardes the bying of a carte and horses to carry awe[y] the fylthe from the cocckys and the swepinges of the market	53s. 4d.

And so restith tobe answered by this accomptaunt £53 3s. 1d. and one obligacion of Thomas Smythe of Yermothe <tol> for the payment of £20 at Christmas next/[81]

Examinatur per nos
[signed] John Aldryche, Christofer Laier, Nycholas Sotherton, Thomas Stokys

[79] Charing Cross: a stone cross in the parish of St Gregory.
[80] See the Introduction, p. 116.
[81] This was Katheryn Rogers' gift. See f. 66r, above.

[1576–77]

[*f. 70v*] Thaccompte of Christofer Layer alderman treasorour and surveyour of all the revenues belonging to the river and streates as well of all souche sumes of mony as he have receyved, as also, of all the payementes made concerninge the same, *vidz.*, from the feaste of thanunciacion of Our Lady *anno* 1576 untill the feast of thanunciac[*i*]on of <of> Our Lady *anno* 1577 beinge one whole yeare as hereafter insuith

/*Arrerages*/ *Inprimis* the sayd accomptant is chardged wyth mony that remayned upon thend and determinacion of his last accompte, and also wyth one obligacion of Thomas Smythes of Yarmothe for the paiment of £20 as in the fote of the same accompte maye appeare   £53 3s. 1d.

Summa patet

Receyved of Peter Peterson c[*h*]amberlyn of the cittie of Norwich *anno* 1576 for mony dew out of the chamberleyns office to the use of the river and streates for one whole yeare ended at the feast of thanunciacion of Our Lady 1577   £14

Receyved of Mathew Plome forreine receivour for mony dew out of the same office to thuse abovesayd for one hole yeare end [*sic*] at the feaste aforesayd   £4

Receyved of George Mann and Nicholas Beston myllers for mony dew from them to the use aforesayd for one hole yeare ended at the feaste aforesayde   53s. 4d.

[*f. 71r*] /*Receiptes*/ Item of John Gygges for the hole yeares ferme of a close boughte of Mr Peade at Saint Stevens gates   66s. 8d.

Item Edmond Style for the hole yeares ferme of an ortchard bought of Mr Peade in St Stevens   20s.

Item of John [*blank*] for the hole yeares ferme of an ortchard bought of Mr Peade in Saint Stevens   22s.

Item of Robert Cockett for the ferme of his tenement for one hole yeare ended at the foresayd feaste   30s.

Item of George Buttry for the hole yeares ferme of his tenement ended at the said feaste   13s. 4d.

Item of Edward Reve for the hole yeares ferme of his tenement ended at the sayd feaste   33s. 4d.

Item of Mrs Bate wedow for the hole yeares ferme of a pece of grounde that is wonne out of the river and dew at the feast of Our Ladye   20d.

Item of Mr Some alderman for the ferme of a parcell of grounde
in the parishe of St Marten at the Oke dewe for one hole yeare
ended at the feast of St Mychall tharchangell within the tyme of
this accompte   3s.

Item of Thomas Ferrour for the hole yeares ferme of twoo peces
of grounde wythout Bisshoppes gates ended at the feast of
thanunciacion of [Our] Lady anno [blank]   7s. 4d.

[f. 71v] Item of Mr John Sotherton for the hole yeares [farm] of a
pece of grounde that is wonne out of the ryver ended at the feast
of thanunciacion of Our Lady anno 1577   2s.

Item of Robert Ezoode for the remaynder of his last colleccion for
the warde of Wymer   29s.

Item of Robert Davye collectour for the warde of Mancrofte uppon
the remaynder of his laste colleccion   6s. 8d.

Item of John Wilkenson collectour for the warde Beyonde the
Water uppon the remaynder of his last colleccion   3s. 9d.

Item receyved of Ebbottes in parte of payment of a dett of 53s. 4d.
which was lent hym as in the last accompte maye appeare   20s.

Item receyved of Mr Smyth of Yarmorth for a legacy that
Mrs Rogers dyd gyve to the ryver and streates   £20

Item received off Mr Ellys Batts wyffe for the arerages off [the]
ferme off 1 pec[e] off ground off 20d. a yere for 5 yere[82]   8s. 4d.

Item of [blank] collectour of Connesforde, Berestrete and Trowes

Item of [blank] collectour for the warde of Mancrofte this yere

Item of [blank] collectour for the warde of Wymer this yeare

Item of [blank] collectour for the warde Beyonde the Water

/ For somoche as ther was greate errors in former yeares in collecting the mony
in thes severall wardes it is agreed by concent of assembly that nothing shalbe
charged but clerly remitted and after tobe charged orderly as in former accomptes
have ben used tobe charged/

/[£54 0s. 5d.]/

   Summa totalis aswell of the arrerages as of the receiptes this yeare   £107 3s. 6d.
/[£107 3s. 6d.]/

[f. 72r] / Paymentes/ Payed to John Smyth laborer beinge hyered for
the ryver for his wages dew to hym for one hole yeare ended at the
feast of thanunciacion of Our Lady anno 1577   £8

Payed to William Granger laborer beinge hyered for the lyke purpose for hys
wages dew to hym for one hole yeare ended at the feaste aforesayde   £8

---

[82] This entry is in a different hand.

Payed to Ebottes for swepinge of the cockis and market place and
for carryinge aweye of the mennor for one yeares wages ended at
the feaste aforesayde   £8

Payed to John Kyddell for his paines taking in overseinge the fiers
and cutters of the ryver for one hole yeare ended at the sayd feaste   53s. 4d.

Payed for one dayes worke of a man in the cuttinge boote in
cuttinge of the ryver   8d.

Payed to Caudell the seconde of June 1576 for fyve dayes worke in
the cutting boote   3s. 4d.

Payed to Keddell at that tyme for thre dayes worke and a halfe in
the cuttinge bote   2s. 4d.

Payed to Caudell the nynth of June for syx dayes worke in the
ryver bote   4s.

Payed to Robert Skott and Richard Clarke laborers for eight dayes
worke in the cutting bote   10s. 8d.

Payed more to the foresayd Robert Skott & Richard Clarke the
syxten of June 1576 for fower dayes in the cuttinge bote   5s. 4d.

Payed to Cawdell the sayd daye and yeare for fower dayes worke
in the river bote at 8d. the daye   2s. 8d.

/£20 2s. 1d. [£28 2s. 4d.]/

[f. 72v] /Paymentes/ Payed to Cann the botewright the 16 of Maye
1576 for 37 foote of borde to mende the bote wythall   2s. 2d.

Item to the sayd Canne for one dayes worke and seaven ledges   17d.

Item for nayle   4d.

Item for an anker stocke   7d.

Item for a baste rope 22d. and packethred 2d.   <14d. > 2s.

Item for a payer of owers   16d.

Item to Clarke and Skott the 23 of June 1576 for 6 dayes a pece
in the cutting bote   8s.

Item payed to Cawdell the 23 of June 1576 for 6 dayes in the
ryver bote   4s.

Item payed by Mr Raffe Marsham, John Sylver and the rest unto
43 men which wrought at the mouthe of the myll   39s. 8d.

Item payed for a bast rope   22d.

Item to fyve men which ded drawe water to make cleane the streates
with when master mayor ded take his chardge   10d.

Item payed to Kyddell for beinge *in* the cutting bote wyth
Granger six dayes and a halfe   4s. 4d.

Item payed for the bringinge up of Stingates kele to the mylles	20d.
Item payed by Mr Morley to divers that wrought at the New Mylles	2s. 6d.
Item payed to Bexwell and his too men for being at the mylles to helpe the workemen there the 25 of June 1576	3s.
Item payed to Skott and Clarke for one dayes worke a pece being in the water	2s.

/[£3 15s. 8d.]/

[f. 73r] /Paymentes/ Payed to Skott and Clarke the 30 of June for fower dayes worke in the cuttinge bote	5s. 4d.
Item payed to Caudell for one dayes worke in the ryver at the New Mylles	10d.
Item payed to the sayd Caudell and Kyddell for fower dayes worke *and a halfe* in cutting of the ryver wyth Granger	6s.
Item geven to the smyth and rest of the workemen for ther paines taking at the mylles	4d.
Item to Caudell the 7 of July for 6 dayes worke in the cutting bote	4s.
Item payed to Skot and Clarke for fower dayes worke in the ryver bote	5s. 4d.
Item payed to the sayd Skott and Clarke the fowertenth of July 1576 for 6 dayes worke in the cuttinge bote	8s.
Item payed to Cawdell the 14 of July 1576 for syx dayes worke in the ryver bote	4s.
Item payed to Skott and Clarke the 21 of July for syx dayes worke in the cuttinge bote	8s.
Item payed to Cawdell the 21 of July 1576 for fyve dayes worke in the river bote	3s. 4d.
Item payed to Granger this yeare for house rometh for the implymentes of the river	6s. 8d.
Item payed to Cawdell the 28 of July 1576 for fyve dayes worke in the ryver bote	3s. 4d.
Item payed to Skott and Clarke the sayd daye and yeare for fyve dayes worke in the cutting bote	6s. 8d.
Item payed to the sayd Skott and Clarke the <sayd> forth of August 1576 for <fower> *syx* dayes worke in the cutting bote	8s.

/£3 9s. 10d./

[f. 73v] /Paymentes/ Paymentes payed to Cawdell the forth of August for syx dayes worke in the cutting bote	3s.

Item payed to Kyddell for one dayes worke & a halfe in cuttinge the ryver wyth Granger 12*d.*

Item payed to Skot and Clarke the seaventh of August for too dayes worke in the cuttinge bote 2*s.* 8*d.*

Item payed for carryinge downe of Stingates kele from the mylles 4*d.*

Item payed to <Smyth> Stanforth the thred of September for too payer of botes for Smyth and Granger 16*s.*

Item payed by<e> Kyddell for three furringe sparres for quantes <2*s.*> 2*s.*

Item payed by Kyddell for a quant iron and the nayles 9*d.*

Item payed to Heyward the smyth for gryndinge and mending the cutting sheres 5*s.* 10*d.*

Item for a towe for the bote 21*d.*

Item payed to John Twesdaye by the commandiment of master mayor as well for his owne paines as for the chardges of other menn that wrought at the stone mynes £4 10*s.*

Item to Mr Marker for writing of this accompt[83] 2*s.* 6*d.*

/[£6 3*s.* 4*d.*] [£41 13*s.* 8*d.*] £6 5*s.* <4> 10*d.*/[84]

[*f. 74r*] *Summa totalis* of all the paymentes aforesayde £41 13*s.* 8*d.*

And so restithe dewe uponn this accompte £65 9*s.* 10*d.*

/ *The which sume of £65 9s. 10d. the sayde accomptaunt delyvered and payed to the handes of Mr Richard Baker alderman lately elected and chosen tobe one of the surveyours of the river & stretes & so charged upon hym as in the accompte followyng maye appere/*

Examinatur per nos
[*signed*] Robert Sucklyng, [*Christofer*] Laier

[1577–78]

[*f. 74v*] Thaccompte of Mr Richard Baker alderman tresorour and surveyour of all the revenues belonging to the river and streates aswell of all souch somes of money as he have receyved, as also of all the paymentes made concernyng the same, *viz.*, from the feast of thannunciacion of Our Lady *anno* 1577 untill the feast of thannunciacion of Our Lady *anno* 1578 being one whole yeare as hereafter insewith

---

[83] This entry is in a different hand.

[84] The first of the three totals given here represents the page total minus the final payment of 2*s.* 6*d.* to Mr Marker, which was added after the initial calculation was made. The second and third totals represent, respectively, the total expenditure for the year and the final page total including the sum to Marker.

/*Arrerages*/ *Inprimis* the said accomptaunt is chardged with money
by him receyved of Christofer Layer late treasorer to the use
aforesaid as mony remayning upon thend and determinacion of
his accompt as in the fote of the same accompt maye appeare   £65 9s. 10d.

Receyved of Peter Peterson chamberlyne of the cittie of Norwich
for mony dew out of the chamberlyns office to the use of the river
and streates for one whole yeare ended at the feast of thannunciacion
of Our Lady 1578   £14

Receyved of Mathew Plombe forreyne receyvour for money dew
out of the same office to thuse abovesaid for one whole yere ended
at the feast aforesaid   £4

Receyved of George Manne and Nicholas Beston myllers for   n[ihil] for that
mony dew <to> *from* them to the use aforesaid for one whole   they ded cut
yeare ended at the feast aforesaid   the ryver
                                                                  them selves

[*f. 75r*] /*Receiptes*/ Item receyved of John Gygges for the whole
yeares ferme of a close bought of Mr Peade at Sainct Stevens gates   66s. 8d.

Item receyved of Edmond Style for the whole yeares ferme of an
ortchard bought of Mr Pead in St Stevens   20s.

Item receyved of John Nylson for the whole yeares ferme of an
ortchard in St Stevens bought of Mr Peade   22s.

Item receyved of Robert Cocket for the ferme of his tenement for
one whole yeare ended at the said feast   30s.

Item of George Buttry for the whole yeres ferme of his tenement
ended at the foresaid feast   13s. 4d.

Item of Edward Reve for the whole yeares fearme of his tenement
ended at the said feast   33s. 4d.

Item of Mrs Bate wedowe for the whole yeares ferme of a pece of
ground that is wonne out of the river and dew at the feast of
thanunciacion of Our Lady   20d.

Item of Mr Christofer Some alderman for the whole yeares ferme
of a parcell of grownde in the parishe of St Marten at the Oke
ended at the feast of St Michaell tharchaungell within the tyme of
this accompt   3s.

Item of Thomas Ferrour for the whole yeares ferme of too peces of
grownde without Bisshoppes gates ended at the feast of Our Lady   7s. 4d.

Item of John Sotherton alderman for the whole yeares ferme of a pece
of ground that is wonne out of the river ended at the foresaid feast   2s.

/[£9 19s. 4d.]/

[*f. 75v*] Item of John Cotwyn collector of Connesford, Berestrete and Trowse — 40*s.*

Item of Nicholas Dannocke collectour of the warde of Mancrofte — 62*s.*

Item of John Sylver collectour of the warde of Wymer — £10

Item of Henry Pye collector of the warde Beyond the Water — 100*s.*

Summa totalis <of> aswell of the arrerages as of the receiptes this yere — £113 11*s.* 2*d.*

Payd to William Granger laborer being hiered for the river for his wages dew to hym for one whole yeare ended at the feast of thanuncia[c]ion of Our Lady 1578 — £8

Item to John Skypper laborer being hiered for the like purpose for his wages dew to him for one whole yeare ended at the aforesaid feast — £8

[*f. 76r*] /*Paymentes*/ Item to Ebbottes for sweping of the cockes and market place and for the carrying awey of the menor for one yeares wages ended at the feast aforesaid — £8

Item to John Kyddell for his paynes taking in overseing the fiers and cutters of the river for one whole yeare ended at the same feast — 53*s.* 4*d.*

Item to Younges the shomaker for too payer of bootes for Graunger and Skipper — 20*s.*

Item to Graunger this yeare for howse rometh for the implementes belonging to the river — 6*s.* 8*d.*

Item to Mr Petwys for a cote cloth for John Kyddell — 15*s.* 2*d.*
/*From this tyme forth no more eny souche allowance to be geven*/

Item for 4 bookes for the collectours & for writing of them — <20*d.*> 4*d.*

Item to Henry Davy for one pece of bast — 2*s.*

Item for one payer of owres for the cutting bote — 18*d.*

Item to [*blank*] for too dayes worke in mending of the cutting bote — 2*s.* 2*d.*

Item for nayles and 3 *li.* of hardes for the same bote — 15*d.*

Item for 18 fote of borde for the same bote — 12*d.*

Item for 7 *li.* of pitche — 8*d.*

Item for lyne and packe thred — 3*d.*

Item to Mr Bate for thre furring spares — 18*d.*

Item for one crome of iron — 8*d.*

Item for too barrowes for the watermen — 4*s.* 8*d.*

Item for too anker ropes for the bote — 3*s.*

Item for too dayes worke of a man in the ryver — 16*d.*

/£13 15*s.* 6*d.*/

[*f. 76v*] /*Paymentes*/ Item to Kiddell for one dayes worke in cutting
the hospitall[85] <river> krickes [*creeks*]   10*d.*

Item to Mrs Tesmond for thre remnauntes of bast rope   22*d.*

Item to Canne for mending of the litle bote   10*d.*

Item to Graunger for nayles & a b[*i*]nde [*binding*] for an ower   4*d.*

Item for towe for the bote   2*s.*

Item to Pickarell for one rope for the great bote   3*s.* 4*d.*

Item for thre cottes for the quantes   6*d.*

Item to Heward for grynding of the cutting sheres 6 tymes   6*s.*

Item to John Smyth laborer for cutting of the river from the comon
stath to Surlyngham for one whole yeare   100*s.*

Item to Robert Force, Henry Allen, Thomas Fillippes & Thomas
Pullam the 16 daye of Marche 1576 either of them for 5 dayes
worke & a halfe at the stone mynges either of them at 8*d.* the daye   14*s.* 8*d.*

Item the same daye to Henry Magges for five daye[*s*] worke there
at 8*d.* the daye   3*s.* 4*d.*

Item to John Rothester for 3 dayes worke at 8*d.* the daye   2*s.*

Item to Peter Keniam for 4 dayes worke & *an* halfe at 8*d.* the daye   3*s.*

Item to Henry Goalte & Peter Giles for 3 dayes worke and a halfe
either of them at 8*d.* the daye   4*s.* 8*d.*

/£7 3*s.* 4*d.*/

[*f. 77r*] /*Paymentes*/ Item to Henry Taylour, Henry Allen, Robert
Forse, Henry Magges, Thomas Pullan, Edward Bannister, Thomas
Phillippes & Henry Gault for 6 dayes worke at the stone mynges
either of them at 8*d.* the daye   32*s.*

Item to John Tewisdaye the younger for 6 dayes worke at 8*d.* the daye   4*s.*

Item to Symond Carmar for 4 dayes worke at 8*d.* the daye   2*s.* 8*d.*

Item to Richard Burges & John Rochester for 4 dayes worke & an
halfe either of them at 8*d.* the daye   6*s.*

Item to Richard Thackster for 5 dayes worke at 8*d.* the daye   3*s.* 4*d.*

Item to Peter Pecocke for 2 dayes worke at 8*d.* the daye   16*d.*

Item to Robert Call for 3 dayes worke at 8*d.* the daye   2*s.*

Item for 6 shovelles   3*s.* 8*d.*

Item for mending of the pickaxes & for nayles & for-lockes   2*s.* 5*d.*

---

[85] Hospital creeks: the Spitaldyke (see *figure* 2) by St Paul's hospital. This medieval institution
was acquired by the city in 1565, and was converted into a bridewell by 1571: *RCN* ii, pp. civ,
347.

Item to John Tewisday sen[ior] & William Blewit for too weekes
worke either of them at 8d. the daye   16s.

Item to Robert Forse, William Thackster, Henry Magges, Thomas
Pullan, Edward Bannister, Richard Rodes, Robert Call, John
Tewisdaye the younger & William Blewit the 23 daye of Marche
1576 every of them for 5 dayes worke at 8d. the daye a pece   30s.

Item to Richard Burges for 3 dayes worke   2s.

Item to Henry Gaulte for 2 dayes worke & a halfe   20d.

Item to John Rochester for 2 dayes worke   16d.

Item to John Tewisdaye sen[ior] for 4 dayes worke   2s. 8d.

/£5 11s. 1d./

[f. 77v] /Paymentes/ Item the 30 daye of Marche to Robert Forse,
Henry Magges, Thomas Pullan, Edward Banister, Robert Browne,
Robert Call, William Thackster, Richard Rodes, John Hill & John
Tewisdaye the younger for 5 dayes worke every of them at 8d. the
daye a pece   33s. 4d.

Item to John Rochester & Henry Gault either of them for 3 dayes
worke at 8d. the daye a pece   4s.

Item to William Blewit for 5 dayes worke at 10d. the daye   4s. 2d.

Item to John Tewisdaye sen[ior] for 4 dayes worke at 10d. the day   3s. 4d.

Item for 6 barrowes   14s.

Item to Robert Forse, Robert Call, William Thackster, Thomas
Pullan, Henry Gault, Edward Bannister, Robert Browne, Richard
Rodes, John Hill, Henry Magges & John Tewisdaye the younger
the 6 daye of Aprill 1577 every of them for 5 dayes worke and an
halfe at 8d. the daye a pece   40s. 4d.

Item to John Rochester for 4 dayes worke at 8d. the daye   2s. 8d.

Item to John Springall for 3 dayes worke at 8d. the daye   2s.

Item to William Blewit for 5 dayes worke and an halfe at *10d.
the daye*   4s. 7d.

Item to John Tewisdaye thelder for 4 dayes worke at 10d. the daye   3s. 4d.

Item to Robert Force, Robert Browne, Robert Call, William
Thackester, Edward Bannister, John Rochester, John Hill, Thomas
Pullam, Richard Rodes and John Tewisday the younger either of
them for 4 dayes worke at 8d. the daye a pece   26s. 8d.

/£5 18s. 5d./

[f. 78r] /Paymentes/ Item to Henry Gault & Henry Magges either
of them for too dayes worke at 8d. the daye   2s. 8d.

Item to William Blewet for 4 dayes worke at 10*d*. the daye   3*s*. 4*d*.

Item to John Tewisdaye thelder for too dayes worke at 10*d*. the daye   20*d*.

Item to Robert Forse, William Thackester, Richard Rodes, John Hill,
John Rochester, Thomas Pullan, Adam Barker, Richard Nedeham
and John Tewisday jun[*ior*] every of them for three dayes worke at
8*d*. the daye a pece   18*s*.

Item to William Blewit & John Tewesday thelder either of them for
3 dayes worke at 10*d*. the daye   <2*s*. 6*d*.> 5*s*.

Item for an yron spendle for a barrowe   8*d*.

Item for nayles   2*d*.

Item for mending of [*a*] spendle   1*d*.

Item <for> to Robert Forse, Robert Browne, Richard Rodes,
William Thackester & John Tewisdaye the yonger every of them
for 4 dayes and an halfe at 8*d*. the daye a pece   15*s*.

Item to John Rochester, Robert Call, Adam Barker and John Hill
every of them for 4 days worke at 8*d*. the daye a pece   10*s*. 8*d*.

Item to Richard Nedehame for 3 dayes worke at 8*d*. the daye   2*s*.

Item to Richard Blewit for 4 dayes worke and an halfe at 10*d*. the daye   3*s*. 9*d*.

Item to Robert Forse, Robert Browne, Robert Call, Richard
Roodes, John Hall, Adam Barker, William Thacker, John Rochester
and John Tewisday the younger every of them for 4 dayes worke
at 8*d*. the daye a pece   24*s*.

Item to Mathew Robynson for 3 dayes worke at 8*d*. the daye   2*s*.

Item to Thomas Pecke for one dayes worke   8*d*.

Item to William Blewet and John Tewisday sen[*ior*] either of them
for 4 dayes worke at 10*d*. the daye   6*s*. 8*d*.

/£4 16*s*. 4*d*./

[*f. 78v*] /*Paymentes*/ Item to Robert Force, William Thacster, John
Rochester, Adam Barker, John Hill, John Tuisdaye the yonger &
Robert Browne every of them 5 dayes worke at 8*d*. the daye a pece   23*s*. 4*d*.

Item to Robert Roodes for 4 dayes worke   2*s*. 8*d*.

Item to William Blewit & John Tewisday sen[*ior*] for 5 dayes worke
a pece at 10*d*. the daye   8*s*. 4*d*.

Item to Robert Browne, Adam Barker, John Hill, Richard Roodes
and John Tuisday the yonger the <20> 18 daye of Maye 1577 every
of them for 4 dayes worke and a halfe at 8*d*. the daye a pece   15*s*.

Item to Robert Force and John Rochester either of them for 4   <4*s*. 8*d*.>
dayes worke at 8*d*. the daye   5*s*. 4*d*.

Item to William Thackster for 3 dayes & a halfe at 8*d.* the daye	2*s.* 4*d.*
Item to Edward Banister for 2 dayes worke	16*d.*
Item to William Blewit and John Tewisday thelder for 4 dayes & a halfe at 10*d.* the daye either of them	7*s.* 6*d.*
Item to Adam Barker, Robert Browne, Richard Roodes, John Tewisdaye, John Hill, Robert Force, John Rochester, Edward Banister, William Thacster the 25 daye of Maye 1577 every of them for 5 dayes worke and a halfe at 8*d.* the daye a pece	33*s.*
Item to John Tewisdaye thelder & William Blewit either of them for 5 dayes worke & a halfe at 10*d.* the daye a pece	9*s.* 2*d.*
Item payd to Henry Palmer for 6 dayes worke at 8*d.* the daye	4*s.*
Item to Anthony Marker for wrighting & ingrossing this accompte	2*s.* 6*d.*

/£5 13*s.*/

[*f. 79r*]	*Summa totalis* of all the paym[*en*]tes aforesayde	£59 19*s.* 2*d.*
	viz., the ryver	£35 11*s.* 2*d.*
	stonemyndes	£24 5*s.* 6*d.*

[*f. 79v blank*]

And so restithe dewe upon the determinacion of this accompte	£53 12*s.*

Examinatur per nos
[*signed*] Roberte Sucklyng, [*Christofer*] Laier

[*1578–79*]

[*f. 80r*] Thaccompte of Mr Richard Baker alderman treasorour and surveyour<s> of all the revenues belonging to the river and streates aswell of all souche somes of mony as he have receyved as also of all the paymentes made concernyng the same, *vidz.*, from the feast of thanunciacion of Our Lady *anno* 1578 untill the feast of thanunciacion of Our Lady *anno* 1579 being one whole yeare as hereafter insewith

/*Arrerages*/ Inprimis the said accomptaunt is chardged with mony <by him receyved of Christofer Layer> which remayned upon thend and determinacion of his last accompte as in the fote of the same accompte maye appeare	£53 12*s.*

Summa patet

/*Receiptes*/ Receyved of Peter Peterson chamberlyne of the cittie of Norwich for mony dew out of the chamberlyns office to the use of the river and streates for one whole yeare ended at the feast of thanunciacion of Our Lady 1579	£14

Receyved of Mathew Plome forreyen receyvour for mony dew out
of the same office to thuse abovesaid for one whole yeare ended
\<ended> at the feast aforesaid   £4

Receyved of [*blank*] Newman the myller for mony dew from him
to the use aforesaid for one whole yeare ended at the feast aforesaid   53s. 4d.

Receyved of John Gygges for the whole yeares ferme of a close
bought of Mr Peade at St Stevens gates   66s. 8d.

Receyved of Edmond Style for the whole yeares ferme of \<a close>
an ortchyard bought of Mr Peade   20s.

[*f. 80v*] /*Receiptes*/ Receyved of John Nylson for the whole yeares
ferme of an ortchyard in [*St*] Stevens bought of Mr Peade   22s.

Receyved of Robert Cocket for the ferme of his tenement for one
whole yeare ended at the foresaid feast   30s.

Receyved George Buttry for the whole yeare ferme of his tenement
ended at the said feast   13s. 4d.

Receyved of Edwarde Reve for the whole yeares ferme of his
tenement at the same feast   33s. 4d.

Receyved of Mrs Bate wedowe for the whole yeares ferme of a
pece of ground that is wonne out of the river and dew at the feast
of thanunciacion of Our Lady   20d.

Receyved of Christofer Some alderman for the whole yeares ferme
of a parcell of ground in the parishe of St Martyn at the Oke
ended at the feast of St Michaell tharchangell within the tyme of
this \<accom> accompte   3s.

Receyved of Thomas Ferrour for the whole yeares ferme of too
peces of grounde without Bisshoppes gates ended at the feast of
Our Lady   7s. 4d.

Receyved of John Sotherton alderman for the whole yeares ferme
of a pece of grounde that is wonne out of the river ended at the
foresaid feast   2s.

Receyved of Nicholas Dannocke collectour for the warde of
\<Manch> Mancroft upon the remaynder of his last accompte   4s.

Receyved of William Blome collectour for the warde of Connesford,
Berestrete et [*sic*] Trowse for this yeares colleccion   52s. 11d.

Receyved of Richard Hooke collectour for the warde of Mancrofte
for this yeare   57s. 11d.

Receyved of Peter Golde collectour for the warde \<of> Beyond
the Water for this yere   £5 7s. 6d.

[*f. 81r*] /*Rec[e]iptes*/ Receyved of William Ives and Mr Fraunces
Morley collectours for the warde of Wymer for this yeare   £9 3s. 3d.

Receyved of Mr Nicholas Layer for 5 loades of small stone at 10d.
the loade   4s. 2d.

Item of him for too loades of great stones at 14d. the loade   2s. 4d.

Item more of him for 3 loades of midle stones at 12d. the loade   3s.

Item of Blyth in St Martins for three loades of midle stones at 12d.
the loade   3s.

Item more of him for too loades of greate stones at 14d. the loade   2s. 4d.

Item of John Hennont the brewer for 5 loades of great stones
at 14d.   5s. 10d.

Item of John Tewisdaye for too loades of midle stone at 12d. the
loade   2s.

Item of Castelowe the reder for one loade of midle stones at   12d.

Item of Cowper for one loade of midle stones   12d.

Item of John Pye for too loades of greate stones at 14d. the loade   2s. 4d.

Item of Thomas Bettes for one load of greate stones   14d.

Item of the wedow Bettes for too loades of greate stones at 14d.
the lode   2s. 4d.

Item of Robert Davy for one loade of small stones   10d.

Item of Richard Skottowe for one lode of great stones   14d.

Item of Henry Elmy for one load of greate stones   14d.

Item of Mr Rugg for 5 loades of greate stones at 14d. the loade   5s. 10d.

Item of John Shovell for too loades of small stone at 10d. the loade   20d.

Item of Water Teynton for one loade of small stones   10d.

Item of John Tewisdaye the 27 of December for certeyne stones
which he sold in *anno* 1577 from the stone mynes   22s. 6d.

Item of the wedow Sellers for one loade of midle stone   12d.

[*f. 81v*] Item for 20 loades of greate stone for St Johns streate[86] at
14d. the loade   23s. 4d.

Item of Mr Chamberlyne for too loades of greate stones at 14d.
the loade   2s. 4d.

---

[86] St John's street: the medieval Holgate, in South Conesford. Kirkpatrick, *Streets and Lanes*,
pp. 10–11 suggests this lane got its name because it was a 'hollow way', gullied by the rain water
running down from Berstreet. The sum due for the transaction mentioned here was in fact not
paid before the end of the accounting year, and a note was made to this effect at the end of the
year's account (see below, f. 84r).

Item of Thomas Ferrour for 4 loads of small stone at 10*d.* the loade   3*s.* 4*d.*
/[£55 12*s.* 9*d.*]/

    Summa totalis aswell of the arrerages as of the receiptes this yere   £109 4*s.* 9*d.*
/£109 4*s.* 9*d.*/

Payd to William Granger laborer being hiered for the river <and
stretes> for his wages dew to him for one <whole> *quarter of a*
yeare ended at the feast of <thanunciacion of Our Lady> *St John
Baptist* *anno* 1578   <£8> 40*s.*

Item to John Skypper laborer being hiered for the ryver for his
wages dew for one whole yeare ended at the <foresaid> feast *of
thanunciacion of Our Lady 1579*   £8

Item to Ebbottes *£4* and Borley *£4* for sweping of the cockeis
and market place and for carrying awey of the menor for one yeres
wages ended at the foresaid feast, *vidz.*, either of them for halfe a yeare   £8

[*f. 82r*] /*Paymentes*/ Item to William Gynney laborer being hiered
for the river from the feast of John Baptist untill the feast of Our
Lady aforesaid   £6

Item to John Kiddell for his paynes taking in overseing the fiers
and cutters of the river<?>[87] for one whole yeares wages ended at
the fest aforesaid   53*s.* 4*d.*

Item to John Smyth laborer being hiered for the ryver from the
comon stath to Surlingham   100*s.*

Item to Yonges the shomaker for too payer of bootes the 10th daye
<daye> <daye> of <Ap<?r>ris> Aprill for Skipper & Graunger   20*s.*

Item to Boreley the 28 daye of Marche for fying and carrieng away
the menour from the cockeis when Ebbottes which [*i.e., was*] sicke   5*s.*

Item to Kidell for 4 litle paper bookes for the collectors   4*d.*

Item to John Tewisdaye, Robert Force, William Gynny and
Richard Baxter for fyve dayes worke the 14 daye of June in the
<cutting boote> ryver at 9*d.* the daye   15*s.*

Item to Canne the botewright for 3 dayes worke in reparing of the
cutting boate the 16 daye of June   3*s.*

Item paid for hardes, thrumes and rede for the bote   7*d.*

Item to Pickarell the 16 daye of June for nayles   6*d.*

Item to him for 21 *li.* of pytche for the boate   3*s.* 6*d.*

Item for a faggot and too pitche barrell staves at the same tyme   3*d.*

Item the 20 daye of June for too cotes for the quantes   4*d.*

[87] An illegible character has been deleted here.

Item for lyne, packe thred and a pinte of tarr for the boate	10d.
Item to Thomas Pickarell for a pece of bast	2s.
Item to Presson the smyth the 19th daye of June for too iron rakes for fying of the ryver	2s. 6d.

/[£34 7s. 2d.]/

[f.82v] /Paymentes/ Item to Presson for mending of them at too sundry tymes	4d.
Item to Henry Davy for too new skopettes	12d.
Item to Richard Sotherton for too new owers	18d.
Item for too new bordes and packe thred for the boate the 30 daye of June	7d.
Item to Mathew Nikerson, John Tewisday and John Battley every of them for a days worke at 9d. the daye	2s. 3d.
Item to John Kiddle for 18 dayes worke in cutting of the ryver at 8d. the daye the 21 daye of July	12s.
Item to William Granger the first daye of August for keping of the citties implementes for halfe a yeare ended at Lammas	3s. 4d.
Item the 2nd daye of August to Henry Yonges for a payer of boates [i.e., boots] for William Gynney	10s.
Item to John Tewisday the 4th daye of August for 5 dayes & a halfe in cutting of the ryver at 10d. the daye	4s. 7d.
Item to John Nikerson the same daye for 4 dayes worke and an halfe in cutting of the ryver	3s. 9d.
Item to Hissam the 6 daye of August for one dayes worke & dimidia in the ryver	15d.
Item to Robert Call for 2 dayes worke & dimidia in cutting of the ryver	2s. 1d.
Item to Thomas Pickarell for a pece of bast the same daye for the cutting boate	22d.
Item the 8 daye of August for too new sith staves	6d.
Item to John Smyth for 4 dayes worke in cutting of the ryver the 12th daye of August at 10d. the daye	3s. 4d.
Item to Walker the same daye for 4 dayes worke in the cutting boate	3s. 4d.
Item to Bexwell the 12th of August for 4 dayes worke in the ryver	3s. 4d.
Item to Granger for too dayes worke in the ryver	20d.

/[£56 7s. 0d.]/

[*f. 83r*] /*Paymentes*/ Item to Kyddell for 18 dayes worke the same
daye in cutting of the ryver at 8*d.* the daye   12*s.*

Item the \<the\> 13 daye of December for drawing upp of the towne
bote into the botewrightes yardes   4*d.*

Item to Mr Johnson for a barrell of pitch   12*s.*

Item to Glover the smith for 4 *C* of nayles   2*s.* 8*d.*

Item to him for clynke nayles   2*s.*

Item for hardes, rede and thrumes for the boate   18*d.*

Item the 18th daye of December for too new quantes   18*d.*

Item the same daye for a hundred and a quarter of borde   7*s.* 6*d.*

Item for halfe a hundreth of planckes   4*s.*

Item for tymber for the boate   12*d.*

Item to Canne for 10 dayes worke about the boate   10*s.*

Item to him for his man six dayes   3*s.*

Item to John Byrche the 28 daye of January at the comaundement
of [*blank*] maior for making of a stath at Fullers Whole[88] in *anno* 1575   50*s.*

Item to William Gynny for keping of the implementes belonging to
the ryver for halfe a yeare due to him at the feast of the purificacion
of Our Lady   3*s.* 4*d.*

Item to Hewerd the smyth for grynding of the cutting sheres 6 tymes   6*s.*

Item for grynding too sithes & 2 caning sickles   4*d.*

Item for a virrell and for-lockes   8*d.*

Item to Newman the 26 daye of June towardes the making of the
crane   40*s.*

Item more to him \<for\> the 26 \<7\> daye of August toward the
making of the same   53*s.* 4*d.*

Item to Thomas Pickarell for 3 lynes waying 15 *li.* at 3½*d.* the pound   4*s.* 4*d.*

Item to Fylde the 27 daye of November for iron worke belonging
to the crane   £3

Item to Clement Herne the 6 daye of December towardes the said
crane as by his bill appeareth   59*s.* 5*d.*
/[£16 14*s.* 11*d.*]/

[*f. 83v*] /*Paymentes*/ Item to Newman the 28 daye of December for
certeyn canvas for the pooke   14*s.* 9*d.*

---

[88] Fuller's Hole: see *figure* 2. It is not clear which mayor is being referred to here. The mayor
in January 1578/9 was Robert Wood. The mayors whose incumbencies covered parts of the year
1575 were Christopher Some (June 1574–June 1575) and William Farrour (June 1575–June
1576): Hawes, *Index*, pp. x, xxiii.

Item for lyne for the pooke	3s.
Item for three staves	12d.
Item for three rake heades	12d.
Item for lyme and sand for bricke and workemanshipp in making upp of the wall at Coslany Brigge	7s.
Item the 19 daye of Aprill 1578 to William Gilbert, John Tewisdaye, John Hall, John Fuller, Simond Browne, William Gynny, John Kiddell and Robert Force every of them for 6 dayes worke at 8d. the daye	32s.
Item to John Browne for 3 dayes worke at 8d. the daye	2s.
Item to Martyne Sithirne for 2 dayes worke at 8d. the daye	16d.
Item to John Browne, Simond Browne, John Moore, John Tewesday, Robert Force & Robert Seadman the 26 daye of Aprill every of them for 5 dayes worke and an halfe at the stone mynges at 8d. the daye	22s.
Item to William Gilbert, John Writh, John Kyddell, Richard Nedham and William Gynny the same daye every of them five dayes workes <in> at 8d. the daye	18s. 4d.
Item to William Wreth, John Glover, Robert Force, John Tewisdaye, William Gynny, Simond Browne, Thomas Taylour, Robert Seadman, Richard Nedham, William Gilbert & John Kiddell the thred weeke every of them for 5 dayes worke at 8d. the daye	36s. 8d.
Item to John Glover, John Tewisdaye, Robert Seadman, Richard Nedham, William Gynny, Thomas Taylour, Simond Browne, John Wreth & John Kyddell the 4th weeke every of them at 8d. the *daye* for 5 dayes worke at the stone mynges	30s.
Item to John Askew and John Hill for 3 dayes worke ther either of them at 8d. the daye	4s.
Item to Robert Force for 4 dayes worke and an halfe at 8d. the daye	3s.

/[£8 16s. 1d.]/

[f. 84r] /Paymentes/ <Item to John Hill for 3 dayes worke there>	<2s.>
Item to Mathew Nicolson for 4 dayes worke ther at 8d. the daye	2s. 8d.
Item the 5th weeke to<o> John Glover, John Tewserdaye, Robert Seadman, Robert Force, William Jenny, Thomas Taylour, Edmond Browne, John Wreth, Mathew Nicholson, Richard Nedham and John Kiddell every of them for 6 dayes at 8d. the daye	44s.
Item to John Rochester for 3 dayes worke	<?>[89] 2s.

[89] An illegible character has been deleted here.

Item to William Emmis for one dayes worke	8*d.*
Item to Robert Blackeborne the 22 daye of Aprill for 6 shovelles	3*s.* 6*d.*
Item to Bretten for too barrowes	5*s.*
Item to Preston the smythe for \<making\> yren belonging to them	2*s.* 4*d.*
Item to him for nayles and spyndells	6*d.*
Item to Robert Force for a lader at the stone mynges	10*d.*
Item to Presson for mending of 4 \<barrow\> barrowes	12*d.*
Item for the yron worke that did belong to the litle howse at the stone mynges to ly in the implementes	6*d.*
Item for a locke to the same howse	6*d.*
Item to Anthony Marker for writing and engrossing of this accompte	2*s.* 6*d.*

/[£3 3*s.* 6*d.*]/

Summa *totalis* of all the paymentes aforesayde   £66 10*d.*

/ *Totalis* *patet* £66 \<18*s.* 4[*d.*]\> *10*d.**/

And so restith dewe upon the determinacion of this accompte   £43 3*s.* 11*d.*

/ *Wherof there is owyng for stones that were delyvered to Mr John Sotherton towardes the pavyng of the strete at St Johns churche*/[90]   23*s.* 4*d.*

And so restith   £42 7*d.*

Examinatur per nos
[*signed*] Christofer Layer, Thomas Stokys

[*f. 84v blank*]

[1579–80]

[*f. 85r*] Thaccompte of Mr Richard Baker alderman treasorour and receyvour of all the revenues belonging to the ryver and stretes, aswell of all souche summes of mony as he have receyved, as also of all the paymentes made concernyng the same. *Viz.*, from the feaste of thanunciac[*ion*] of Our Lady *anno* \<158\> 1579 untyll the feaste of the anunciacion of Our Lady *anno* 1580 beyng one hole yeare as hereafter ensueth

/ *Arrerages*/ *Inprimis* the sayde accomptaunt is charged with mony which remayned upon thende and determinacion of his laste accompte as in the fote of the same accompte maye appeare   £42 7*d.*

summa patet

[90] St John's church: St John Sepulchre. (See f. 81v and n. 86 for St John's Street, which led up to near the church.)

/*Receiptes*/ Receyved of Peter Peterson chamberlyne of the citie for
mony dewe oute of the chamberlyns office to the use of the ryver
and stretes for one whole yeare ended at the feaste of thanunciacion
of Our Lady *anno* 1580 £14

Receyved of Mathew Plombe forren receyvo[*ur*] for mony dewe
owte of the same office to the use abovesayde for one hole yeare
ended at the feast aforesayde £4

Received of [*blank*] the myller for mony dewe from hym to the use
aforesayde, *viz.*, for cutting the wedes in the ryver for one whole   nothing
yeare ended at the feaste aforesayde   this yeare

Received of John Gygges for the whole yeares ferme of a close
boughte of Mr Pede lying in the parisshe of St Stephan 66s. 8d.

Received of Robarte Cocket for the ferme of his tenement for one
whole yeare ended at the sayd feaste 30s.

[*f. 85v*] /*Receiptes*/ Received of Edmonde Stile for the whole yeares
ferme of an orteyarde bought of Mr Pede 20s.

Received of John Nylson for the hole yeares ferme of an other
orteyarde in St Stephans bought of Mr Pede 22s.

Received of George Buttery for the whole yeares ferme of his
tenement dewe at the sayd feaste 13s. 4d.

Received of Edwarde Reve for the whole yeares ferme of his
tenement dewe at the sayd feaste 33s. 4d.

Received of Mrs Bate wedow for the whole yeares ferme of a pece
of grownde that is wonne owte of the ryver and dewe at the feaste
of the anunciacion of Our Lady 20d.

Received of Lambe the glover for the whole yeares ferme of a
parcell of grownde in the parisshe of Saynt Marteyne at the Oke
for the yeare ended at the feaste of St Michell tharchaungell within
the tyme of this accompte 3s.

Received of Thomas Farrour for the ferme of too peces of grownde
withoute Bisshopps gate for the hole yeare endyd at Our Lady 7s. 4d.

Received of John Sotherton alderman for the hole yeares ferme
of a pece of grownde that is wonne owte of the ryver 2s.

Received of William Peter collectour for the warde of Mancrofte
for this yeares colleccion 60s.

Received of John Cotwyn collectour for the warde of Berestrete for
this yeares colleccion 40s.

Received of William Pyckeryng collectour for the warde of Wymer
this yeres colleccion £7 4s. 2d.

Received of Mathew Plombe collectour for the warde Beyonnde
the Water for this yeres colleccion   102s. 7d.

/[£72 2s. 6d.]/

[f. 86r]   Summa totalis aswell of the arrerages as of the receiptes this
                                                         yeare   £87 6s. 8d.

/[£87 6s. 8d.]/

/Paymentes/ Payed to Thomas Thetforde laborer beyng hyred for the
ryver for his wages dewe unto hym for halfe a yeare ended at the
feaste of St Michell tharchaungell anno 1579   £4

Item to William Gynne laborer beyng lykewise hyryd for the ryver
for his wages dewe unto hym for 3 quarters of a yere ended at the
sayde feaste of Cristemas anno 1579   £6

Item more to hym for his wages for one quarter of a yeare ended at
Our Lady 1580   40s.

Item to Peter Wyet laborer beyng hyred for the ryver for his wages
dewe to hym for one halfe yeare ended at Our Lady   £4

Item to Thomas Hewarde beyng hyred to feye the cockyes for his
quarters wages dewe to hym at the feaste of the natyvetie of
St John Baptiste anno 1579   40s.

Item William Abbot beyng hyred for skavenger and feyer of the
cockyes for his wages dewe to hym for 3 quarters of a yeare ended
at Our Lady   £6

Item to John Kyddell for his paynes taking in overseyng the feyers
and cutters of the ryver for one whole yeare ended at the feaste of
thanunciacion of Our Lady   53s. 4d.

Item to John Smythe beyng hyred to cutt the ryver from the comon
stathe to Surlingham   100s.

/[£31 13s. 4d.]/

[f. 86v] /Paymentes/ Item payed to Younges the shomaker for too
payer of botes for the laborers in the ryver   20s.

Item to William Gynne for keping of the implementes and gere
belonging to the bote for one whole yeare ended at the feaste of
the <anunciacion> purificacion of Our Lady   6s. 8d.

Item to John Smyth and Walter Taillour for wydenyng of the ryver
betwen Mr Grenes and Surlingham churche by the appoyntment
of Mr Some 15 dayes at 20d. a daye betwen them   25s.

Item to Thomas Chapman botewrighte for thre dayes worke at 16d.
the daye   4s.

Item to hym more for thre dayes worke of his man at 10*d.* the daye	2*s.* 6*d.*
Item to Cowper for reparing the littelbote one daye and halfe	18*d.*
Item more to hym for his boye a daye & halffe	9*d.*
Item for too stone of pytche	3*s.* 4*d.*
Item for a pynte of terr	2*d.*
Item for 3 pounde of hardes	6*d.*
Item for twybordes	2*d.*
Item for reede	2*d.*
Item for thrumes	1*d.*
Item for too fagottes	3*d.*
Item for nayles	10*d.*
Item for a pece of baste	22*d.*
Item for packe threde	1*d.*
Item for lyne	3*d.*
Item to Thomas Pykerell for a towrope	19*d.*
Item for a payer of new owers	16*d.*
Item to Edwarde Curtes for carreyng awaye 24 lodes of mucke that laye in Saynt Margaretes lane[91]	8*s.*
Item for a payer of sheres stelyng	20*s.*
Item for mending a payer of sheres that were broke in the backe	4*s.*

/[£5 3*s.* 0*d.*]/

[*f. 87r*] /*Paymentes*/ Item for 3 payer of sheres grynding	3*s.*
Item for a sythe pecyng	4*d.*
Item fo[r] gryndyng of the cane syckelles	4*d.*
Item payed to Roberte Force for 8 dayes working at the stone mynes at 8*d.* the daye	5*s.* 4*d.*
Item to John Kyddell for 8 dayes working at the same mynes at 8*d.* the daye	5*s.* 4*d.*
Item to John Tewesdaye for 6 dayes working at the same mynes	4*s.*
Item to John Staff for 6 dayes working there	4*s.*
Item to Thomas Plomerton for 6 dayes working there	4*s.*
Item to Jackeson for 5 dayes at 8*d.* the daye	3*s.* 4*d.*
Item to Thomas Askew for 3 dayes at 8*d.* the daye	2*s.*
Item to Joh<e>n James for 2 dayes	16*d.*

[91] St Margaret's lane: in the parish of St Margaret Westwick.

Item to Bull for too dayes	16*d.*
Item to William Thaxter for too dayes	16*d.*
Item to William Garwoode for 3 dayes	2*s.*
Item to William Granger for 6 dayes	4*s.*
Item to Robert Force for 5 dayes	3*s.* 4*d.*
Item more to John James for 6 dayes	4*s.*
Item to Roberte Jackeson for 6 dayes	4*s.*
Item to John Staff for 6 dayes	4*s.*
Item to Thomas Ashen for 5 dayes & halfe	3*s.* 8*d.*
Item to John Tewesdaye for 6 dayes	4*s.*
Item to Thomas Plomerton for 6 dayes	4*s.*
Item to Prior for 4 dayes	2*s.* 8*d.*
Item more to John Kyddell for too dayes	16*d.*
Item more to Robert Forse for 4 dayes & halfe	3*s.*
Item to William Granger for 4 dayes & halfe	3*s.*
Item to John Staff for 4 dayes & halfe	3*s.*
Item to Thomas Astoo for 4 dayes & halfe	3*s.*
Item to Thomas Plomerton for 4 dayes	2*s.* 8*d.*
Item to Lawrence Chambers for 4 dayes & halfe	3*s.*
Item to William Thacker for 4 dayes & halfe	3*s.*
Item to William Ducker for 3 dayes & halfe	2*s.* 4*d.*
/[£4 15s. 8d.]/	
[*f. 87v*] /*Paymentes*/ Item to William Garrard for 4 dayes and halfe	3*s.*
Item to John Tewesdaye for 4 dayes & halfe	3*s.*
Item more to Robert Force for 4 dayes & halfe	3*s.*
Item to William Granger for 4 dayes & halfe	3*s.*
Item to John Staff for 4 dayes & halfe	3*s.*
Item to Thomas Astoo for 4 dayes & halfe	3*s.*
Item to Thomas Plomerton for 4 dayes	2*s.* 8*d.*
Item to Lawrence Chambers for 4 dayes & halfe	3*s.*
Item to William Thacker for 4 dayes & halfe	3*s.*
Item to William Ducker for 3 dayes & halfe	2*s.* 4*d.*
Item to William Garrarde for 4 dayes & halfe	3*s.*
Item to John Tewesdaye for 4 dayes & halfe	3*s.*
Item for the wrighting and ingrossing this accompte	2*s.* 6*d.*

<Item to Edwarde Curtes for carryngawaye 24 lodes mucke that
laye in St Margaretes lane> /allowed before/   <8s.>

Item to Presson the smythe for making a new pickeax that did waye
8 pounde   2s.

Item to Presson for new making a nother olde pickeax   12d.

Item to Prior for makyng thelves for too pickeaxes   3d.

/[£2 8s. 9d.]/

                    Summa totalis of all the paymentes aforesayde   £43 12s. 9d.

/<£44 9d.>/

/<£43 5s. 11d.> And so resteth dewe upon the determinacion of
this accompte   £43 13s. 11d.

Examinatur per nos
[*signed*] [*Christofer*] Layer, Thomas Pettus, Clement Hyrne

/*Totalis* *patet* <£47 9d.>/

APPENDIX

Probable location of cockeys
mentioned in the text

All Hallows'/All Saints' (1559–60): situated in the parish of All Saints Timberhill in the sub-ward of Berstreet. This was probably part of the Great Cockey.

Blackfriars' (1575–76): this is presumably the outflow of the Great Cockey which entered the Wensum at Blackfriars' bridge close to the site of the former Dominican friary. The accounts show that access to this cockey was restricted by a locked door.

Market cockeys (1557–58): these were presumably large gutters, but may also have included sections of the Great Cockey.

Great Cockey (1573–74): the largest and most important of all the city's streams. Its source was at 'Jack's Pit' (*figure* 2), and its course skirted the castle and the market place to enter the Wensum near Blackfriars' bridge.

St Andrew's: the surveyors were given a special warrant by the mayor to construct a new cockey (or large drain) in the parish of St Andrew in the sub-ward of Middle Wymer, in 1563–64.

St Austin's (1557–58): probably part of the Dalymond dyke in the parish of St Augustine in the sub-ward of Colegate, north of the river (*figure* 2).

St John's (1557–58, 1559–60): probably part of the Great Cockey in the parish of St John Timberhill in the sub-ward of Berstreet, by the castle.

St Lawrence's (1557–58, 1559–60): situated in the parish of St Lawrence in the sub-ward of West Wymer.

St Margaret's (1559–60): situated in the parish of St Margaret Westwick in the sub-ward of West Wymer.

St Martin's (1557–58): situated in one of the city's three parishes dedicated to St Martin.

St Michael's (1559–60): probably part of the Great Cockey in the parish of St Michael at Thorn in the sub-ward of Berstreet.

St Simon's (1557–58): situated in the parish of St Simon and St Jude in the sub-ward of East Wymer.

St Swithin's (1557–58): this was probably part of the cockey arising from the Pit Lane pit in the parish of St Swithin's in the sub-ward of West Wymer (*figure* 2).

GENERAL GLOSSARY
with Saints' Days and Festivals

C.R. Cheney, *Handbook of Dates* (1978)

J.A. Simpson and E.S.C. Weiner, eds., *Oxford English Dictionary* (Oxford, 1933, reprinted 1961); also accessed at www.oed.com

J. Wright, ed., *The English Dialect Dictionary* (1898)

D. Yaxley, *A Researcher's Handbook* (Fakenham, 2003)

acquittance acknowledgement of receipts or discharge

ale aisle

allercarres a carr was a bog or marshy piece of ground on which willows or alders (allers) grew

alterage revenue derived from gifts made at the altar

amercement fine at the discretion (mercy) of the mayor's court

anker stoke anchor stock: heavy wooden cross-bar of an anchor

anno, anno predicto in the year, in the aforesaid year

annoying damaging

arrears (arrerrages) an unpaid amount; balance carried over from previous year

assise rents fixed rents

astlell wood comprising small splints or shingles of thin board

bast rope, bast rope made from the inner bark of the lime tree

boken wooden pail with upright handle

brace timber placed at right angles or diagonally across a gate in order to strengthen (brace) the structure

bradde thin, flat, tapering nail

brent(e) burnt

brigg(e) bridge

brynnyng burning

burthen burden or load

bushell, *bz* measure of volume containing eight gallons (although local variations existed)

butt the end of a piece of timber

C, centum   one hundred. *C* may also stand for the 'long hundred', *i.e.*, 120, particularly with regard to quantities of timber. See also *hundredweight*, below. For more information on *C*, see Yaxley, *Researcher's Glossary*, pp. 29, 107

caning sickle   reaping-hook with serrated edge for removing reeds (canes)

capital messuage   main dwelling within a range of properties

capon   castrated cock

carr   see **allercarres**

carreyn   carrion

caytour   person who supplied provisions, mainly food, to the household

chalder   measure of capacity, originally 32 bushels though regional variations existed before 1695 when the weight was fixed by an Act of Parliament.

chamberleyne, chamberlyng   chamberlain – principal city financial officer

chene   chain

Christchurch   Norwich cathedral

clynke nayles   clench nails: type of nail provided with a rove (see **roffe**) for clinching in boatbuilding, *i.e.*, where the nail is beaten back over the rove as a fastening

cockey (cockes, cockeis, cokkes)   stream or gutter

combe   dry measure for capacity for grain equating to 32 gallons

compasse, compace, cumpasse   compost: mixture of materials used for fertiliser; prepared manure or mould

concealed lands   lands held from the king without a proper title

coovering   roughcasting, *i.e.* covering walls with a coarse plaster similar to daubing

coquies   female cook

cot   cottage, shed or shelter, as in bellcote or a pigsty

cottes, cotes   probably the cross-part of a handle

crome hook   long-shafted tool with three or four tines at right angles for drawing out muck, weeds *etc*

crosse house   a projecting wing

crowe   an iron bar with one end bent and sharpened to a beak, used as a lever or prise; tool to lift heavy burdens

cuppell sparres   lengths of timber of medium cross-section, providing a pair of inclined beams meeting at the top; rafters.

curtilage   small courtyard or piece of land attached to a dwelling

dawber   one who applies daub, a clay mix

deanyng   meaning unknown. Perhaps deneing (*i.e.*, beaching on a bare sandy tract)

demesne lands   home farm

di., dimidia   half

didall (**didole, didle**)   sharp triangular spade used for cleaning water-courses; a long pole with a metal scoop, net or dredge fixed to the end

didall or didle boat   boat from which bottom of the river is cleaned out using a didall

dike   bank or a ditch but can also refer to excavation during building work

dooles   dooles were boundary markers though a 'dole' can refer to a strip of land in open fields, or a share or portion

dorestall   doorpost or doorframe

dormond   horizontal beam or sleeper

engrossing   arranging and writing out in fair

examinatur per nos   examined by us

exhibition   fixed sum given to a scholar for a term of years

fadom   fathom: measure of distance equalling six feet

faldergate   entrance gate

farm, ferme   fixed yearly amount of rent

farren receyver, forren receyvour   foreign receiver (Norwich civic official)

feedings   pasture for grazing

fermor   holder of a lease

fey, fye   to clean out, clear, dredge

foldcourse/foldage   the right of foldage, the practice of grazing sheep in moveable pens or 'folds'

forelock   wedge driven through the end of a bolt to keep it in place

forrell   type of parchment

free and copyholders   freeholders were manorial tenants whose obligations were light. Copyholders were subject to more onerous duties. A copy of the court record was their title deed

furryng sparre, fyrren, firren, furringe   an undressed stem of fir wood

fye see **fey**

fyers, fiers   cleaners, clearers

fylth(e)   unclean matter, dirt

gallon   8 pints

grinding   sharpening

groundselyng   laying the foundation (groundsel) of a timber building

hamper   treasury

hardes hards   flax or hemp fibres; linen made from these

haryette   see **heriot**

hasp   hinged plate that fits over a staple (see below) to enable a gate, lid or door to be secured

helve   a handle

helving   fit with a **helve**

hengles   hinges

herbage   pasture

heriot   best beast or possession payable on death

hoghed, dry   a cask of sufficient capacity to hold a hogshead (approx. 63 gallons) of dry material

hookewood   ?oakwood

hosier   maker of or dealer in hose, *i.e.*, stockings, socks

hundred   100 or 120. See also *C*

hundredweight   8 stone or 112 *lb*. See also *C*

in primis   first

in supra   above

ingrossing   see **engrossing**

jemer, jemowe   a gimmer: a type of hinge

Jhus   Jesus

joined   jointed, that is with a mortise and tenon frame

kele   flat-bottomed vessel

krickes   creeks

kyll   kiln

lading   small, lightly constructed building

ledges   small timbers, fixed across a boat's length

li., libra   one pound, 16 *oz*

liberties   privilege or right granted to a subject, or the district over which the privilege or right extends

lock and a staple   bolt and bolt fastening

long entry   entry point or passageway between houses

loop   an opening in a wall

mark   13s 4d

meanor   manure, dung

meslin   mixture of wheat and rye

messuage/meeses   plot of land with a building on it. **Meeses** is a plural form

milne, myle   mill

mocke, mokke   muck: dung, mud, filth

nether   lower or bottom part

nihil/hoc anno/hic/quia primus annus   nothing/this year/here/because it is the first year

orteyarde   orchard

osyeryerde   land where willows (osiers) were grown for their tough but pliable branches

packthread, packe thred   twine or thread, used either for binding or as a bricklayers plumb line

pale   thin short piece of timber used to make fencing or a gate with rails

parre   enclosure for animals

pavemente   paving stones

pecyng   piecing: joining together, repairing

penner   meaning unclear. It may refer to a case or cylinder (such as might be used for pens or needles), or to a bodkin (*i.e.*, a long pin)

pightle   small field or enclosure

plauncher   flooring, putting in a wooden floor

pooke   poke: bag or sack

popple   poplar (tree)

proxies and sinages   procurations and synodals: church fees

pynnyng   underpinning foundations, general repairs, or filling in joints of masonry with stone chips

quant (qwante)   a pole for propelling a barge or punt

quanthok   prong or flange at the end of a quant to prevent it from becoming embedded in mud

quare   quire: copybook or writing book, especially one composed of four folded sheets making eight leaves

quarrell   diamond-shaped pane of glass

quarter   (weight) 2 stone or 28 *lb.*; (time) one of four periods in the year separated by quarter days, *i.e.*, Lady Day, Midsummer, Michaelmas, Christmas

quere   choir (in the architectural sense)

recipitur per me   received by me

rent hen   a hen paid as rent

rentes resolute   fixed rents

roffe   a small metal plate or ring through which a nail is passed and clinched to form a rivet, used in clinker boatbuilding. See **clynke nayles**

rood   measure of land containing a quarter of an acre. Also, in the context of hedging and ditching, used for a 'rod', a linear measure of around eight yards

rowel   wheel or disc; short flat board

rygg   to cover the top of a wall

ryving   to split wood, specifically to make lathes by splitting wood along the grain into thin wooden strips

scythe stave   rod or pole for a scythe

seelyng board   panelling

sheres, sheris, sherys   shears

sheriff's tourn (shreves turne)   special session of the Hundred Court presided over by the sheriff and held twice a year at Easter and Michaelmas

sherman   one who shears the nap off woollen cloth

shod(d) shoovel/sholves   wooden shovel with an iron or steel edge to the blade

shruff   either rubbish or small fragments of wood or other dry material used as fuel

sinages   see **proxies**

sith(e)   scythe

skep   large basket

skopette   shovel with a narrow blade for cleaning out ditches

slite   wear and tear

Spanish iron   iron imported from Spain, considered superior to English iron

spar   length of timber or a cross bar. See also **cuppell sparres** and **furryng sparres**

spindle (spyndel, spendle)   a rod of iron or other metal serving as an axis

staith (stath, stathe)   landing stage or wharf; embankment

staple   U-shaped piece of iron driven into a post or piece of timber to hold a hook or bolt. See also **lock and staple**

staunch   upright stay or support

stave   rod or pole

steeling (**stelyng**)   sharpening

stockeng   to furnish with a stock. See **anker stoke**

stondle   tub slung on a pole and carried by two people

stone   14 *lb.*

stopp   waterbucket

stud   wood strips used as the upright section of lath and plaster buildings or, more generally, small upright timbers between the principal posts of a wall

stulpe   post or main post of a paling fence

summa/summa totalis/summa patet   sum/sum total/the sum is apparent *i.e.* is shown above

tenters (**taynters**)   wooden frame over which wet cloth was stretched to encourage even drying and thus resist shrinkage

thake tile   roofing, not paving, tiles. The manufacture and dimensions of such tiles were regulated in 1477

thelves   see **helve**

thrums, throm(e)s   waste wool or hemp yarn, used for making mops/rough brushes

tracte ... tyme   waste time

trimming (**trymmyng**)   fitting out, repairing or cleaning the bottom of a ship

tryce   mobile crane used to lift and move timber

twye bord   meaning unknown

tylte   awning or cover (probably for a boat, but possibly for a cart); a tent

unche bord   inch board: board that is one inch thick

virrell   virl: ring, band or ferrule (*i.e.*, ring or cap of metal to strengthen wood, or prevent splitting or wearing)

visitor   priest charged with visiting the prisoners in the Guildhall

viz., vidz.   *videlicit*: namely

waifs and strays   ownerless piece of property, typically a wandering animal, which if unclaimed within a fixed period fell to the Lord of the Manor

water baly/baylyff   water bailiff (civic officer)

wharfage   payment for use of a wharf

wronge(s)   rungs: boat floor timbers

Money

Throughout the accounts, pounds, shillings and pence (*libre, solidi* and *denarii*) were abbreviated to *li.*, *s.* and *d.* An *ob.* (*obolus*) was ½*d* and a *q.* (*quarta*) ¼*d*. There were twelve pence to a shilling and twenty shillings to a pound.

Saints' Days and Festivals

All Hallows – 1 November

Annunciation of the Blessed Virgin Mary – 25 March

Candlemas – 2 February

Christmas/birth of Our Lord God – 25 December

Crouchmas – 14 September

Easter – a moveable feast falling on the Sunday following the first full moon on or after 21 March

Ladyday – see Annunciation

Lammas Day – 1 August

Michaelmas – 29 September

Mid-Lent Sunday – the fourth Sunday of Lent

Midsummer – 24 June

Nativity of St John Baptist – 24 June

Our Lady in Lent – see Annunciation

Passion week – the fifth full week in Lent, beginning with Passion Sunday

Purification of the Blessed Virgin Mary – see Candlemas

St Hillary the Confessor – 13 January

St Mathias day – 24 February

St Michael the Archangel – see Michaelmas

St Peter in Chains – 1 August

St Thomas day – 21 December

Whitsuntide – the seventh Sunday after Easter (Whitsunday) and the days immediately following

Index